THE DREAM AND THE UNDERWORLD

THE DREAM
AND THE
UNDERWORLD

JAMES HILLMAN

HarperPerennial

A Division of HarperCollinsPublishers

A word of thanks to Lyn Cowan for her index; to James Gerald Donat, Judith Kipnis, and Caroline Weening, and to Gabriella: *Genio loci ignoto.*

A shorter version of this book was published in the *Eranos Yearbook*–42, 1973 (Netherlands: Brill, 1975).

FIRST EDITION

Designed by Eve Kirch

Library of Congress Cataloging in Publication Data

Hillman, James.
    The dream and the underworld.

    A shorter version of this book was published in the Eranos yearbook–42, 1973.
    Bibliography: p.
    Includes index.
    1. Dreams. 2. Mythology. 3. Death. I. Title.
BF1078.H63   1979   154.6'34   78–4733
ISBN 0-06-011902-0
ISBN 0-06-090682-0 pbk.

HB 06.01.2022

CONTENTS

The dread and resistance which every natural human being experiences when it comes to delving too deeply into himself is, at bottom, the fear of the journey to Hades.

C. G. Jung,
Psychology and Alchemy,
CW 12 §439.

And by the way let us recount our dreams.

. . . I have had a most rare vision. I have had a dream, past the wit of man to say what dream it was: man is but an ass, if he go about to expound this dream. . . . The eye of man hath not heard, the ear of man hath not seen, man's hand is not able to taste, his tongue to conceive, nor his heart to report, what my dream was. . . . It shall be called 'Bottom's Dream,' because it hath no bottom; and I will sing it in the latter end of a play. . . . to make it the more gracious, I shall sing it at her death. *Exit.*

Wm. Shakespeare,
A Midsummer-Night's Dream,
act 4, sc. 1, 205–26.

1

BRIDGE

It is sometimes said that most ideas can be put into a few words—like one of those pre-Socratic fragments—and these few words condensed into a title, so that what one calls a book is no easy matter. Among the possible titles for this work have been "The Dream Bridge," or "The Dream Between World and Underworld." Freud had already used a similar metaphor; he called the dream a royal road, the *via regia* to the unconscious. But because this *via regia,* in most psychotherapy since his time, has become a straight one-way street of all morning traffic, moving out of the unconscious toward the ego's city, I have chosen to face the other way. Hence my title, which is a directional signpost for a different one-way movement, let us say vesperal, into the dark. So, at the beginning, I must admit to working this bridge with a certain singleness of intent.

This little book attempts a different view of the dream from those we are used to. Its thesis does not rely on ideas of repression (Freud) or of compensation (Jung), but imagines dreams in relation with soul and soul with death. I have come to believe that the entire procedure of dream interpretation aiming at more consciousness about living is radically wrong. And I mean *"wrong"* in all its fullness: harmful, twisted, deceptive, inadequate, mistaken, and exegetically insulting to its material, the dream. When we wrong the dream, we wrong the soul, and if the soul has the intimate connection with death that tradition has always supposed, then mistaken dream interpretation deceives our dying. What this dying and this death is in relation to dreams will be explored in the following pages.

We begin by asking an obvious, though overlooked, question: To what mythological region, to what Gods, do dreams belong? The assumption in the question is: were we to know "where" dreams belong, then we would know better what they want, what they mean, and what we are to do with them. The consequences of the answer put the dream theory in this book on the base of myth—it is no secret that dreams belong to the underworld and its Gods, for our title announces this, and the short second chapter shows that a mythic base for dreams is an old story. Freud, more or less unwittingly, made exactly this move, turning to the mythical underworld for grounding his theory of dreams.

What is new in what follows is the attempt to re-vision the dream in the light of myth. Theories of dreams there are aplenty. Any well-stocked analytical community—uptown Manhattan, Harley Street or Hampstead, Beverly Hills, Zürich—can display wares of all sorts: Freudian, orthodox Freudian, neo-Freudian, modified psychodynamic Freudian, Jungian in various contours and pastels, Gestalt-dramatical, transcendental-mystical, scientific-empirical, ego-behavioral, primal-parapsychological, as well as existential and phenomenological approaches that reach back to the romantics and earlier. Yet, none I know asks the mythic question; none tries to suggest a theory, and a praxis with it, derived from an archetypal approach to the whole business of dreams. Others have seen myths in dreams and have used myths for amplifying dream motifs. It is, however, another vision altogether to look at dreams as phenomena that emerge from a specific archetypal "place" and that correspond with a distinct mythic geography and then, further, to reflect this underworld in psychological theory. By connecting psychological theory with mythological theoria ("viewing," "speculation"), we are essaying a psychology of dreams that tries to keep a sense of underworld always present in our work with them.

This move backwards from logos to mythos, this move against the historical stream of our culture, has been taking me quite some time. I first presented themes of this essay in a lecture in 1972 in New York City to the American Society of Arts, Religion, and Culture, under the genial chairmanship of Stanley Romaine Hopper, at the invitation of David Miller and James Wiggins. It was next expanded into my contribution to the Eranos Conference in Ascona, Switzerland, for the year 1973 and published in *Correspondences in Man and World,* * edited by Adolf Portmann and Rudolf Ritsema. Though now much wider and fuller, it yet bears the marks of Eranos, where for several years I have been elaborating specific archetypal themes and the ways they influence our consciousness, particularly the ideas and attitudes of psychology.

I have looked at the psychology of ego development and growth in terms of the child archetype (1971), at the psychology of age versus youth in terms of the puer-senex pair (1967), at the diagnosis of hysteria and inferior femininity by means of the archetypal configuration of Dionysos (1969), and at the therapeutic concern with changing abnormality into normality through the figures of Ananke and Athene (1974). Each of these has been an attempt to see through accepted

* Eranos Jahrbuch 42 (1973) (Leiden: E. J. Brill, 1975).

psychological positions by placing them against a relevant mythic background. The hope has been that archetypal perspectives can rectify our vision of the psyche and give a more psychological (i.e., self-reflective, imaginal, and deeper) account of what psychology is saying and doing.

This essay, like those, is therefore an essay in epistrophe, reversion, return, the recall of phenomena to their imaginal background. This principle—regarding phenomena in terms of their likenesses—derives more immediately from the work of Henry Corbin, a friend at Eranos, and the method of *ta'wil* that he has so profoundly explained and illustrated in his own immense work.*

Reversion through likeness, *resemblance,* is a primary principle for the archetypal approach to all psychic events. Reversion is a bridge too, a method which connects an event to its image, a psychic process to its myth, a suffering of the soul to the imaginal mystery expressed therein. Epistrophe, or the return through likeness, offers to psychological understanding a main avenue for recovering order from the confusion of psychic phenomena, other than Freud's idea of development and Jung's of opposites. Besides, this method has two distinct advantages. First, it makes us look again at the phenomenon: what is actually dreamed, actually stated, actually experienced, for only by scrutinizing the event at hand can we attempt to find which of many archetypal constellations it might resemble. "Which of many" is the second advantage: a single explanatory principle, regardless how profound and differentiated its formulation, such as Jung's Self and its opposites or Freud's development of the libido, does not offer the psyche's native variety a diversity of resemblances. Epistrophe implies return to multiple possibilities, correspondences with images that can not be encompassed within any systematic account.

---

* *Ta'wil* means literally, he says, " 'reconduire, ramener' une chose à son origine et principe, à son archetype" ("to lead something back to its origin and principle, to its archetype").[1]

The image has been my starting point for the archetypal re-visioning of psychology. This emphasis upon images is carried further and worked into more detail in this book. In fact, this book becomes the main bridge—or tunnel—into my other writings. For here the psychology of the image is placed more definitely within a psychology of dreams and of death. A depth psychology which relies upon the shadowy images of fantasy, upon deepening and pathologizing, and upon therapy as a cult of soul is referring mythologically to the underworld. To start with the image in depth psychology is to begin in the mythological underworld, so this book provides the mythical perspective to our psychology of the image. The claim that images come first is to say that dreams are the primary givens and that all daylight consciousness begins in the night and bears its shadows. Our depth psychology begins with the perspective of death.

The shifts of perspective aim not only to criticize and rectify what has already been said in psychology, in this case about the dream. More: the sudden shaft of insight that occurs when the bridge is struck between an ordinary event or a concept and its mythic resemblance can yield startling new perspectives in the taken-for-granted psychology of our own experience, as well as the all too familiar psychology of our contemporary theory.

Despite my penchant for the radical and the scandalously new and my childish delight in seeing through the Emperor's clothes, I have tried to keep strict limitations. I would like to make these principles of limit clear at the outset, for they are as much a description of scope and method as they are a statement of faith.

First, no matter how far up or down we go in the psyche with our speculations and soundings, we shall try to stay within the bounds of the Western psyche, its cultural, geographical, and historical roots in our tradition. The romantic endeavor to explore and disclose is possible only within the classic confines of the old, the known, and the limited. Newness from this perspective means nothing more than renewal, renascence, recuperation—not creation; what is said is addressed to the dead and the past—not to the future, which will do what it will; it is a commentary, a footnote, upon what others have done before and better, a bridge backward.

So, second, we shall try to stay within the field of psychology. As Freud and Jung abjured anatomy, biology, natural science, and theology for their psychic premises, so the tradition of depth psychology is to stay at home and to create its own ground as it proceeds. This ground—psychodynamics, psychotherapy, psychopathology—is surely well trodden by now, even if the field is only 80 years old. But I do not imagine the grass to be greener in the other fields—it can be green right under our feet, providing we work it afresh, which in depth psychology means digging ever deeper, a bridge downward.

Third, to make my limitations even more strict, that part of the psychological field we till is the very same field worked by Freud and by Jung. It is, in fact, their field. We shall plow it, however, from another angle, not with their plow or in their furrows, but turning their soil in our style. The contours that emerge may differ, but the field is the same limited one: the psyche of Western man in his historical tradition and cultural predicament; and the intention is the same as theirs: to articulate a psychology that reflects the passionate importance of the individual soul. A bridge inward.

2

FREUD

FREUD AND MY THESIS

The question we start with arises from Aristotle. It is a practical question, one that bears on each of us in the morning in regard to interpreting our own dreams. Aristotle said, "The most skillful interpreter of dreams is he who has the faculty of observing resemblances."[1] Now what does the dream itself resemble? I do not mean dream images and thoughts, but the dream as dream. What is its likeness, so that in terms of what myth or universe could dream images be interpreted? With what world do dreams correspond? If we had an answer here, would it not help us to place all dream contents more truly and deeply against their right background?

In response to my question, I wish you to entertain a prolonged fantasy that is romantic, Renaissance, and Greek. I want to turn the clock back. I want to take up the dream anew by going back before the age of Freud.

Freud's great work on dreams appeared on November 4,

1899 (*ID*, p. xii), although the 1900 on its title page announced the new century. The book does indeed represent the turning point. It both opened our era's relation to the psyche and closed the era preceding.

There were then three dominant views of the dream: romantic, rationalist, and somaticist.[2] Freud took strands from each and wove them together into an elegant system. From the romantics, he took the idea that the dream contained a hidden but important personal message from another world. From the rationalists, Freud accepted the idea that the manifest dream, dream language as it appeared, was a worthless jumble of nonsense—for Freud, however, it was decipherable into a latent value and meaning. With the somaticists, he agreed that the dream reflected physiological processes—for Freud, however, these had mainly to do with sexuality and sleep.

Of the three positions, the romantic one was nearest to Freud's, and therefore it is this romantic position, by having been most assimilated, that most disappeared from the post-Freudian era in which we all live and dream. Like the romantics, Freud built a world upon the dream and connected the dream primarily with the realm of sleep (*TD*, pp. 137–38), the nightworld, and with classical myth, giving to it a separate region with its own topography. By saying it was "absolutely egoistic" (*TD*, p. 138), "not a social utterance, not a means for making oneself understood" (*NIL*, p. 17), he insisted on its private significance, again a romantic viewpoint. The dream is a wholly intrapsychic phenomenon, un-understandable even to the dreamer who dreams it and who seems to walk around in it and there play a part.

Freud did, however, introduce two concessions to the rationalists. First, he equated the dreamworld with a temporary psychosis, because both nightworld and the psychotic world represent "a turning away from the real external world" (*NIL*, p. 27). Freud took his stand with the dayworld view of sanity, where reality meant external, social, material.[3]

The second concession is still more significant—and ruinous to his achievement. I refer to the idea that residues of the day *(Tagesreste)* are the building stones of the dream: ". . . experience has taught us that in almost every dream is incorporated a memory trace of, or an allusion to, an event . . . of the previous day; and if we follow up these links we often discover all of a sudden the bridge from the apparently remote dreamworld to the real life of the patient" *(NIL,* pp. 20–21). Likewise, ". . . every dream without any possible exception goes back to an impression of the past few days . . . or . . . of the day immediately preceding the dream, of the 'dreamday' " *(OD,* p. 31).

Here begins the one-way bridge I mentioned. "If we follow up these links . . . ," we cross back over from the dreamworld into the "real life of the patient," into the "dreamday." That the dream could contain images left over from the day, yet images which we do not remember ever having perceived, was soon established experimentally by Otto Pötzl in Vienna.[4] Thus the old *tabula rasa* view of the mind, the view of rational empiricism, remained essentially unthreatened by the new Freudian theory of the dream. Dreams could be shown to consist of subliminally perceived images from the dayworld. There was still nothing in the mind that was not first in sense. The dream may mean something, yes, but it was basically only a rearrangement of daylife residues in accordance with the instinctual needs of sleep and sexuality. In the end, the dream becomes a "compromise," as Freud called it, between the demands of the nightworld and the dayworld. Or is it rather that Freud's view of the dream is a compromise between the positions of the romantic nightworld and the rationalist dayworld? Under final scrutiny, however, the compromise breaks apart. The rationalists win out.

The rationalist position defeats the romantic one because Freud returns the dream to the upperworld. This happens first through the day-residues and the return to the previous day (*CP* 5:136), and it happens through Freud's idea of interpretation as "translation into the language of waking life" (*CP* 5:150).

Now Freud fully recognized, even in the most romantic sense, that the *dream itself* belonged to the underworld. He says that the day residues "are not the dream itself. . . . They could not of themselves form a dream. They are, strictly speaking, only the psychical material which the dream work employs . . ." (*CP* 2:138). The dayworld is only the material cause of the dream; its formal, efficient and final causes are the wishes of Eros working upon the psyche in the night to keep it sleeping (*OD*, p. 66; *ID*, p. 160n.).[5]

Moreover, he is unequivocal and adamant about the final cause, the dream's purpose. It has nothing to do with the dayworld. Freud says, ". . . it would be misleading to say that dreams are concerned with the tasks of life before us or seek to find a solution for the problems of our daily work. . . . Useful work of this kind is remote from dreams. . . . There is only one useful task . . . that can be ascribed to a dream, and that is the guarding of sleep . . ." (*CP* 5:150–51). Everything about the dream is foreign to waking life, its speech, its morality (*CP* 5:154), its logic, its time, so foreign, in fact, is the dream that Freud speaks of it in the language of psychopathology: narcissism, hallucination, psychosis (*CP* 4:38, 145; *NIL*, p. 27; *TD* p. 145); hysterical symptoms and obsessional ideas (*OD*, p. 72).

The conflict now stands out clearly. On the one hand, the *dream* belongs wholly to sleep; on the other hand, the *interpretation* of dreams is to bring them over into the dayworld, shall we say rescuing or "reclaiming" (Freud's own metaphor) the dream from its underworld madness and immersion in the pleasure principle. Freud would wake up Psyche from its embrace in the nightworld of erotic pleasure, its narcissistic delight in its own imagery. This is his ambition. His book is not called The Nature of Dreams, or The Study of Dreams, or The World of Dream. It is called *Die Traum-deutung* ("The Interpretation of Dreams"), and by interpretation Freud means, as he says often and again, "translation" (*CP* 5:139–40, 152; *OD*, p. 69) into the language of waking life.

Thus the aim of therapeutic interpretation has been to take the *via regia* of the dream *out* of the nightworld; as Freud says, this "work which proceeds in the contrary direction . . . is our *work of interpretation*. This work of interpretation seeks to undo the dream-work" (*IL*, p. 170), "to unravel what the dream-work has woven" (*OD*, p. 71).

The dream itself resists being awakened into this translation (*ID*, p. 525). In fact, the concept of resistance and that of interpretation are directly connected through an inverse relationship (*CP* 5:137–38, 152; *NIL*, pp. 23–5). The *more* resistance between the "awakened ego" and the "unconscious," the less possible a dream interpretation; the *less* the resistance between dream and dayworld, the more successful the translation of the dream into waking language. In other words, there is a definite resistance on the part of the dream to be converted into the dayworld and put to its uses.

Yet this conversion has become the main effort in the therapeutic use of dreams. We turn the light on them in the morning, take them to the typewriter, bring them to the analyst, and together we read them for messages about living situations, choices, and relationships of our conscious life, its problems, feelings and thoughts. By means of the dream we may remember what was forgotten in the past, perceive what we missed in the present, or decide about the future, reading the dream prophetically, oracularly, for tendencies in the underworld that will help us to cope better with our lives.

Our thesis (against dreams being translated into the ego's language) must here meet two objections, from the Freudians and the Jungians. The Freudians would insist that this "reclamation work" (*NIL*, p. 106) is precisely the work of therapy.

"Psycho-analysis is an instrument to enable the ego to achieve a progressive conquest of the id" (*EI*, p. 56). The interpretation of dreams is a daily part of the reclamation work.

The Jungian objection has two horns. Following Freud, the interpretation of dreams is indeed the work of ego-consciousness and part of the overall conquest of the id or of making the unconscious conscious, which alchemical Jungians understand as the *opus contra naturam*. For Jungians, however, nature itself wants this opus, for "becoming conscious" is itself an archetypal process buried in the dream's own wish. Hence the dream comes back in the morning and itself asks for interpretation, even as it resists interpretation. Interpretation serves nature, even as it interferes with it.

The second Jungian objection to our thesis against therapeutic translation of dreams into the waking-world of life is yet more subtle. A Jungian analysis follows the individuation process. It takes the dream into the waking ego only for the sake of the psyche as a whole. It is not for the sake of life that Jungians focus so intensely upon dreams. We Jungians, so the argument would go, read dreams for their information regarding the process of individuation, for their symbolic, not literal content. We relate them to the ego *only in compensation,* to fill out its inadequate attitude. Dream interpretation makes a bridge between day and night, creating a new midway standpoint, more whole, that includes both dream and ego, both inner and outer life.

The remainder of this essay meets these Freudian and Jungian objections, which can be summarily condensed into one statement: *the dream requires translation into waking-language* either to extend waking-consciousness' domain or to serve nature's demand for the more broadened and balanced quality of consciousness. In developing my thesis further, I shall follow Freud and Jung both—but not only: Freud by insisting that the dream has nothing to do with the waking world but is the psyche speaking to itself in its own language;

and Jung by insisting that the ego requires adjustment to the nightworld. I shall *not* be following them in bringing the dream into the dayworld in any other form than its own, implying that the dream may not be envisaged either as a message to be deciphered for the dayworld (Freud) or as a compensation to it (Jung).

By dayworld and daylight, I do not mean the daily world. I mean rather the literal view of any world where things seem as they appear, where we have not seen through into their darkness, their deadly nightshade. It is this dayworld style of thinking—literal realities, natural comparisons, contrary opposites, processional steps—that must be set aside in order to pursue the dream into its home territory. There thinking moves in images, resemblances, correspondences. To go in this direction, we must sever the link with the dayworld, foregoing all ideas that originate there—translation, reclamation, compensation. We must go over the bridge and let it fall behind us, and if it will not fall, then let it burn.

FECHNER, FREUD, AND THE UNDERWORLD

The attempt to interpret the dream into the context of life has often enough been savagely criticized. Here is one example:

> Out of this sick condition of our times arose the silly attempts to explain the dream, the positive product of sleep, in terms only of waking consciousness. This method of explanation saw nothing in dreams except the half repressed thoughts and images of the day.[6]

These words were written by Heinrich Steffens and published in Leipzig in 1821, as far before Freud as we are after him. Steffens' statement represents the romantic critique of waking consciousness, a critique, whether before Freud or after him, that is based on the ontological disjunction between dayworld and nightworld. Drawn to extremes, each world tries to deny the other, and a diagnosis of madness or of evil is placed by each on the other.

When Freud went into the dream and the relations between sleeping and waking consciousness, he entered into one of the major archetypal fantasies of the nineteenth century. For Gustav Theodor Fechner, to whom we shall soon turn, this relation between sleep and waking was what life was all about, its very definition.[7] Because of the romantics—as has been so thoroughly and so beautifully exposed by Albert Béguin in his work *L'âme romantique et le rêve,*[8] a work that should be on the syllabus of all schools of depth psychology—sleeping and waking, day and night, had become depositories of every possible sort of thought. These "diurnal and nocturnal regimes," to use the language of Gilbert Durand,[9] had become the main carriers of opposites: ontological, psychological, symbolic, ethical. When we place a problem into this language, as we are doing here, we are at once reentering a tradition about night and day, sleeping and waking, that begins at least with Heraclitus, continues through Plato and the cave, through Neoplatonism and romanticism, through Freud's two systems of mental functioning, issuing into Jung's lunar and solar consciousness.

No one made more of this metaphor than G. T. Fechner of Leipzig, who lived the fantasy of a *Tagesansicht* ("day-face") and a *Nachtansicht* ("night-face") in his actual life. He was, on the one hand, the founder of psychophysics, a sensitive experimenter, using a quantitative and physiological approach to psychological problems, while, on the other hand, under the name of Dr. Mises, he wrote treatises, serious and satirical, on such subjects as "The Comparative Anatomy of Angels," "The Soul-Life of Plants," "The Zend Avesta," various ridicules against medicine,[10] and he wrote on life after death.

Fechner illustrates better than anyone of the time the reality of the two worlds, for in him they came apart. At the age of thirty-nine, after years of intensive reading and experimental work, especially on the psychophysics of color perception, his eyes failed. He took to wearing blue glasses, and then he went blind. He fell into melancholic isolation, lost control over his thoughts, hallucinated tortures, and his alimentary tract broke down. Fechner remained in this tormented night-world state for three years. Twice he was miraculously healed: once when a woman friend dreamed of preparing him a meal of *Bauernschinken,* heavily spiced raw ham cured in lemon juice and Rhine wine. This she did, took it to him, and he, against his better judgment, ate it, which restored his appetite and digestion. The second and final time came suddenly one morning at dawn when he found he was able to bear the light and even hungered for it, and then he began recuperating. He lived another forty-four years, until age eighty-six.[11]

With his recovery Fechner was a converted man. He exchanged his university chair in physics for one in philosophy. Dayworld and nightworld took on a meaning different from his romantic forebears. Dayworld was the realm of light, spirit, God, and beauty; nightworld, of matter, pessimism, godless secularism. The idea of the unconscious he put into the nightworld.[12] Despite shifting the valences, the archetypal fantasy of the two regimes remained fundamental to him, as it still remains fundamental in all depth psychologies.

In turning to Fechner, I take my cue from Freud, who wrote in a letter to Fliess (*OPA,* Letter 83, 9 February 1898): "I am deep in the dream book. . . . If only one did not have to read! The literature on the subject, such as it is, is too much for me already. The only sensible thing on the subject was said by old Fechner. . . ."

This "sensible thing" that old Fechner said is paraphrased and italicized by Freud (*ID,* pp. 48, 536), *"the scene of action of dreams is different from that of waking ideational life."*

This idea Freud draws from a quotation from Fechner's *Elemente der Psychophysik* (ed. 1889) :

> If the scene of action of psychophysical activity were the same in sleeping and waking, dreams could, in my view, only be a prolongation at a lower degree of intensity of waking ideational life and, moreover, would necessarily be of the same material and form. But the facts are quite otherwise.

It is this idea, that the scene of action of dreams is essentially different, which Freud developed into the "psychical locality" of the unconscious. The "psychical locality" of the dream, he goes on to say "will correspond to a point . . . at which one of the preliminary stages of an image comes into being."

Freud's thinking here, like Fechner's, is a *topos* thinking. By saying "a topographical regression takes place in dreams" (*TD,* p. 144), Freud has moved the dream, and with it psychology itself, from a functional and descriptive cosmos to a topographical cosmos. He has restored to psychotherapy the realm of inner space. Here Freud begins to write interior geography and to make a voyage in the imaginal.[13] Through the dream, he rediscovers the underworld. This is stated in the *Traumdeutung*'s motto taken from the *Aeneid* of Virgil: "Flectere si nequeo superos, Acheronta movebo" ("If I cannot bend the higher powers, I will move Acheron" [the most dreadful and sinister river of the netherworld]).[14]

This bold, this heroic move of Freud into unknown lands was made without cognizance of its consequences for psychology. While it opened new ground for psychological thinking, giving it the new dimension of depth, this depth was fixed into a fantasy of structural levels. Although Freud was aware of the dangers of confusing the *topos*-thinking of psychology with that of physiology (cortical and medullary brain regions), he was less aware of the other dangers inherent in this metaphor. Imaginary space is not a mere receptacle but comes already loaded with significances about "up" and "down," "surface" and "deep," "close" and "remote." It brings with it ontological, esthetic, and moral considerations that are reflected in many spiritual topographies of religions. "The unconscious" has itself been influenced by Freud's placing it below; its description, like that of "the id," is never able to free itself from an inherent feeling that the unconscious is both the base of conscious life and also "basely" subversive to its ontology and its values.

Soon, we shall be making our own "descent to the underworld" in detail. I am assuming that its general geography is already somewhat familiar from myths, religions, painting, and literature, where the horrors of hell and the sufferings of the deep, the waters one crosses to get there, the guardians at the gates, the figures who reside there, have been relayed to us through centuries of our common lore. As I recount Freud's topography of the unconscious, let us listen to his descriptions against that general background in your memory, a background which will be substantiated more carefully in the next chapter.

First of all, says Freud, the unconscious is a region below consciousness. Owing to this region, there is intense psychic suffering, neurosis, and psychosis, and from this region come dreams.

Between the two areas—and Freud has drawn maps (*NIL*, p. 105; *EI*, p. 24)—there is a threshold or "barrier" (*NIL*, p. 103) that prevents easy passage and even a forbidding "censor" (*CP*4:105 f.; *IL*, p. 140 f.) Repression is the concept psychology uses for describing the fact that a host of *eidola* or "images" are kept on the other side. What takes place in this other "mental province" (*NIL*, p. 96) gives our waking life anxiety.

Freud often referred to this other side in an apotropaic manner, by means of an "impersonal pronoun" (*NIL*, p. 94). *Das Es*, the id, in his later theory replaces the topographical unconscious. *Das Es* seems to have a background in philosophical thinking—Nietzsche and Schopenhauer—but Freud's manner of naming and his descriptions point rather to a background in mythical thinking, where apotropaic and euphemistic words were frequent for Hades and the underworld. (Guggenbühl-Craig once remarked: "The Freudians cannot properly understand Freud because they take him at his word. The Jungians may be better at understanding Freud because they can read him for his mythology.")

So Freud speaks of the "psychological underworld" (*NIL*, p. 79) in describing the unconscious, of the repressed as a "foreign territory" (*NIL*, p. 78), and of the energy of the id as "fluid" (*NIL*, p. 100). (Still today many psychotherapists identify bodies of water in dreams, e.g., bathtubs, swimming pools, oceans, as "the unconscious.") Freud goes on to say that the space of the id should be imagined as incomparably greater than that of the ego (*NIL*, p. 104), and what little we know of it is mainly from hypnosis (named after Hypnos), from suffering, and from the study of dreams (*NIL*, p. 98).

We also know of it through falling into it through slips, cracks, and crevices in consciousness. These Freud called the psychopathology of everyday life, and Jung, disturbances in attention. Mythology recognized these lacunae in the continuity of ground underfoot, these caves and holes, as entrances to the underworld. Furthermore, like the classical underworld, the unconscious receives mainly a negative description (*NIL*, p. 98), because by definition it is invisible and not directly knowable.

Freud says, "We can come nearer to the id with images, and call it a chaos, a cauldron of seething excitement" (*NIL*, p. 98). But "it cannot say what it wants" (*EI*, p. 59), any more than can the dead in the mythological underworld speak except in a whisper.[15] "It would be possible to picture the id," suggests Freud, in the last sentence of his essay that introduced the "id," to psychology, "under the domination of the mute but powerful death instincts . . ." (*EI*, p. 59).

Like the classical idea of death, Freud's death instinct is "elusive," difficult to see (*EI*, pp. 40, 42, 46). In the id, the laws of logic do not obtain; and the id knows no values, no good and evil, no morality (*NIL*, p. 99; *EI*, p. 54; *CP* 5:155). Above all, in the id there is no recognition of the passage of time (*BPP*, p. 33). Impulses that remain there are "virtually immortal and are preserved for whole decades as though they had only recently occurred" (*NIL*, p. 99). Because of its immortality, Freud links it with heroes (*CP* 4:313), and there "in the id . . . are harboured residues of existence of countless egos." These "reviving shapes of former egos" are resurrected in a personal life (*EI*, p. 38). The mythological underworld (say, of Homer) also shows heroic figures, who go on immutably in a timeless state, perhaps still reviving in our personal lives, not only in literature.

The ego, in Freud's fantasy, "stands for reason and circumspection" (*NIL*, p. 102; *EI*, p. 25). We may imagine its relation to the id like that of the hero's relation to the underworld, for the hero too must use "tricks" (*NIL*, p. 102)—the word is from Freud—for gaining energy for itself. And if it does not use tricks, it uses "musculature" (*EI*, pp. 41, 56; *TD*, p. 148; *CP* 4:148; *OTL*, p. 7)—again the word is from Freud's description of the ego. Ego, like hero, must meet the raging demands of the repressed, where "wishes appear to rise up out of a positive Hell" (*IL*, p. 143). The denizens of the underworld are, in Freud's language, "instinctual cathexes seeking discharges—that, in our view, is all the id contains" (*NIL*, p. 100). These cathexes make immense demands upon the ego. (Remember the clamoring dead assaulting Ulysses?) And finally, this id, like the Homeric underworld, is completely cut off from the external world, dealing with it only "through the medium of the ego" (*NIL*, p. 104; *OTL*, p. 69).

Even Freud's early description of therapy as "the talking-cure" and his method of doing it—persons so positioned that they do not look at each other, whose gaze is ritually averted—finds its pattern in antiquity: "Sacrifice to the deities of the dead was made with averted face; no looking, only the voice, was allowed in the realm of the departed. That could work miracles . . . ,"[16] says Kerényi (in regard to Orpheus who looked and lost).

It is not difficult to transpose psychology's conceptual mythology into the mythology of the underworld, nor is it difficult to envision the relationship between dayworld and nightworld as the hero's descent[17] and our modern notions of the unconscious as reflections of Tartaros and Styx, Charon and Cerberus, Hades and Pluto. Pluto, especially, is important to recognize in our euphemistic references to the unconscious as the giver of wholeness, a storehouse of abundant riches, a place not of fixation in torment, but a place, if propitiated rightly, that offers fertile plenty. Euphemism is a way of covering anxiety. In antiquity, Pluto ("riches") was said as a euphemistic name to cover the frightening depth of Hades. Today, the "creative" unconscious euphemistically conceals the processes of destruction and death in the deeps of the soul.

Freud's own midlife breakdown took place while he was working on the dreambook. Ellenberger calls it a "creative illness" and compares it with those of Jung and Fechner. Freud's breakdown was his breakthrough into the realm of depth which his previous attempts via hypnosis, cocaine, and therapy with hysterics had not achieved.

We must remember here that Freud's *Traumdeutung* is based almost entirely upon his own dreams, that it is a personal descent and a personal report and a personal myth of the underworld, turned into a work of art with a body of teaching which has had validity for others, as did the *nekyia* of Dante and the other imaginal trips of the classics. They used images; Freud, concepts. Freud's feeling about his theory of dreams, however, attests to its archetypical significance.

The theory of dreams "marks a turning point," he says, "analysis passed from being a psychotherapeutic method to being a psychology of the depths of human nature." His dream theory was for him "a new found land, which has been reclaimed from the regions of Folklore and Mysticism." Freud goes on to say that when he was often in doubt and confused about his work, it was to the dream and his theory of dreams that he turned, gaining thereby renewed confidence (*NIL*, pp. 15–16).[18]

Ernest Jones, in writing about Freud's self-analysis (which constitutes the book on dreams), is also seized by the myth of the heroic descent to the underworld: ". . . Freud undertook his most heroic feat—a psycho-analysis of his own unconscious . . . the uniqueness of the feat remains. Once done it is done for ever. For no one again can be the first to explore those depths. . . . It was daring much, and risking much. What indomitable courage. . . ." On the next page, Jones calls it a "Herculean labour."[19]

Freud's underworld experience, like Jung's own descent later, was the touchstone for an entire life. So, Freud wrote of his *Traumdeutung*: "Insight such as this falls to one's lot but once in a lifetime."[20] And the reason for this personal significance also resonates against the myths of the underworld. Freud writes: "It [the book] was, I found, a portion of my own self-analysis, my reaction to my father's death—that is to say, to the most important event, the most poignant loss, of a man's life."[21] Listening to him metaphorically and against the background of the *nekyia,* or the archetypal descent—remember Aeneas and his dead father in the underworld—we see more readily how Freud's dream theory could be his sustaining vision and "shibboleth" (*NIL*, p. 15). It was not merely a theory composed of hypotheses—repression, wish-fulfilment, dream-work, etc. It was a *revelation* of the underworld, formulated in the faith language of his time and of his personal code: the metaphors of rational science.

Freud summons up "the great Fechner" (*ID*, p. 536) once more in regard to a principal idea. This idea is no less significant for our understanding of the underworld in psychoanalysis than his theory of dreams. I refer to Freud's little book *Beyond the Pleasure Principle,* where he again builds upon Fechner (pp. 3–5). Freud says: ". . . we have conceived the principle which governs all mental processes as a special case of Fechner's *tendency to stability.* . ." (*CP* 2:255). The mythical descriptions of the figures of the underworld fixed in their repetitions, unredeemable, unredressed, correspond metaphorically with Fechner's principle of stability to which Freud connected the death drive. We shall return, toward the close of this book, to this unchanging component of the psyche in regard to that pressing social problem called psychopathy or the sociopathic personality.

Freud's deference to Fechner suggests to me more than a respect for his ideas.[22] "Old" and "great" Fechner with his miserable midlife breakdown and underworld experience, his passionate struggle between science and mysticism, observation and speculation, was probably for Freud an interior mentor, as Jung looked back to Carus and Paracelsus, Dorn and Goethe. The psychological tradition builds on its own tradition, not only in its ideas but in the figures we choose to illumine, and to help us carry, our own personal biography.

3

PSYCHE

These parallels, which expose the mythology in a psychological conceptual system, bear witness to the thesis that classical myths are not simply part of the past, belonging to another age or only to specialist scholars of Greek and Latin. Myth lives vividly in our symptoms and fantasies and in our conceptual systems. Myth is precisely that which gives these concepts, such as Freud's "unconscious" or "id," their vitality and credibility. We believe Freud, not only because of the reasoning of his logic or the empirical demonstration of his evidence. We feel conviction because of the metaphorical substructure in the theory, which evokes in our memorial psyche the archetypal realm of the underworld.

Thus our work on Freud brings out a fundamental tenet of archetypal psychology: the interchangeability of mythology and psychology. Mythology is a psychology of antiquity. Psychology is a mythology of modernity. The ancients had no psychology, properly speaking, but they had myths, the speculative tellings about humans in relation with more-than-human forces and images. We moderns have no mythology, properly speaking, but we have psychological systems, the speculative theories about humans in relation with more-than-human forces and images, today called fields, instincts, drives, complexes. This tenet of archetypal psychology—perhaps a hallmark distinguishing it from other psychologies—is also an operation. It offers the opportunity to reflect every psychological position as a fantasy or mythologem. It works as a self-critique of positivisms by means of myths. Our tenet also operates upon every mythic tale and figure, removing them from the realm of story only and pulling them down and in, showing how a myth precisely works in the psyche, in its habits of mind and heart. We seek to reflect back and forth between the two, myth and psyche, using them to provide insights for each other, preventing either from being taken on its own terms only.

DEPTH

The relationships between mythology and psychology appear strikingly in the term *depth psychology (Tiefenpsychologie)* proposed early in this century by Eugen Bleuler, the Zürich psychiatrist, as the appropriate name for the new science of psychoanalysis.[1] This move shifted attention from the activity of taking things apart to the vision of seeing them in depth. The new field was now on a different ground, one that was less physically scientific, because less oriented toward analytic reduction into parts, and more metaphysically philosophical, because the reduction now aimed toward more profound understanding. This different ground, however, was not a new ground. It was very old, for in the choice of this word, and its acceptance, there appears again an ancient image connecting psychology and depth.

Heraclitus (frg. 45) first brings together *psyche, logos,* and *bathun* ("depth"): "You could not find the ends of the soul though you travelled every way, so deep is its logos." As Bruno Snell says, "In Heraclitus the image of depth is designed to throw light on the outstanding trait of the soul and its realm: that it has its own dimension, that it is not extended in space."[2] Ever after Heraclitus depth became the direction, the quality, and the dimension of the psyche. Our familiar term *depth psychology* says quite directly: to study soul, we must go deep, and when we go deep, soul becomes involved. The logos of the soul, *psychology*, implies the act of travelling the soul's labyrinth in which *we can never go deep enough.*

Here we see that the metaphors we believe we choose for describing archetypal processes and ideas, such as Freud's "unconscious" and Bleuler's "depth psychology," are inherently part of those very processes and ideas themselves. It is as if the archetypal material chooses its own descriptive terms as one aspect of its self-expression. This would mean that 'naming' is not a nominalistic activity, but realistic indeed, because the name takes us into its reality. We might even submit that there is an archetypal selective factor involved in the invention of terms. Let us call this an archetypal semantics or phonetics on which archetypal hermeneutics is based. After all, to lead archetypal significance out of the language of psychology suggests that the significance is already 'there' in the words, their roots or their sounds.[3]

Much as Freud at the beginning of depth psychology resonates back to the underworld of mythology, so Heraclitus at the beginning of philosophy foreshadows the unconscious of psychology. One is obliged to turn to Heraclitus, as we shall be doing all along the way, to provide background and insight to depth psychology. Aristotle said that Heraclitus took soul as his *archon*, his first principle, which makes him the first depth psychologist in our tradition.[4] This means as well that we are obliged to read his fragments from that same perspective, one that places psyche first. As we read Freud mythologically, we read Heraclitus psychologically.

So, his statement about the depth of the soul also hints that visibilities—what is only natural—are never enough for the soul. It desires to go beyond, to go ever inward and deeper. Why? This too he answers, saying (frg. 54), "Invisible connection is stronger than visible." To arrive at the basic structure of things we must go into their darkness. Again, why? Because, says Heraclitus (frg. 123), "The real constitition of each thing is accustomed to hide itself," which has also been translated: "Nature loves to hide" (Burnet, p. 10: Wheelwright, p. 17). Shortly, we shall be examining the notions of hiding and invisibility in relation with Hades, but even before we do, we can grasp what Heraclitus implies. When we put together the few fragments we have just cited, we may realize that the depth dimension is the only one that can penetrate to what is hidden; and since only what is hidden is true nature of all things, including nature itself, then only the way of soul can lead to true insight. Heraclitus suggests that true equals deep, and he is opening the way for a psychological hermeneutic, a viewpoint of soul toward all things. It is as if he knew our English word *understand*, exploring it as if he had read Heidegger.

From Heraclitus we learn that soul is not only a region in Freud's topographical sense, or even a dimension in Heraclitus' own sense; it is an operation of penetrating, an insighting into depths that makes soul as it proceeds. If soul is a prime mover, then its primary movement is deepening, by which it increases its dimension, just as Freud added caverns and components to psychology by his topographical explorations. The pursuit of hidden connections in a dimension without limit accounts for the latent imperialism of psychology. There is no end to depth, and all things become soul. The basic elements of all things compose and decompose, generate and degenerate into soul (frg. 36), the first and last term of our moving world.

Elsewhere at some length, I have described this endless activity of soul-making and called it "psychologizing."[5] Now we are able to give a more distinct mythologem to the activity. The innate urge to go below appearances to the "invisible connection" and hidden constitution leads to the world interior to whatever is given. This autochthonous urge of the psyche, its native desire to understand psychologically, would seem to be akin to what Freud calls the *death drive* and what Plato presented (*Cratylus* 403c) as the desire for Hades. The urge shows itself in the analytical mind, which makes psyche by taking things apart. It works through destruction, the dissolving, decomposing, detaching, and disintegrating processes necessary both to alchemical psychologizing and to modern psychoanalyzing. We are able also now to understand the necessity of such terms as *psychoanalysis* (Freud) and *analytical psychology* (Jung) for soul-making. They describe a "disintegrative" *method* of depth referring to the mythologems of Hades.[5a]

HADES

Hades was of course the God of depths, the God of invisibles. He is himself invisible, which could imply that the invisible connection is Hades, and that the essential "what" that holds things in their form is the secret of their death. And if, as Heraclitus said, Nature loves to hide, then nature loves Hades.

Hades is said to have had no temples or altars in the upperworld[6] and his confrontation with it is experienced as a violence, a violation (Persephone's rape; the assaults on simple vegetative nymphs, Leuce and Minthe;[6a] and *Iliad*

5, 395 or Pindar *Ol.* 9, 33). He is so invisible in fact that the entire collection of Greek antique art shows no ideal portrait of Hades, such as we are familiar with of other Gods.[7] He had no representative attributes, except an eagle,[8] which brings out his shadowy affiliation with his brother, Zeus. He leaves no trace on earth, for no clan descends from him, no generations.[9]

Hades' name was rarely used. At times he was referred to as "the unseen one," more often as Pluto ("wealth," "riches") or as Trophonios ("nourishing"). These disguises of Hades have been taken by some interpreters to be covering euphemisms for the fear of death, but then why this particular euphemism and not some other? Perhaps Pluto is a description of Hades, much as Plato understood this God. Then, Pluto refers to the hidden wealth or the riches of the invisible. Hence, we can understand one reason why there was no cult and no sacrifice to him—Hades was the wealthy one, the giver of nourishment to the soul. Sometimes, he was fused with Thanatos ("Death")[10] of whom Aeschylus wrote, "Death is the only God who loves not gifts and cares not for sacrifices or libation, who has no altars and receives no hymns . . ." (frg. *Niobe*). On vase paintings when Hades is shown, he may have his face averted,[11] as if he were not even characterized by a specific physiognomy. All this 'negative' evidence does coalesce to form a definite image of a void, an interiority or depth that is unknown but nameable, there and felt even if not seen. Hades is not an absence, but a hidden presence—even an invisible fullness.

Etymological investigations into the root word for *death demon* show it to mean "hider."[12] To grasp better the ways in which Hades hides invisibly in things, let us take apart this concept, listening for the hidden connections, the metaphors, within the word *hidden* itself: (1) buried, shrouded, concealed from eyesight, whether a corpse or a *mysterium;*

(2) occult, esoteric, concealed in the sense of secret; (3) that which per se cannot be seen: non-visible as non-spatial, non-extended; (4) without light: dark, black; (5) that which cannot be seen on inspection, i.e., blocked, censored, forbidden, or obscured; (6) hidden, as contained within (interior) or as contained below (inferior), where the Latin *cella* ("subterranean storeroom") is cognate with the Old Irish *cuile* ("cellar") and *cel* ("death"), again cognate with our *hell;* (7) that which is experienced with dread and terror, a void, a nothing; (8) that which is experienced as hiding, e.g., withdrawing, turning away from life; (9) stealth, surreptitiousness, deceit, such as the hidden motives and unseen connections of Hermes. In short, Hades, the hidden hider, presides over both the crypt and cryptic, which gives to Heraclitus' phrase (frg. 123): "Nature loves to hide" *(physis kryptesthai philei),* a subtle and multiple implication indeed.

Some say that the cap or helmet Hades wears belongs primarily to Hermes and may have little or nothing to do with Hades.[13] This hat is a curious phenomenon: Hermes wears it, Hades wears it; Athene puts it on to beat Ares, and Perseus to overcome the Gorgon. It makes its wearer invisible. Evidently the explicit image of connection between Hermes and Hades (announced in the Homeric "Hymn to Hermes") is the headdress. Hermes and Hades share a certain style of covering their heads that both hides their thoughts and perceives hidden thoughts. It is their intentions that become invisible. We cannot perceive where their 'heads are at,' though we may have the sense of a hidden watch over our inmost thoughts. Because we can never discover what their covert minds intend, we consider them deceptive, unpredictable, frightening—or wise.

When we consider the House of Hades, we must remember that the myths—and Freud too—tell us that there is no time in the underworld. There is no decay, no progress, no change of any sort. Because time has nothing to do with the under-world, we may not conceive the underworld as "after" life, except as the afterthoughts within life. The House of Hades is a psychological realm now, not an eschatological realm later. It is not a far-off place of judgment over our actions but provides that place of judging now, and within, the inhib-iting reflection interior to our actions.

This simultaneity of the underworld with the daily world is imaged by Hades coinciding indistinguishably with Zeus, or identical with Zeus *chthonios*. The brotherhood of Zeus and Hades says that upper and lower worlds are the same; only the perspectives differ. There is only one and the same universe, coexistent and synchronous, but one brother's view sees it from above and through the light, the other from below and into its darkness. Hades' realm is contiguous with life, touching it at all points, just below it, its shadow brother *(Doppelgänger)* giving to life its depth and its psyche.

Because his realm was conceived as the final end of each soul, Hades is the final cause, the purpose, the very *telos* of every soul and every soul process. If so, then *all* psychic events have a Hades aspect, and not merely the sadistic or destructive events that Freud attributed to Thanatos. All soul processes, everything in the psyche, moves towards Hades. As the *finis* is Hades, so the *telos* is Hades. Everything would become deeper, moving from the visible connections to the invisible ones, dying out of life. When we search for the most revelatory meaning in an experience, we get it most starkly by letting it go to Hades, asking what has this to do with 'my' death. Then essence stands out.

Here too Hades has bearing on psychological theory. A psychology that emphasizes the final point of view—Jung's, for instance, and Adler's—is restating the Hades perspective, even if these psychologies do not go right to the end of their ends. I mean by this that the finalism in psychology seems to shy away from the full consequences of mythology, in which the finalism is not a theory only but is the experience in soul of its call to Hades.

Now hold here a moment. Let us beware of taking this call as literal death, of which so much is spoken and written today, that we begin to believe we know all about what we know nothing about. Literal death is becoming a clichéd mystery, that is, we have best-seller evidence about the unknowable.

Rather, by the call to Hades I am referring to the sense of purpose that enters whenever we talk about soul. What does it want? What is it trying to say (in this dream, this symptom, experience, problem)? Where is my fate or individuation process going? If we stare these questions in the face, of course we know where our individuation process is going— to death. This unknowable goal is the one absolutely sure event of the human condition. Hades is the unseen one and yet absolutely present.

The call to Hades suggests that all aspects of the process of the soul must be read finally, not only as part of the general human process toward death, but as particular events of and in that death. Each facet then is a finished image in itself, completing its purpose that is at the same time unending, not literally unending in time but limitless in depth. In other words, we can stop nowhere—and anywhere—because the end is not in time but in death, where death means the *telos* or fulfillment of anything, or, we can stop anywhere, because from the final point of view everything is an end in itself. The goal is always now.

A true finalistic psychology will show its ends in its means. We will be able to see its end goal of death in the methods it uses to work towards it. Therefore, to live fully into the consequences of the finalistic view means to bear the perspective of Hades and the underworld toward each psychic event. We ask: what is the purpose of this event for my soul, for my death? Such questions extend the dimension of depth without limit, and again psychology is pushed by Hades into an imperialism of soul, reflecting the imperialisms of his kingdom and the radical dominion of death.

THE BROOD OF NIGHT

The strong contrast between day and night, as well as the housing of dreams only with the nightworld of sleep and with death, begins before Heraclitus. Already in Homer's *Iliad* (14.321; 16.454,671,681; 11.241; cf *Od.* 13.79 f.), Hypnos ("sleep") and Thanatos ("death") are twin brothers. They are not mere poetic allegories of abstract ideas. "Hypnos in Homer is already a real person able to decide whether to grant sleep to someone or not."[14] These very vivid, very powerful persons, who govern our darkness, are sons of Night, according to Hesiod's *Theogony* (211 ff.). They are part of her great brood, which includes Old Age, Envy, Strife, Doom, Lamentation, Destiny, Deceit—and Dreams *(oneiroi)*.[15]

In the Odyssey, Homer locates dreams either in the House of Hades as part of his realm or close by in their own house in the Western ocean, where the sun goes down. For Virgil the entire brood of Night resided in the underworld, and this remained a convention in Roman poetry. Ovid says in his *Metamorphoses* (11.614) that dreams appear like creatures of the underworld, without bodily life. Homer (*Od.* 11.204–22) had put the same thought in reverse: the psyche of the dead flits about and hovers to and fro, like a dream. Orphic mythology also groups dreams with death and with sleep, which is there called the brother of death and of forgetting.[16] A more distant parallel comes from the Hindu *Athar'va-Veda*, where it is said that the dream comes from Yama's world. Yama is the lord of the dead.

We see that the archetypal cluster to which dreams belong, according to this most ancient and continuous model in our tradition, is the world of Night. Each dream is a child of Night, affiliated closely with Sleep and Death, and with Forgetting (Lethe) all that the daily world remembers. Dreams have no father, no call upwards. They come only from Night, and they have no home other than in that dark realm. Such then is the genealogy of dreams, the myth of their origins, describing their archetypal kinship, telling us where they belong.

I have stressed both the historical length of the tradition and its poetic strength, believing that the mythopoeic presents archetypal truth through its imaginative power, just as the historical exhibits archetypal truth through its power to endure. Freud again is witness. When he said that dreams protect sleep and that is their sole purpose, he put dreams and sleep into their ancient fraternal connection. In the same context, when Freud said that the architect of dreams is Eros (*OD*, p. 66; *NIL*, p. 28), because dreams by fulfilling erotic wishes also protect sleep, he was again imagining Eros as part of the brood of Night, just as Cicero did.[17]

If we follow this notion of Eros, then it is the brother of death and not the principle that will save us from it. There would then be a closer bond between what goes on in dreams and a love that fulfills itself in darkness, in the intangible bodies of psychic images. Thus there is a downward love, and not only an Eros stretching its arms towards the horizon of others. This downward love appeared all through later antiquity as statues of Amor, wings folded, his torch pointing downward. The same yearning for the depths becomes literalized in romanticism and even enacted in suicidal love pacts.

We may realize here that Eros is not so simple, neither in life nor in myth. Is Eros the connecting life principle, a libido that wants unions, as Freud says, and does it pertain more to 'the feminine' as Jung says? Is Eros an ever-needy child of Want (Plato), a sleepy languorous little boy, or a son of Venus, arrowing straight into our life her desires and her pleasures? Does he come 'first' as a progenitor of every-thing, as some myth held, or 'first' as a virtue in the Christian sense? Or is Eros a brother of Hades himself, as Schelling said? Myth leaves the definition of Eros in perplexity—or rather it only speaks of Eros *within a specific context,* such as this one, which puts Eros into the bed of Sleep, Death, and Dreams among the brood of Night. Modern statements about Eros, of which contemporary psychology is so romanti-cally resplendent, carry no validity unless these statements be developed against one or another of the precise archetypal backgrounds to Eros. What a person says about love tells more about the person than about love. It tells within which fantasy his or her experience of Eros is being enacted.

The brood of Night gives to the dream an atmosphere that is far from the happy optimism of growth psychology or the secret delight of sexual desire. We are not being told that our dreams help us, that they round out our lives by indicating the direction of our creative tendencies. Nor are we being told that dreams pour out of an id-pool of libidinal pleasure, a wishing well. Instead, they are akin to deceits and conflicts, to the lamentations of ageing, to the doom of our destiny—in a word: depression. The dream takes us down-ward, and the mood that corresponds with this movement is the slowing, saddening, introspective feeling of depression.

This depression has different faces. To the heroic conscious-ness of the very ancient world, Night was the source of evil, while to the mystic consciousness of the Orphics, Night was a depth of love (Eros) and light (Phanes). Our consciousness today is less mystic than heroic, and we need incantations to summon Hypnos or Hermes to help us drop off to sleep, a ritual of prayer, toothbrushing and teddy bear, of masturba-tion, food cramming, and the late show, of nightcap and sleeping pill. The basic bedtime story of our culture is that to sleep is to dream and to dream is to enter the House of the Lord of the Dead, where our complexes lie in wait. We do not go gentle into that good night.

UNDERGROUND AND UNDERWORLD

When using the word *underworld*, it is imperative to keep in mind a distinction made by some classicists.[18] This distinction is of great psychological importance, because it frees the psychic realm from nature. *Chthōn* and *gē* ("underworld" and "underground") do not necessarily refer to the same region or evoke identical feelings. "Chthōn with its derivatives refers in origin to the cold, dead depths and has nothing to do with fertility."[19] This kind of deep ground is not the same as the dark earth; and the Great Lady *(potnia chthōn)*, who sends black-winged dreams[20] and who can also be called Erinys,[21] cannot simply be merged into the single figure of the Great Earth Mother.

Psychology's great-mother complex has swallowed even her own differentiations. Small wonder that this complex is also called "uroboric consciousness," for even she herself vanishes into an interpretive monotony that makes me believe that the monotheistic psychology I so often belabor is less a mimesis of ancient Hebrewism (within and alongside of which there was much space for imaginal variety) than it is a mimesis of the Great Mother. Monism as Momism. Be this as it may, when we read analytical psychology today to discover about the 'chthonic,' we find it has taken on her meaning of primitive earthiness. Moreover, as primitive and earthy, it must mean matriarchal and feminine. Thus our instinctual body, whether in flesh or image, in men or women, in the past or now, belongs to her, and we must become murderous heroes to get it back. The great-mother complex hangs the trinket of female gender on agriculture and fertility, as well as on the earth, body, instinct, and on depth. This move ignores that *chthonic* is an epithet belonging also to Hermes, Dionysos, and to Zeus himself; and it ignores, in the sense of "is ignorant about," a chthon that cannot be identified with instinctual body or earthy soil.

Let us be clear: the chthonic is not only female, not only instinctual, not only physical, and it does not have to do with fertility rites. As Wilamowitz-Moellendorf said, "If modern scholars, who talk so much about chthonian cults, think in this connection of agriculture and all that goes along with Demeter in that sphere, they have not accustomed their ear to the overtones of Greek words."[22] The two words *gē* and *chthōn* imply two worlds, the first of the earth and in it, the second below the earth and beyond it.

There are even *three* distinctions here which have been imagined as levels of earth: an earthed imagination in keeping with Ge herself, whose name we still find in ge-ography, ge-ology, and ge-ometry. The first of these distinctions is between Demeter's horizontal green plain with its activities of growth and Ge, the earth below Demeter. This second level, Ge, may be imagined as the physical and psychic ground of an individual or community, its 'place on earth,' with its natural rights, rituals, and laws (Ge-Themis). Here, Ge serves as a fundament on which human life depends even more deeply than on food and fertility. Ge would be like the rituals and laws that guarantee fertility, like a governing maternal principle that makes material fertility possible and is its spiritual ground, and then beneath these the third, chthon, the depths, the dead's world.

Of course, a polytheistic mind does not firmly divide these "levels," and so Demeter-Ge-chthon frequently merge in epithet and cult.[23] (What scholars imagine about the Greeks does not correspond, nor must it, with what the Greeks imagine about the Gods.) Also against my distinctions is the fact that one can as well view the entire complex of the underworld from the perspective of Ge, as does Patricia Berry.[24] She then is able to see much of the chthonic spirit that I meet in Hades to be equally present in Ge, and that Gaia (Ge) is both material, maternal earth, and chthonic void with its own spirit.

The question here partly turns on how one regards earth.

The strata of meanings which I have just laid out in terms of Demeter-Ge-chthon imagines a nonphysical earth or *terre pur,* below or beyond and maybe prior to the ground that we touch. Some etymologists and classicists try to relate the three "levels" culturally, believing one level of meaning to be prior in the sense of historically earlier than another; as if in a genealogy fantasy themselves, they try to derive one level from another, tracing the historical development of these three concepts. For example, Kirk refers to the very early pre-Socratic Pherecydes of Syros (frg. 1), who placed Chthon at the beginning with Zeus and Chronos, "but Chthonie acquired the name Ge. . . ."[25]

Rather than enter the arguments of historical fantasy, I would keep to the psychological distinctions reflected in the three words and three personifications. Ge herself shows two aspects. On the one hand, she has to do with retributive justice, with the Fates, and she has also mantic, oracular powers. (Ge *chthōnia* was worshipped on Mykonos, together with Zeus *chthōnios* and Dionysos Leneus, as she was linked with the chthonic Pluto and Hermes and the Erinyes at Athens [Areopagus].) This is the "great lady" who sends the black-winged dreams and is appropriately the mother of Themis ("Justice"). This spiritual side of her can be distinguished, on the other hand, from the physical Ge to whom grains and fruits were given (Ge-Demeter). Demeter too has a mystery aspect; her daughter Persephone belongs to Hades and has an underworld function. The spiritual significance may not be reduced to the physical (death cult to fertility rites, sense of justice to agricultural rituals) without ignoring the blatant fact that there are different figures with different epithets. In other words, even the earth and nature have their *psychic* function as well as their terrestrial ones, and one may serve the earth and be on the ground in more ways than one, i.e., through *psychic activities,* and not only through natural ones.

The distinction between chthonic and earthy, between invisible fundaments and tangible ground, between darkness of soul and blackness of soil, between psychical depths and concrete depths, initiation mystery and fertility rite, finds a comparison in a distinction between three Egyptian hieroglyphs, one for earth, another for Aker or entrance to the underground at the edge of existence, and yet another for the realm of the dead of Anubis, the blue-black jackal-dog.[26] Once again, the distinctions are presented in terms of distance. The most radical classicist of the late nineteenth century, Erwin Rohde, friend of Nietzsche, said in his great work *Psyche* that the underworld of Hades and Persephone is so remote from our world that those removed there "can have no influence upon the life and doings of men on earth."[27] He further emphasized the distinction between the underground of Ge and the chthonic underworld by saying that Ge "in actual worship was seldom found among the groups of male and female deities of a chthonic nature such as were worshipped together at many places."[28]

The spiritual quality of the underworld stands forth most clearly in descriptions of Tartaros, which, from Hesiod onward, was imagined to be at the very bottom of Hades, its farthest chasm. Tartaros was compared with the sky—as distant from the earth as the heaven above, and it was personified as the son of ether and of earth,[29] that is, a realm of dust, a composite of the most material and immaterial.

As the fantasy of Tartaros developed, it became more and more a pneumatic region of air and wind.[30] Unlike the Christian hell of fire,[31] in the imagination of late antiquity Tartaros was a region of dense cold air without light.[32] Hence, Hades often was spoken of as having wings, just as in the Gilgamesh Epic, Enkidu dreams of his death as a transformation into a bird, his arms covered with feathers. The dead are clad like birds, their element evidently air.[33]

The volatilization of the underworld contrasts it sharply with the ground under our feet. In the Alexandrian age, the netherworld lost its localization in the earth altogether—that is, it became free of natural literalism—and was geographically transposed to the underside of the world.[34] There was now a lower hemisphere. The word subterranean *(hypogeios,* or "below ge")* referred to the whole celestial hemisphere curved below our earth and which, like Hades, must necessarily be invisible from our perspective. It cannot be seen from our usual standpoint. Already then the dayworld and the nightworld, the two sides of the romantic soul, were conceived in a geographical theology of upperworld and netherworld. In "this theology the world is divided into two halves by the line of the horizon; the upper hemisphere is the domain of the living and the higher gods, the lower that of the dead and the infernal gods."[35] The Egyptians had carried into extreme detail this reversed world below our feet. The dead walked upside down, feet up, heads down. "People there walk with their feet against the ceiling. This has the unpleasant consequence that digestion goes in the reverse direction, so that excrements arrive in the mouth."[36] The Underworld is converse to dayworld, and so its behavior will be obverse, perverse. What is merely shit from the daytime perspective— or what Freud called day-residues—becomes soul food when turned upside down. The way we go about there, the way we ruminate, even logic is stood on its head, for there our heads are in another place. (In Chapter 6 we shall look at some contemporary examples of this "upsidedownness," including excrements in dreams.)

Might there be an archetypal figure within Freud's "day residues" that are the material of the dream? Could these leftover scraps refer to the household garbage that was sacrificed to Hekate (*Cults* 2:515)? Hekate has long been implicated in dream interpretations. Both the magical view that considers dreams to be foretellings and the nineteenth-century mechanistic view that attributes them to waste products of physiological sensations (garbage) show Hekate's influence. When she becomes equated with Nyx (night), as in Spenser and at times in Shakespeare, then dreams become her province and our interpretative ideas reflect her perspectives.

We may continue this tradition, although in a different manner. Yes, the dream is made of scraps that belong to the Goddess who makes sacred the waste of life, so that it all counts, it all matters. Offering the dream to "the mysteries of Hekate and the night" (*King Lear,* act 1, scene 1) means giving back the regurgitations that "come up" in dreams without attempts to save them morally or to find their dayworld use. The junk of the soul is primordially saved by Hekate's blessing, and even our trashing ourselves can be led back to her. The messy life is a way of entering her domain and becoming a "child of Hekate." Our part is only to recognize that there is a myth in the mess so as to dispose of the day residues at the proper place, that is, to place them at Hekate's altar. Ritually, the garbage was placed at night at a crossroads, so that each dream may lead off in at least three directions besides the one we have come from. Hekate, who has traditionally been represented with three heads, keeps us looking and listening in many ways at once.

Because the underworld differs so radically from the underground, that which has its home there, dreams, must refer to a psychic or pneumatic world of ghosts, spirits, ancestors, souls, daimones. These are invisible by nature, and not merely invisible because they have been forgotten or repressed. This world is fluid, or dusty, fiery, muddy, or aetherial, so there is nothing firm to hold to—unless we develop intuitive instruments for seizing impalpables that slip through our fingers or burn at the touch.

By locating the dream among these impalpable fundamentals in Hades, we will begin to find that dreams reflect an underworld of essences rather than an underground of root and seed. They present images of being rather than of becoming. We will learn that a dream is less a comment on life

and an indication as to where it is growing, than it is a statement from the chthonic depths, the cold, dense, unchanging
state—what we so often today call psychopathic because, as
Freud saw, the dream does not show morality, human feelings, or the sense of time. We can no longer turn to the
dream in hopes of progress, transformation, and rebirth.

I think too that the underworld teaches us to abandon
our hopes for achieving unification of personality by means
of the dream. The underworld spirits are plural. So much
is this the case that the *di manes* (underworld spirits), who
were the Roman equivalent of the Greek *theoi chthōnioi,* have
no native singular form. Even individual dead persons were
spoken of plurally, as *di manes.*[37] "The ancient Egyptian
was thought to live after death in a multiplicity of forms,
each of these forms was the full man himself" (*Ba,* p. 113).
The underworld is an innumerable community of figures.
The endless variety of figures reflects the endlessness of the
soul, and dreams restore to consciousness this sense of multiplicity. The polytheistic perspective is grounded in the
chthonic depths of the soul. A psychotherapy that reflects
these depths can therefore make no attempt at achieving undi-
vided individuality or encouraging a personal identity as a
unified wholeness. Instead, psychotherapeutic emphasis will
be upon the disintegrative effects of the dream, which also
confronts us with our moral dis-integrity, our psychopathic
lack of a central hold on ourselves. Dreams show us to be
plural and that each of the forms that figure there are "the
full man himself," full potentials of behavior. Only by falling
apart (*RP,* pp. 53–112) into the multiple figures do we extend
consciousness to embrace and contain its psychopathic potentials.

We get into difficulties when we try to read the deep
chthonic level from the viewpoints of Demeter or of Ge.
To perceive the chthonic with Demeter's eyes is to take the
dream as signal for literal action and to translate it with

naturalistic ethics into a moralized world. To take a dream as containing an immoral implication or a moral indication for setting matters right and redressing a balance is to read it from the Ge-Themis-Dike perspective. Perhaps we need the intervention of another lady of the underworld, Hekate, who was especially adept with ghosts, who both brought and banned fear, and who had nothing to do with the round of human life (marriage, birth, agriculture), herself without brother or sister or any descendants. "Her worship was without morality."[38] Hekate's underworld perspective reaches to the chthonic depth of the dream, which, on the one hand, is a simple statement of essence—how spectral things look when stripped of their human context—and, on the other, elicits our psychopathy.

The region of the soul in which dreams have their home is deeper than flesh-and-blood urges, which we have been, mistakenly, calling chthonic, as if it were the same as natural, as if the underworld referred to *ira* and *cupiditas*, the blood-soul, the *thymos*. This all is earthy; the natural, physical, somatic soul of emotions. Our modern word *unconscious* has become a catch-all, collecting into one clouded reservoir all fantasies of the deep, the lower, the baser, the heavier (depressed), and the darker. We have buried in the same monolithic tomb called The Unconscious the red and earthy body of the primeval Adam, the collective common man and woman, and the shades, phantoms, and ancestors. We cannot distinguish a compulsion from a call, an instinct from an image, a desirous demand from a movement of imagination. Looking into the night from the white light of the dayworld (where the term *unconscious* was fashioned), we cannot tell the red from the black. So we read dreams for all sorts of messages at once—somatic, personal, psychic, mantic, ancestral, practical, confusing instinctual and emotional life with the realm of death.

The pronounced distinction between emotion and soul, be-

tween emotional man and psychological man, comes out in
another of Heraclitus' fragments (85): ". . . whatever it
[thymos] wishes it buys at the price of soul." *Thymos,* the
earlier Greek experience of emotional consciousness or moist
soul, did not belong in the underworld.[39] So, to consider
the dream as an emotional wish costs soul; to mistake the
chthonic as the natural loses psyche. We cannot claim to
be psychological when we read dream images in terms of
drives or desires. Whatever counsel an analyst gives about
emotional life, supposing it drawn from dreams, refers to
his experience, which he reflects from the dreams. It is not
in the dreams. He is "sup-posing" about them, that is, he
is "putting onto" them what he knows about life.

What one knows about life may not be relevant for what
is below life. What one knows and has done in life may be
as irrelevant to the underworld as clothes that adjust us to
life and the flesh and bones that the clothes cover. For in
the underworld all is stripped away, and life is upside down.
We are further than the expectations based on life experience,
and the wisdom derived from it.

Again, we can follow Heraclitus (frg. 27): "When men
die there awaits them what they neither expect nor even imagine." The word translated here as "expect" is related in Greek
to "hope" *(elpis),* so that the specific hope that is abandoned
(Dante, *Inferno 3*) on entering the underworld perspective
is the fantasy of daylife expectations and flesh-and-blood illusions. Souls in Hades are "incurable" said Plato. There is
no alteration to be hoped for. Such hope would be hope
for the wrong thing. We need more the hope of St. Paul,
which is a hope of invisibles and for invisibles, than the hope
of Pandora, who, as the wife of Prometheus, contains a hidden
hope, which he makes evident in his mission to help mankind.
To go deep into a dream requires abandoning hope, the hope
that rises in the morning and would turn the dream to its
purposes. At the Hades level of the dream there is neither

hope nor despair. They cancel each other out; and we can move beyond the language of expectations, measuring progressions and regressions, ego strengthening and weakening, coping and failing.

Let me once more try to draw this distinction between the underground of vital, emotional life and the underworld. Heraclitus said (frg. 15):

If it were not in honour of Dionysus
that they conducted the procession and sang
the hymn to the male organ, their activity would be
completely shameless.
Hades and Dionysus are the same, no matter
how much they go mad and rave celebrating
bacchic rites in honour of the latter.

The passage has given scholars—those who accept this phrasing at all—so much trouble partly because it juxtaposes, even identifies, the very different realms we are keeping distinct: psychic essences and emotional nature.[40]

This fragment refers to the mystery of a sacred procession, and it must be read with a similar reverence, even as a revelation of something profound in acts that seem shamelessly pornographic, raving, and mad. It is therefore not enough to pass it off with a moral generality, as some interpreters do, that Heraclitus means that even the wildest life forces also lead to death, or to let it go by, as other interpreters do, as another of his metaphysical generalities about the sameness of life and death (frgs. 62, 88). We are still left with the vivid imagery of this mystery in the sexual language that is so fundamental to psychology. So, Heraclitus, as one psychologist to another, across the centuries I read you to be saying that for this troublesome distinction between emotion and soul, between the perspective of vitality (Dionysos) and the perspective of psyche (Hades), sexual fantasy holds a secret. In what seems most evident, public, and concrete, there is also something covered in shame, hidden and invisible.

The Hades within Dionysos says that there is an invisible meaning in sexual acts, a significance for soul in the phallic parade, that all our life force, including the polymorphous and pornographic desires of the psyche, refer to the underworld of images. Things in life, no matter how full of life, are not only natural. Dionysos is also a "downer."[41] We may believe we are living life only on the level of life, but we cannot escape the psychic significance of what we are doing. Soul is made in the rout of the world. What has meaning for life has meaning for soul at the same moment, so consider your living in the light of the Hades within it.

The other side of the mysterious identity, the Dionysos within Hades, says that there is a *zoe*, a vitality in all underworld phenomena. The realm of the dead is not as dead as we expect it. Hades too can rape and also seize the psyche through sexual fantasies. Although without *thymos*, body, or voice, there is a hidden libido in the shadows. The images in Hades are also Dionysian—not fertile in the natural sense, but in the psychic sense, imaginatively fertile. There is an imagination below the earth that abounds in animal forms, that revels and makes music. There is a dance in death. Hades and Dionysos are the same. As Hades darkens Dionysos toward his own tragedy, Dionysos softens and rounds out Hades into his own richness. Farnell describes their fusion as a "mildness joined with melancholy."[42]

UNDERWORLD AND PSYCHE

In the Homeric imagination, the dead lack both *phrenes* and *thymos*, and thus they ask Ulysses for the blood of life. Achilles in the *Iliad* (23. 100; cf. 11. 204–22) tells just what is and what is not present in the underworld: "Ah me, then there is even in the halls of Hades a *psyché* and *eidolon* [a "soul" and a "phantom shape"], but *phrenes* there are not therein at all" (*OET*, p. 59). According to Onians, the *phrenes* refers rather to the breath consciousness of the lungs and its voice. The dead (with the exception of Teiresias) do not have this kind of consciousness derived from the daily in-and-out exchange with life. The *thymos* that the dead seek from the living is the blood vapour which they get from sacrificed animals. (Remember Fechner's 'return from the dead' after eating the meat of the pig?)[43] Even as late as Ovid, the dead are shades who wander "bodiless, bloodless and boneless."[44]

But psyche remains. The underworld is a realm of only psyche, a purely psychical world. What one meets there is soul, as the figures Ulysses meets—Ajax, Anticleia, Agamemnon—are called psyches, and the way they move is compared with dreams; or to say this in another way, underworld is the mythological style of describing a psychological cosmos.

Put more bluntly: underworld is psyche. When we use the word *underworld,* we are referring to a wholly psychic perspective, where one's entire mode of being has been de-substantialized, killed of natural life, and yet is in every shape and sense and size the exact replica of natural life. The underworld Ba of Egypt and the underworld *psyché* of Homeric Greece was the whole person as in life but devoid of life. This means that the underworld perspective radically alters our experience of life. It no longer matters on its own terms but only in terms of the psyche. To know the psyche at its basic depths, for a true depth psychology, one must go to the underworld.

It would be a rewarding venture now to make one descent after another, like a culture hero, through Etruscan tombs, across the Činvat bridge of Iran, following the Babylonian descents of Ishtar and Enkidu, in the steps of the Hellenistic-Christian *nekyia* described by Dieterich,[45] and come back up with authoritative reports. This would be heroic, hubristic, and too much.[46] Also it is not the aim of this book, which is not a comparative mythology of the underworld, but a revision of the dream in terms of it.

Jung superbly summed up the primary message imparted by the guidebooks (Egyptian and Tibetan[47]) to the "land of the dead," saying that they teach us "the primacy of the psyche, for that is the one thing which life does not make clear to us" (*CW* 11, § 841), or, as Burnet said of the Homeric *psyché:* "It is not of the slightest importance during life" (*ERE* 11:738b),[48] just as the Egyptian Ba-soul "never means life" (*ibid.*, p. 752b), appearing only in connection with death.[49] Robert Lowie states: "the 'psyche' (i.e., the entity which functions after death or in dreams or trances) . . . —instead of actively functioning in living and conscious human beings—is quite dormant in the conception of most primitive peoples."[50]

It is in the light of psyche that we must read all underworld descriptions. Being in the underworld means psychic being, being psychological, where soul comes first. Underworld fantasies and anxieties are transposed descriptions of psychic existence. Underworld images are ontological statements about the soul, how it exists in and for itself beyond life. So we read all movements towards this realm of death, whether they be fantasies of decay, images of sickness in dreams, repetitive compulsions, or suicidal impulses, as movements towards a more psychological perspective. We are making a closer connection between psyche and Thanatos, in fact, taking up again Freud's main line of thought at the end of his life.

Freud's preoccupation with Thanatos had begun much earlier and more personally. He was obsessed with his own death. As he approached it, and as Thanatos emerged in his theoretical imagination, his stoic patience with his own dying became more and more exemplary. As we are reading underworld descriptions in a psychological light, we also may read psychology's concern with death in light of the underworld. Ever since Freud, death has haunted the profession, first in Freud, then in the suicides of his early associates (Silberer and Tausk), and of Jung's (Honegger).[51] Psychiatric suicide still goes on. According to Walter Freeman, physicians are more prone to suicide than men in other occupations, and at the top of the suicide list of medical specialists are psychiatrists.[52] His figures show that between 1895 and 1965, 203 American psychiatrists were officially reported to have killed themselves—81 of whom were still in their twenties or thirties.

Death is the fundamental fear of the profession, actively working as its fundamental metaphor. The contemporary growth cult of optimistic therapies that focus on peaks, freedom, cures, and creativity is a manic defense against psychotherapy's own ground, an acting-out promulgated as therapy. To be a *psycho*therapist and work in depth, one must in some way or another cooperate with Hades.

The intervention of Hades turns the world upside down. The point of view of life ceases. Now phenomena are seen not only through the eyes of Eros and human life and love, but also through Thanatos, their cold unmoving depths unconnected to life. By turning matters upside down in this way, we participate in Hades' rape, which is, let us remember, not just psychopathy, but a central initiatory mystery in the Eleusis myths. This rape threatens the intact psychological system that takes its strength from life, holding to human relationships and the natural ways of Demeter's daughter.[53] Rape moves the Persephone soul from the being of Demeter's daughter to the being of Hades' wife, from the natural being of generation, what is given to a daughter by mothering life, to the psychic being of marriage with what is alien, different, and is not given. The experience of the underworld is overwhelming and must be made. This style of the underworld experience is overwhelming, it comes as violation, dragging one out of life and into the Kingdom that the Orphic Hymn to Pluto describes as "void of day." So it often says on Greek epitaphs that entering Hades is "leaving the sweet sunlight."[54]

The archetypal psychology of the Hades-Persephone-Demeter triangle did not cease in Greece.[55] Aspects of the psychological mystery of Eleusis still take place in the soul today. The Persephone experience occurs to us each in sudden depressions, when we feel ourselves caught in hatefulness, cold, numbed, and drawn downward out of life by a force we cannot see, against which we would flee, distractedly thrashing about for naturalistic explanations and comforts for what is happening so darkly. We feel invaded from below, assaulted, and we think of death.

To be raped into the underworld is not the only mode of experiencing it. There are many other modes of descent. But when it comes in this radical fashion, then we may know which mytheme has encased us. We are dragged into Hades' chariot only if we are out in Demeter's green fields, seductively innocent with playmates among flowers. That world has to open up. When the bottom falls out, we feel only the black abyss of despair, but this is not the only way to experience even this mytheme.

For instance, Hekate was supposedly standing by the whole time, listening or watching.[56] There is evidently a perspective that can witness the soul's struggles without the flap of Persephone or the disaster of Demeter. In us is also a dark angel (Hekate was also called *angelos*), a consciousness (and she was called *phosphoros*) that shines in the dark and that witnesses such events because it already is aware of them a priori. This part has an a priori connection with the underworld through sniffing dogs and bitchery, dark moons, ghosts, garbage, and poisons. Part of us is not dragged down but always lives there, as Hekate is partly an underworld Goddess. From this vantage point we may observe our own catastrophes with a dark wisdom that expects little else.

May I point out in passing that the references to ancient Greece are not aimed at reconstructing historically how the Greeks took the Hades-Persephone mytheme, or death, or dreams. To place dreams with Hypnos, Nyx, Hekate, Thanatos, and Chthon is not to give them a cult or ritual location in Greek culture, but to give them imaginal location in ours. We are constructing their imaginal background, their home, the world in which they find their likeness. The only imaginal location we have had until now has been Freud's topology of the unconscious, which we are here reestablishing as a psychological *topos*.

Furthermore, to place dreams with the chthonic underworld does not assume that dreams may not refer to Gods other than Night and her brood. We know, for instance, that it is to Hermes that one turns for dreams, indicating that they could be sent through him from any of the Gods, since he carried their messages.[57] Many Gods and heroes have chthonic aspects and epithets, so that we may descend through many archetypal styles, not only as does Persephone. That Hermes brought dreams and that Hermes is the sole way to Hades, as that same Homeric Hymn states, leads us back to the same *topos,* for even if the activity of dreaming refers to Hermes, it is this God's *chthonic* aspect from which comes the dream activity. Dreams themselves are neither Gods, nor even messages from the Gods except as transmitted through Hermes, whose peculiarly twisted ways are as unfathomable and deceptive as the psyche's depths.[58] That dreams come via Hermes may help us to keep from divinizing them in psychotherapy, or taking them as divinations, or believing that, by brilliant interpretations, we can outwit the God after whom is named both their hermetic closedness and the hermeneutics by which we would reveal them.

IMAGES AND SHADOWS

"Entering the underworld" refers to a transition from the material to the psychical point of view. Three dimensions become two as the perspective of nature, flesh, and matter fall away, leaving an existence of immaterial, mirrorlike images, *eidola.* We are in the land of soul. As Nilsson says, "*Eidolon . . .* signifies simply 'image' and always keeps this sense. . . . for the Greeks the soul was an image."[59]

We have to be careful about the words we use for describing these *eidola.* They are not substantial, and so we may not use our convenient substantializing language. We may not just say they *are* this or that, or say that existence in the underworld *is* so and so. We may speak of *eidola* only as they "seem," "appear to be," or what they "liken unto." Our statements must be prefixed by an "as," as if that little word is the coin we offer Charon for taking us across the separating waters between two kinds of speech. The dead speak differently: they whisper. Their talk has lost its positive substance, its natural certainty. We must lean in close to hear this kind of speech.

Eidola may be distinguished from ikons, which are better compared with pictorial copies, visible things out-there that we can touch, even make. The word *eidolon* relates with Hades himself *(aidoneus)* and with *eidos,* ideational forms and shapes, the ideas that form and shape life, but are so buried in it that we only "see" them when pulled out in abstractions. So, we are speaking of images that are at the same time invisible. We are inside the imaginative mind.

Another way of putting this underworld would be to stress the shadowy or shade aspect. *Skia* was another word the Greek imagination used for underworld figures. The persons there are shades. So, we must imagine a world without light in which shadows move. Yet how can we speak about shadows in the dark, since, for upperworld consciousness, shadows result only from physical things blocking the light. How can there be shadows in the dark? The problem is very much like trying to sense the movement of one's own shadow. Trying to catch a glimmer of the shape behind the scenes, to tune into what else is going on in what seems to be a natural action or simple conversation is precisely "trying to see shadows in the dark." It is to notice the fantasy in the moment, to witness the psyche's shadow play in our unconscious daily living.

Consciousness of this sort is reflective, watching not just the physical reality in front of the eyeballs and by means of them, but seeing into the flickering patterns within that physical reality, and within the eyes themselves. It is a perception of perception, or as Jung said about images: they are the self-perception of instinct. Our blind instinctual life may be self-reflected by means of imagining, not after or before events in the closet of introspection, but as an eye or ear that catches the image of the event while it occurs.

So again, entering the underworld is like entering the mode of reflection, mirroring, which suggests that we may enter the underworld by means of reflection, by reflective means: pausing, pondering, change of pace, voice, or glance, dropping levels. Such reflection is less willed and directed; it is less determinedly introspective like a heroic descent into the underworld to see what's going on there.

Let us rather imagine it to be more Hermetic, a cocked ear, a sideways look, a suspicious fish eye, or intuitional feelings and thoughts that appear in the midst of life and twist life into psyche.

The movement from three-dimensional physical perception to the two dimensions of psychical reflection is first felt as a loss: *thymos* gone, we hunger, bewailing, paralyzed, repetitive. We want blood. Loss does characterize underworld experiences, from mourning to the dream, with its peculiar feeling of incompleteness, as if there is still more to come that we didn't get, always a concealment within it, a lost bit. A life that is lived in close connection with the psyche does indeed have an ongoing feeling of loss. It would be noble to believe this to be the enduring sacrifice that the soul required, but it does not feel so noble. Instead, we experience the humiliating inferiority of uncertainty and an impairment of potential. Socrates, who considered his main task to be care of soul, regularly stated that he didn't really know anything. A sense of infirmity goes with soul, which does not mean taking the loss literally as in neurasthenic, depressive, and hysterical neuroses, where one escapes the soul's work by identifying with it. The experience of loss in its various forms and the literalizing of the experience in theory (the negative mother, absent father, deprived childhood) remain fundamental to psychology.[60] This phenomenon again points to the underworld and its absent dimension.

Loss is not the whole of it, however, because the dimension sensed as loss is actually the presence of the void. Actually, we are experiencing a different dimension, and the price of admission to it is the loss of the material viewpoint. From one perspective, a dimension is given up, but this is to gain Hades and the chambering echoes that are his Halls. Even if we have lost a certain extension of ourselves into physical space and the world of action, here in depth there is space enough to take in the same physical world but in another way. Here we gain contact with the soul of all that is lost in life and with the souls of the lost. Hades is also Pluto; the "void-of-day" with only two dimensions is also a richness and nourishment and vast receptivity. Pictures of Pluto show his cornucopia, like a great ear, spilling over with fruitful possibilities of understanding.

The transition from the material to the psychical perspective often presents dream imagery of sickening and dying. The hospital and doctor's office are not only dream places of getting better. They are also places where the collapse of the corporeal is given refuge. The rotting and blackening processes of alchemy, dreadful wounds and suppurating sores, the ritual butchery of animals or their contagion and poisoning, and other such shocking imagery point to where something material is losing its substance and thrust, where a physical impulse or animal drive is descending toward the underworld. Just here change is taking place within one's materialistic and naturalistic attitudes. To consider the wounded animal or sick flesh only as the part of personality needing cure takes the wound literally and naturalistically, restoring it to the upperworld, strengthening the ego's energy, thereby preventing the pathologizing process that is going on. Such strengthening puts a stop to the *opus contra naturam*.

Underworld images are nonetheless visible, but only to what is invisible in us. The invisible is perceived by means of the invisible, that is, psyche. Psychic images are not necessarily pictures and may not be like sense images at all. Rather they are *images as metaphors*. An image in poetry and the entire imaginative process of music, of course, must be *heard* with the ear, but they are listened to with a third or inner ear.

According to Plato (*Sophist* 266c), dream images are comparable with shadows, "when dark patches interrupt the light," leading us to see a kind of "reflection," "the reverse of the ordinary direct view."[61] This useful analogy presents dreams as dark spots, the lacunae or ab-senses of the dayworld, where the dayworld reverses itself or converts its sense to metaphorical significance. This is not merely the dayworld repeated in a thinner silhouette of two dimensions. Like any visual shadow, these images shade in life, giving it depth and *twi*-light, duplicity, metaphor. The scene in a dream (the root of the word scene is akin to *skia*, "shadow") is a metaphorical version of that scene and those players of yesterday who have now deepened and entered my soul.

The difficulty with understanding images is due partly to our language. Unfortunately in English, we have but one word, "image," for after-images, for perceptual images, dream images, illusory images, and for imaginative metaphorical ideas. We also use the same word for false fronts and collective fantasies. To be imaginative should not be restricted to mean seeing imagery with the eyes closed or to paint or model images. We tend to literalize, to idolize, the image into a visibility, forgetting that the *eidolon* is a psychic phenomenon perceivable only by means of the same psychic consciousness as they are themselves composed. We perceive images with the imagination, or, better said, we imagine them rather than perceive them, and we cannot perceive with sense perception the depths that are not extended in the sense world. The error of empiricism is its attempt to employ sense perception everywhere, for hallucinations, feelings, ideas, and dreams. "To perceive and to imagine are as antithetic as presence and absence."[62] Because the dream speaks in images, or even *is* images—which is what the Homeric *oneiros* meant[63]—because dreaming is imaging, our instrument for undistorted listening can only be the imagination. Dreams call from the imagination to the imagination and can be answered only by the imagination.

These quick-moving images were also called shadows in Egypt and in Rome, where funerals were held at night.[64] They were black; one's underworld being is black—something we shall return to in the final chapter. The shadow world in the depths is an exact replica of daily consciousness, only it must be perceived differently, imaginatively. It is this world in metaphor. Our black being performs all actions just as we do in life, but its life is not merely our shadow. From the psychic perspective of the underworld, only shadow has substance, only what is in the shadow matters truly, eternally. Shadow, then, in psychology is not only that which the ego casts behind, made by the ego out of its light, a moral or repressed or evil reflection to be integrated. Shadow is the very stuff of the soul, the interior darkness that pulls downward out of life and keeps one in relentless connection with the underworld.

Plotinus attempted an account of the relation between the heroic ego and the underworld shade when he spoke of the Shade of Hercules. Plotinus says (4. 3, 27): ". . . this 'shade' . . . remembers all the action and experience of the life . . . of the hero's personal shaping . . ." (cf. 1. 1, 12). In Lucian's dialogue *Menippus, or The Descent into Hades* the dead are prosecuted by their own shadows *(skias)*. "The shadows that our bodies cast in the sunshine . . . are considered very trustworthy because they always keep us company and never leave our bodies."[65] This experience of having one's soul judged by one's shadow makes life in the upperworld seem "as if it had been a dream."[66] Lucian converts the relation of upperworld and dream. What goes on in the life of the ego is merely the reflection of one's deeper essence contained in the shadow.

The shade is thus a cumulative deposit made simultaneously with the ego's career. This shade remembers all the actions of our Herculean life and its physical perspective. If we will have an ego modeled upon Hercules,[67] so we will have its shade. We will always have to walk in the company of our own negative judgments about ourselves, the ego shadowed, driven, by self-criticism.

Plotinus and Lucian indirectly raise the question of guilt: why does a person engaged in the ego's heroic course through the upperworld at the same time feel shadowed by guilt. Furthermore, why does the heroic construction of reality necessitate this fundamental division between life and shade, which gives rise to being shadowed by guilt.

This way of putting the question changes radically our usual notion of super-ego. No longer may we assume it is imposed from above as a later development, as if it comes only from sunlight and as if the small child casts no shadow. Rather, we are watched from within our actions by the shadow of the body, that which is its closest witness. Since the movements of the body and its shadow are simultaneous and inseparable, that is, co-relatives, who is to say which comes first, the act or the shadow? As we project the cause of guilt on to super, more solid, carriers (our parents and society), so we project the cause of our shadow formation on to the more solid heroic ego. But perhaps it works as well the other way around. I and my shadow are born together and act together always. It is just as valid to convert our usual way of thinking, "I cast a shadow," into the proposition, "my shadow casts me."

Consequently, the shadow may be reconceived. Let us now say it creates the heroic endeavors of the day-ego as a sort of expiatory function for its psychic torment 'below.' Usually we conceive the soul as paying for our sins in an afterlife, i.e., subliminal expiation in psychosomatic symptoms and neurotic mechanisms depicted in the accounts of Hell. However, Plotinus (1. 1, 12) says, "The life and activities of the Soul are not those of the Expiator." Rather than viewing the soul as expiating in a nightworld for our shady actions in the dayworld, we may imagine dayworld actions to be expiations for shadows we have not seen. As long as we act in the heroic mode, we are driven by guilt, always paying off. Our doings are more likely undoings, and our visible achievements are driven by an invisible image that either cannot rest (like Sisyphus ever on his hill) or cannot move (like Theseus stuck on his throne), because its desire can never be reached (like Tantalus' unslaked thirst).

The convertibility of underworld figures into upperworld actions nowhere shows better than in the image complex of Styx.[68] The frigid river Styx (whose name, "hateful" or "hatred," derives from *stygeo*, "to hate") is the deepest source of the Gods' morality, for on its water they swear their oaths, implying that hatred plays an essential part in the universal order of things. Besides such originating and ordering principles as Eros, and Strife (Eris or Polemos), and Necessity (Ananke), and Reason (Nous), we must also make a place for Hatred in the scheme of things.[69] Styx's children are called Zellus (zeal), Nike (victory), Bia (force), and Cratos (strength.) Their mother's cold hatefulness is converted by them into those implacable traits we have come to accept as virtues. Her children provide the prototypes for that crusading morality which accompanies the ego on its righteous tasks of destroying in order to maintain itself.

Hateful mother Styx and her hyperactive children did not escape the notice of Freud, who puts them into the conceptual language of hate and ego. First he distinguishes between hate and love, saying that hate is older than love (*CP* 5:82) and that they "did not originate in a cleavage of any common primal element, but sprang from different sources" (*Ibid.*, p. 81). Hate, in other words, derives from its own ground and serves a distinct purpose in 'the ego': "The ego hates, abhors, and pursues with intent to destroy all objects which are for it a source of painful feelings . . . the true prototypes of the hate-relation are derived not from the sexual life but from the struggle of the ego for self-preservation and self-maintenance."

Freud's fantasy that the ego must preserve itself by struggle (for which strength, force, zeal, and victory become requirements), and the moral justification with which these qualities support the fantasy, is a Stygian enactment in the upperworld. The ego here becomes Styx's instrument, a Child of Hatred, icily preserving itself against all enemies, the greatest of which will be warmth, hence our usual notion that hate and love are contraries. Actually, hate has the same objective as love, according to Freud. Both seek pleasure, for which hatred uses the ego to destroy pain. Each of us becomes a child of Styx when we embark on the pain-killing course, justifying

our victories and zeal in destruction in terms of "self-preservation" and "ego-development."

The dissolution of these attitudes would mean reconverting
the zeal and force of our ego-strength back into the hatred
that is its source. Then we would see the hatred in our heroics.
Insight into the prototypes in myth for the actions in life is
an act that returns the children to their mother. Her primordial hatred belongs in the underworld, and there it has another
meaning. There, her implacable coldness gives absolute order
to the Gods themselves, maintaining their own psychic realm,
the underworld, intact. Styx is the limit setter, maintaining
the psychic region to which even the Olympians must descend,
preserving, not the ego, but the underworld from the pain
caused it by invading attitudes of life.

DREAM PERSONS

Owing to the 'convertibility' between upperworld actions
and underworld configurations, shadow figures in dreams offer us a new way of considering the life of the waking-ego.
We will regard it less through its relations with the world
of its realities and more as a reflection of the shades. A dream
psychology that is based on the mythic phenomenology of
the underworld will imaginatively convert the realities of the
daily world into their shadows. These now become the realities within our actions. No longer: Ego casting Shadow after
it; instead, a shade literalizing an ego in front of it and behind
which it can remain hidden.

The shadow figures or shades we meet in dreams are not
the people themselves (Jung's objective level), nor even are
they their characterologic essence (Jung's subjective level),
that is, my own traits that I can integrate. My brother with
whom I worry about my father's business in a dream is neither
my actual objective brother nor the older, sombre, responsible

traits that slow and weigh me down. My dream-brother, because he is now a shade in the underworld, is an *eidola,* a purely psychic form, and our interpretation of him must also make this move from the everyday to the mythic. Jung has said this clearly:

> During the process of integrating the unconscious contents into consciousness, undoubted importance attaches to the business of seeing how the dream symbols relate to trivial everyday realities. But, in a deeper sense and on a long-term view, this procedure is not sufficient, as it fails to bring out the significance of the archetypal contents. These reach down, or up, to quite other levels than so-called common sense would suspect. As *a priori* conditions of all psychic events, they are endured with a dignity which has found immemorial expression in godlike figures. No other formulation will satisfy the needs of the unconscious. . . . This calls for the all embracing vision of the myth. . . .
>
> [*CW* 11: § 280]

To get to this "all embracing vision of the myth," we are going to have to push beyond Freud's method of association, as well as Jung's own method of interpretation on the subjective level. This push belongs in Chapter 5, "Dream," but already here we have to observe that Freud's method projects the persons in a dream back over the bridge into the dreamday, even if for the sake of their latent meaning. We associate my dream-brother and dream-father to my day-brother and day-father and, by this association, return the dream to the day. Jung's method of interpretation on the subjective level takes the dream persons into the subject of the dreamer. They become expressions of *my* psychic traits. They are introjected into my personality. In neither method do we ever truly leave the personal aspect of the dream persons, and thus they and we remain in the upperworld.

Dare I say it loud and clear? The persons I engage with in dreams are neither representations *(simulacra)* of their living selves nor parts of myself. They are shadow images that fill archetypal roles; they are personae, masks, in the hollow of which is a *numen*.

Dodds expresses our point here as follows: "In several Homeric dreams the god or *eidolon* appears to the dreamer in the guise of a living friend, and it is possible that in real life dreams about acquaintances were often interpreted in this manner."[70]

There is a somewhat similar idea in the Egyptian cult of the dead, where the shadow soul is also the image of one or another God. So these shadow images were spoken of as Hathor, Chnum, Ity, etc. In the realm of death, that is, at the psychic level of existence, the essential image of our personal self, who is our shadow soul, is at the same time the image of a God. Our human person is shadowed by an archetypal image in the likeness of a God, and the God appears as the shade of a human person. The dream image of a human person cannot be taken in terms of his actuality, since the image in a dream belongs to the underworld shades and therefore refers to an archetypal person in human shape.

In the example above, the male triplicity of two brothers and a father, even an absent father, their being worried about the father business, the connection through worry to the father, and the other intricacies of this very simple image reach toward configurations that not only sustain but require mythic reflection. Something archetypal is going on, as in every image.

The former teacher, or my professor, in a dream is not only some intellectual potential of my psychic wholeness. More deeply, this figure is the archetypal mentor, who, for now, in this dream, wears the robes of this schoolteacher or that professor. The childhood love in my dreams is not only a special feeling tone that I may rediscover and unite with now as I age. More deeply this youth from then, living in remembrance, is the archetypal *kore* or *puer* who comes in the shape of this or that personal memory. In dreams, we are visited by the *daimones*, nymphs, heroes, and Gods shaped like our friends of last evening.

Our friends have names. The persons in myths also come with names, and Greek mythic personalities not only had each his, her, or its own name, but had a long chain of them. These "epithets of the Gods,"[71] which have been listed by scholars, present a better picture of how the Gods appeared. They did not appear as monolithic statues or as single-word abstractions (Hercules, Hera, Zeus), such as we look up in a dictionary of mythology. These persons of myth were always named so as to give a particular context. The cults of the Gods are *cults of epithets* that image the divine figures in concrete terms: Aider Hercules, Protector-from-Evil Hercules, Warlike Hercules, Victor Hercules—the name gives an image and suggests a mytheme. It reveals the neighborhood, the kinship, the function, the look and the character of the divinity. Epithets, or nicknames, still enliven the imagination of today's underworld: the street gang, mafiosi, prisoners, children, and the American Indians. The essence of the person is in the name.

Part of the name is its *etymon*, its hidden truth buried in its root. The search for the roots of words, the etymological fantasy, is one of the basic rituals of the imaginative tradition, because it seeks to recover an image within a word or to reattach a word to a name of a thing, an action, a place, or a person. One of the ways of restoring the "embracing vision of the myth" to the persons of last evening who have entered the dream is to look at their names.

In their names are their souls—an individual's name and his Ba were interchangeable (*Ba*, p. 99), as if we only get our true names from the underworld in relation with death. To see through a dream-person into his or her psychic reality requires an attentive ear to names.

Even when they have no names or are named only functionally or situationally, these names can be imagined as epithets.

So we get "the unknown woman," "the cashier," "the mechanic," "the owner."

We get figures doing things: the running-boy; the driving-woman; the worrying-brother. Then, should we put capital letters on these figures, we approximate the epithets of the Gods: The Man in the Shirt; The Sunburnt Girl; The Huge Black Cop.

In Hindu thought, there is the idea that in certain states of mind, such as dreaming, names are things in themselves. They do not represent something elsewhere embodied by the name, but they are presentations of the mind to itself of its own presences. The name is then the divine logos clothed in the person of the dream. We watch the mind move its thoughts in the subtle bodies of dream-persons. The way we ourselves are being imagined can also be revealed by nicknaming oneself in the dream: behind-time-I; shopping-I; beauty-parlor-I; pantsless-I. To get to the essential idea of what is going on in the mind, we must find names for the figures or look more deeply into the names that are given, even the banal personal ones (Mister White, the little Fisher girl, Peter Gross). Often enough, the name is the oddity that stands out when one racks one's brains to discover why the dream recalls this insignificant, fleeting ghost from last night's meeting or the school yard of forty years ago.

We may compare three approaches to dream persons. The first, let us call it Freudian, takes them back to the actuality of the day by means of association or by means of the objective level of interpretation. Other people are essential for understanding dream persons. The second, which we may call Jungian, takes them back to the subject as an expression of a person's complexes. My personality is essential for understanding dream persons. The third, archetypal method, takes them back to the underworld of psychic images. They become mythic beings, not mainly by amplifying their mythic parallels but by seeing through to the imaginative persons within the personal masks. Only the persons of the dream are essential for understanding the persons in the dream.

THE DEATH METAPHOR

When I use the word *death* and bring it into connection with dreams, I run the risk of being misunderstood grossly, since death to us tends to mean exclusively gross death—physical, literal death. Our emphasis upon physical death corresponds with our emphasis upon the physical body, not the subtle one; on physical life, not psychic life; on the literal and not the metaphorical. That love and death could be metaphorical is difficult to understand—after all something must be real says the ego, the great literalist, positivist, realist. We easily lose touch with the subtle kinds of death. For us, pollution and decomposition and cancer have become physical only. We concentrate our propitiations against one kind of death only, the kind defined by the ego's sense of reality. The death we speak of in our culture is a fantasy of the ego, and we take our dreams in this same manner.

Our culture is singular for its ignorance of death. The great art and celebrations of many other cultures—ancient Egyptian and Etruscan, the Greek of Eleusis, Tibetan—honor the underworld. We have no ancestor cult, although we are pathetically nostalgic. We keep no relics, though collect antiques. We rarely see dead human beings, though watch a hundred imitations each week on the television tube. The animals we eat are put away out of sight. We have no myths of the *nekyia*, yet our popular heroes in films and music are shady underworld characters. Dante's underworld was our culture's last, and it was imagined even before the Renaissance had properly begun. Our ethnic roots reach back to great underworld configurations: the Celtic Dagda or Cerunnos, the Germanic Hel, and the Biblical Sheol. All have faded;

how pale the fire of the Christian Hell.[72] Where have they
gone? Where is death when it is no longer observed? Where
do contents of consciousness go when they fade from attention? Into the unconscious, says psychology. The underworld
has gone into the unconscious: even become the unconscious.
Depth psychology is where today we find the initiatory mystery, the long journey of psychic learning, ancestor worship,
the encounter with demons and shadows, the sufferings of
Hell.

The person who goes into analysis is therefore not an analysand, a client, a pupil, a trainee, or a partner—but a patient.
This word is retained, not because of its historical origins
in nineteenth-century medicine, as much as because it bespeaks the actual condition of going into the depths of soul.
The *soul* is the patient of *psycho*-therapy, and a person (client,
partner, analysand) is immediately constellated as soul the
moment he or she becomes a patient. The underworld experience turns us each into patients, as well as giving us a new
feeling of patience. "In your patience is your soul," was a
religious alchemical maxim, saying that soul is found in the
reception of its suffering, in the attendance upon it, the waiting
it through. From the soul's viewpoint, there is little difference
between *patient* and *therapist*. Both words in their roots refer
to an attentive devotion, waiting on and waiting for.

Waiting for what? One answer could be: death. Psychotherapy as waiting attendance upon death, dreamwork as death-
work. But this answer would literalize death and lose its
metaphorical sense. The Egyptian Ba never dies; the Christian
soul is immortal—which means that physical death as the
medically and legally defined cessation of life is not the background of dreamwork. This sort of death is again the literal
viewpoint of the ego that can't get out of its own life except
by dying, which it takes in that same physical manner as it
takes everything else. Death is not the background to dream-
work, but soul is. Soul, if immortal, has more to it than

dying, and so dreams cannot be limited to attendance upon death. The psychic perspective is focused not only on death or about dying. Rather, it is a consciousness that stands on its own legs only when we have put our dayworld notions to sleep. *Death* is the most profoundly radical way of expressing this shift in consciousness.

Yet how difficult it is to maintain the underworld perspective; how unnatural! After all, we are in life, and we do look at dreams in "sweet daylight." The price of this sunny viewpoint, however, is that death and the fear of it become the fount of psychology's negative predications: 'evil,' 'shadow,' 'unconscious,' 'psychopathic,' 'regressive,' 'stuck,' 'destructive,' 'cut off,' 'unrelated,' 'cold,' as well as the familiar minus sign pasted onto one side of each complex—do these words and signs not mean "tinged with death," as enemies of life and of love? By declaring a situation or a complex negative, do we not truly mean that it is stopping life, that it is death bound, going to Hell; that now we are engaging hopelessness and a primordial coldness that shuns life, or a darkness that wills the worst, impenetrable to reason's clear sight? The negative signs in psychology seem to me to be really a shorthand for the prejudice of a dayworld's Eros against Thanatos. We can therefore only see negatively, the destructive, pessimistic, suicidal components of the psyche and cannot meet with our understanding the depth to which contents would go in Stygian hatred, or when they prefer separations to unions, or take the downward path of inertia into withdrawal, forgetting, and still reflection.

Depth psychology has been the modern movement within our culture that returns to it a sense of the underworld. Since its inception with Freud, depth psychology has been a "movement," driven by a mission. Some of that mission has been the Resurrection of the Dead, the recall of life of so much forgotten and buried in each of us. It did not go far enough, however. It believed that lifting personal or cultural repression of the instinctual id was its end. It opened the tomb, imagining that a mummified body would rise up; but the id as the underworld is not the instinctual body. It is the chthonic psyche. What is most dead and buried in each of us is the culture's neglect of Death. Hades only now begins to reappear in ominous new concerns with the limits to growth, the energy crisis, ecological pollution, ageing and dying.

Not the dead shall rise, but the Resurrection of Death itself; for depth psychology brings back to us not only the persons of the dream and the memorial psyche of the underworld. It has also brought Death back from its exile in the parapsychology of spiritism, the theology of afterlife, the morality of rewards, and the scientific fantasies of biochemical chance or evolution—back to its main place in the midst of the psychological life of each individual, which opens into depth at every step. Our footfalls echo on its vaults below. There is an opening downward within each moment, an unconscious reverberation, like the thin thread of the dream that we awaken with in our hands each morning leading back and down into the images of the dark.[73]

4

BARRIERS

There are three habits of mind that impede grasping the idea of the underworld as the psychic realm. Let us look at each of these barriers briefly.

MATERIALISM

I have stressed the distinction between underground and underworld, and we have seen that the word *unconscious* tends to gloss over this distinction, giving a naturalistic cast to psychic events. There is an archetypal figure behind this perspective, one with as much historical influence upon our attitudes in psychology, as in law, government, and language. We are Roman in mind, as well as in civilization. In ancient Rome, the Goddess Tellus, who later became *terra mater*, was both maternally earthy and one of the lowerworld Gods, presiding over both the fields of nature and the realm of the dead.[1] The psychological source of the general idea that

Roman culture was materialistic and nonimaginative may well lie in Tellus, for what a difference between an underworld ruled by an invisible Hades and one belonging to Tellus, *terra mater.*

Tellus has some curious characteristics. For one, she was not paired with a sky God, as is so often the case in myths. In fact, she had hardly any male associates at all. She was "inseparable from Ceres," however, whose name connects with creation and increase and not only with cereals.[2] The two together intervene in all funeral rites, as well as being Goddesses of agricultural and human fecundity, including marriage. Most sacred to Tellus was a pregnant cow—a sacrifice with few parallels in the rituals of the world. The slaughter of the animal took place in mid-April, a festival of butchery, blood, meat, bowels, gestation, and increase amid the rich green growth of the rising crop. Death is here wholly envisioned within the cycle of fertility. No pneumatic world of spirit or essence opens below the earthy ground in which the body is inhumed.

The great mother is not merely a stone statue in a museum. She is a modality of consciousness moving through the habits of our thought and feeling. She is our materialism; the common derivation of both matter and *mater* (mother) is neither an accident nor a joke.[3] She is that modality of consciousness which connects all psychic events to material ones, placing the images of the soul in the service of physical tangibilities. Each time we take a dream up into life, we reinforce her domination. Every translation of a dream into the bread-and-butter issues of "real" flesh and blood is a materialism.

Her role in psychology has been extraordinary, as if she were its sole God. I do not mean here only the continual return to the mother-child image as key to understanding the human soul, but even the sophisticated interpreters of generation or two ago attributed everything to her: river; oceans, vegetation and animals, love, life and death.[4] Howev(

now, using the careful application of Aristotle's method with dreams—the search for correct resemblances, we are able to recall that oceans and rivers belong to Okeanos and Poseidon; that Eros is also a male figure and force; that a lord of vegetation and zoetic life, and of childhood too, is Dionysos; and that even the earth itself can have, as in Egypt at the historical roots of our symbolisms, a masculine personification.

Not only religion begins, as many have said, as a reflection upon death. Psychology does too, for it is in the face of death that we ponder and go deep and sense soul, and then build our fantasies for housing it, whether these be the ancient pyramids and sepulchres of religion or the rituals and systems of modern psychology. If the soul is imagined to be an epiphenomenal vapor secreted by the brain or by nervous systems or to result from a microscopic biochemical combination, and the dream is a reflection of the inside behavior of the body that is inside the behavior of social, historical, and physical fields of energy, then the philosophical perspective that best suits the soul and its dreams is materialism. The converse follows: when we give an account of the dream's images and language by referring to other influences—other persons, sense impressions, past memories—we are in a materialism, although we may never have used reductive terms. Materialism may be sophisticated beyond hedonism, sensationalism, associationalism, behaviorism, and the other telltale signs by which we have been taught to recognize it. It occurs whenever we cannot accept a dream as an autochthonous image, a *sui generis* invention of the soul. A dream is not made by something other elsewhere. Rather, the "we" who searches for the causal conditions of the dream is himself of such stuff as dreams.

Materialism in psychology cannot be countered with individual subjectivism, or the private ownership of the self, which is psychological capitalism. For it too is just another materialism. It too posits a transcending ground on which the soul depends and to which dreams ultimately refer. Nor can materialism be adequately met with Christianism, which omits dream, soul, and underworld, as we shall soon see. The pantheistic psychology of the growth and ecology movement is also no answer, for it invites a new cult of the great mother that begins with worship of the physical body and *thymos.*

Materialism in psychology can be met, however, with a wholly different way of making life "matter," making it "count" and have "sense." I mean here the quality of depth that replaces the physical significance. I mean that nothing matters more than death, and when we start our psychological reflection from there, materialism loses its maternal ground. Materialism begins with neither Democritus nor Marx; its starting point is the archetype ruling our perspective toward psychic events, that is our view of death, the underworld, and dreams.

As long as the archetypal mother dominates our psychology, we cannot help but see dreams from her perspective and read the dream's message as corresponding with her concerns. For instance, the dream corresponds with Hera's concerns with social realities, the problems of husbands and wives and families in the daily world; or the dream corresponds with Cybele's concrete visibilities and is to be read as a mantic source for resolving problems so that life may flourish. The archetypal mother also would strengthen the heroic consciousness of the ego by challenging it with huge tasks, as Hera did in so many myths. Dead Roman gladiators left the arena through the "Gate of Ceres," back to the mother who had sent them out in the first place.[5] One of the ways in which the archetypal mother challenges us shows when we consider the dream to be a riddle that must be untied, puzzled out, solved. When the dream is a riddle, there is a Sphinx, and where there is a Sphinx, there is a hero eternally married to mother.

"The Great Earth Mother" is a way of doing psychology that attempts to return dreams to nature through naturalistic interpretations. But "nature" too is only a psychological perspective, one of the fantasies of the soul and itself an imaginal topography, whose description changes through the centuries in accordance with shifting archetypal dominants.[6] Western history shows many such fantasies: nature as a clockwork machine; as an enemy; as wild and beautiful asking to be tamed or to be left unspoilt, virginal; as a harmonious rhythm; as red in tooth and claw, everything competing for survival; as the very face of God. We cannot speak of dreams as nature or as taking them naturally until we have at least first ascertained which view of nature is being assumed.

Another way the great mother works on our dreams is by materializing them into the personal world. As Jung (*CW* 9, i:§ 159) pointed out, psychologies of the mother never can leave the personalistic viewpoint. But the dead are not persons, and the *eidola* of the underworld are not parts of anybody's personality. They are bloodless, bodiless, boneless images, souls no longer fused with personal lives.

A personalistic reduction of the underworld was fundamental to Epicureanism, a major philosophy of Roman civilization.[7] Again we find the effects of Tellus. Although death was an important focus to the Epicurean mind in its concern for how to live the good life, the entire underworld was but a moralistic allegory about personal fears (of death, mainly) and desires (to overcome it). What Freud later saw as the omnipotence fantasy and immortality drive are already adumbrated. Epicureanism teaches that we can do without the afterlife allegory if we learn to discern our emotions, not taking the fantasies *(simulacra)* they project as underworld figures to be actualities. Only the material world presented in felt sensations is actually real and only the sage management (coping) with this world a sensible aim. To be happy, we must live into a future without illusion, especially the illusions of the supernatural, epitomized at their worst by the superstitions of the underworld. All is atoms, passing moments. The best we can do is find peaceful retreat in a community of like-minded friends.

This rationalistic materialism bears comparison with Freudian dream theory—dream figures as introjections of fears and desires ultimately reducible to sensations of pleasure and pain—and much more widely with the philosophy of death pervading our civilization. To the Epicurean Roman, death meant simply the absence of all sense-feeling, and what is not felt is not real or simply does not exist. His modern equivalent makes a similar statement: "Death has no reality for me. Where I am (alive), it isn't; and where or when it is, I am not (dead). So why worry? Get on with life." Rome or here, we find similar concern with practical management of personal life in a universe that is either only chance or only determined (two sides of the same rational, material coin). So the most adequate psychology is ego psychology, alleviated by friendship with like-minded persons (other egocentrics), once the depths beyond the ego are considered its projection.

We can draw a conclusion about the materialistic view that derives a psychology of death from Tellus rather than from Hades. There is a curious correlation between feelings of reality about the underworld and feelings of value about the soul. It is as if, when we have no vivid imagination of the underworld, a flattening takes place, even a depersonalization that must be made good by Epicurean community and friendship—or what today is called "relating." The less underworld, the less depth, and the more horizontally spread out becomes one's life. The materialistic view ends in a kind of void, the very Halls of Hades now only a spiritual vacuum, for its myths and images have been called irrational *simulacra,* fantasies of fear and desire. The end is depression—and this suggests that the pervading, though masked, depression in our civilization is partly a response of the soul to its lost underworld. When the depressed person goes into therapy to analyze the unconscious, he may rediscover there—thanks to Freud—the underworld again. Depth psychology, despite professing scientific materialism and paying hourly homage to the great mother, nonetheless performs the chief function of religion: connecting the individual by means of practical ritual with the realm of death.

In sum, the battle for the deliverance from the mother occurs each time we can move through to a less personal, less natural, less moralized, less related and social conception. The *opus contra naturam* by which psychological work can be defined is thus at first an *opus contra maternam,* not the personal mother, which would be again her snare, but the materialistic philosophies of naturalism and personalism. To free the psychic realm from her natural mind requires first distinguishing the underworld of Hades from Tellus and the underground.

OPPOSITIONALISM

The next barrier across our way into the underworld perspective is our habitual thinking in opposites: oppositionalism. This "ism," like any other, is an ideological frame imposed upon life by our minds and is usually unconscious to our minds. Even when we are somewhat aware of oppositionalism, as I am trying to be in this book, it is nevertheless so bedrock to the thought of our culture, from the pre-Socratics, Aristotle and Neoplatonism, through Scholasticism, to Kant, Hegel, and information theory, that we will not be able to escape its underlying influence. This book too falls often into opposing pairs like nightworld and dayworld, underworld and upperworld, psychical and natural, and the like.

We cannot move to another planet with another universe of discourse, or even to another cultural habit. Since we must remain where oppositionalism is in our very ground, the best we can do is enlighten ourselves about it, hoping for two things: to shift oppositions, so that we may be less caught by them and more able to use them, and to find out what archetypal perspective is most served by this "ism," that is, for what sort of mind wrestling with what sort of question are oppositions necessary.

The logic of oppositions[8] and all their kinds (contradictories, contraries, polarities, complementaries), whether the opposites are formal only or material as well, and then whether the pair of terms together are exhaustive, all this, as well as the metaphysical structure of dualism that seems both to require and imply oppositional logic, extends far beyond an essay on the dream and the underworld. Yet oppositionalism does bear on this essay, because our topic has been conceived by Freud and even more by Jung in terms of opposites. In order to move dream theory from their positions, we need to work through their oppositions, especially the Jungian.

Jung's psychology is thoroughly oppositional. Without significant exception, all his major concepts—eros/logos, ego/self, introversion/extraversion, first half/second half, image/instinct, individual/collective, conscious/unconscious, ethics/morals, anima/animus, and still more—are arranged in pairs. These oppositions are material and functional, but not logical. That means, opposition in Jungian psychology has to do with the *content* of terms and how they *work*. Introversion is opposed to extraversion in its nature and function, not merely formally. A tension of substance operates between the terms, not a logic of contradiction. So it is a mistake to treat Jung's opposites with logical tools, as if he were making logical moves. Because his oppositions are not logically exclusive contradictories, anima does not exclude animus, and we can be conscious and unconscious at the same time, and so on. That is why Jung so often rejects "either/or thinking" in preference to "both." His pairs are antagonistic and complementary at the same time, but never contradictories.

In this sense, Jung is more a follower of the romantic use of opposites. He sees them as constitutive of things more than modes of arguing about things. He would less likely employ oppositions in an Aristotelian-Scholastic manner and more likely agree with Coleridge, who speaks of a law "which reigns through all Nature, viz., the law of polarity, or the manifestation of one power by opposite forces," and who also said, "There is, strictly speaking, no proper opposition but between two polar forces of one and the same power."[9] Here, oppositionalism is mainly a vision of reality, a universal law, and only secondarily an epistemological procedure of ordering.

Jung (*CW* 7:§ 111) refers his grounding principle to Heraclitus' doctrine of enantiodromia,[10] by which Jung understands the "regulative function of opposites." The word itself means "counter" *(enantio)* "running" *(dromia)*, which Jung adapts to mean *les extrêmes se touchent.* If you go far enough with any one movement, a countermovement will set in. Even the clash of opposing directions is understood in the manner of Heraclitus (frg. 30): "The way up and the way down are one and the same," or as Coleridge says, "the manifestation of one power by opposite forces." Jung's whole opus is an elaboration of this view.[11]

As Jung's psychology extended, so did his notion of enantiodromia. In fact, his analytical psychology speaks of opposites in four main ways: (1) Conversion into the opposite (enantiodromia); (2) Regulation of one of a pair by its opposite (self-regulation); (3) Union of opposites (conjunction); (4) Identity of opposites *(coincidentia oppositorum).* The third, and especially the fourth, are the main theme of Jung's alchemical psychology.

Now we come to the dream. It too is approached by means of opposites, for the dream is a compensation.[12] Compensation is the one overall construct which Jung applies to dreams, much as Freud's overall construct of wish-fulfilment. Because it is a compensation, a dream is always partial, one-sided, unbalanced. To be comprehended, it calls for the other member of the pair: the dayworld context, the ego position, the collective situation, the preceding dream series. Theory of compensation forces the dream across the bridge back into links with others, outside itself, elsewhere. A dream is not complete per se.

This theory has consequences in dream analysis. If the dream is incomplete, it is left to analysis to compensate it. So, the Jungian analyst looks within the dream for figures and symbols that will balance out the onesidedness which his Jungian training assures he will espy. Positions taken by the dream ego will be compensated by op-positions. If the ego-figure is passive, the analyst will search for a strengthening shadow, if the ego-figure acts aggressively and self-sure, the analyst attempts to sensitize it with other, more 'feminine' symbols in the dream.

Perhaps, however, there is no compensatory opposite within the dream, as, say, one with 'only' men it it; then the analyst is driven to ask for the missing feminine, that which the theory of compensation requires. Or in a dream in which one is alone in snow and ice, metal blades, and sinister machines, where are human warmth or vegetative and animal life? Elements that the dream does not have must be introduced as compensation to the one-sided picture, much as if one were hearing a brass band and asked, "but where are the violins?" Oppositionalism soon runs away with Jungian practitioners. Inflation is dosed with depression and earth: they attempt to land planes; to move the dreamer out of fancy hotels and high-rises and away from the company of important people (persona), toward wood and wool and cottage cheese. "Masculine traits" are compensated by anima,

anima, by developing the animus. There is always something to add.

If we could examine what goes on in the practitioner's mind in terms of Jung's four kinds of oppositions, I believe we would find something like this. The analyst imagines the opposites in the model of the first case, conversion, and attempts to achieve the second case, regulation, and eventually the third, conjunction. The supposed one-sidedness of the dream is countered by the interpretation. At best, this works like a symbol, transcending the opposites of "ego and unconscious." As the dream is a compensation, so is the work on it compensatory to the dream. The aim is to redress a supposed lost balance. The analyst wants to get the patient on a bridge and to keep him there.[13]

This procedure is medical. The compensatory use of opposites is what goes on in allopathic medicine—our official, academic Western medicine. Healing there means running counter to, reversing the direction of, a disease process by combatting it or by introducing what is missing. The aim is to restore lost balance. The allopathic physician stimulates native elements or introduces foreign ones opposite to the illness in order to reestablish an original harmony, a proper *krasis* or harmonious mixture of elements.

What is this "original harmony," this ideal balance that must be restored, this fantasy in which the dream and its interpretation has become entangled? The philosophical fantasy is one thing and certainly worth discussing, but the result of it in the consulting room of the analyst is that it requires the interpreter to "do something" and appeals to the dreamer to "correct something." And who then is the do-er and the corrector, if not our old protagonist, the ego. Theory of compensation inevitably takes one back to this figure, which is the fundamental other element, the allopathic factor that runs counter to the dream. It feels *(pathos)* other *(allo)* than the dream. Theory of compensation appeals to the dayworld per-

spective of ego and results from its philosophy, not from
the dream. From this perspective the dream of course compensates, because the ego-perspective is a literalism that takes
things from one side only and so is always in need of compensation.

If, however, we do not start from that inadequate position,
we do not need that compensatory theory.

In practice, the compensatory approach constellates the
hero, whose notion of enantiodromia is literal conversion and
literal self-regulation. He takes himself straight into the opposite. He really does put on earth-shoes and chop wood after
a flying dream. The allopathic procedure practically achieves
a new literal opposition, just as one-sided as the former, neces-
sitating another dream, another visit to the doctor, and the
interminable analysis of ego addiction.

If we do speak in terms of opposites, then there is only
one absolute material opponent to any position in life, and
that is its death. If we now deliteralize that statement, we
are saying that 'death' is the way through the opposites, that
is, it is the self-regulation of any position by psyche, by nonliteral, metaphorical perception. In this sense, (3) conjunction
and (4) the identity of opposites mean the simultaneous perception by the perspectives of life and death, the natural and
the psychic. Conjunction, then, is a peculiar union of inner
viewpoints. Through this union, an identity of opposites becomes apparent. We see the hidden connection between what
had hitherto been oppositions. This is the usual way Jung's
alchemical psychology works.

When an analyst has to divide in order to analyze, that
is, has to construct the images and figures in a dream as
opposites or has to introduce the opposite into the patient—
as more gut to balance thought, more reflection to oppose
impulse, more attention to detail to compensate inspired generalities—then it is the analyst who has failed at conjunction.
He has failed to perceive that the opposite is already present,

that every psychic event is an identity of at least two positions and is thus symbolic, metaphorical, and never one-sided. Only by taking it from one side does it become so; by trying to balance it, we break its hidden harmony.

The more fundamental fault here is reading Jung's four varieties of oppositions as stages, from 1 to the goal of 4, that overcome opposites. But, if we base ourselves in the fourth mode, the identity of opposites, we have bypassed one-sidedness, ego, compensation, allopathic treatment—the whole lot. The coincidence of opposites means that nothing has to be introduced by anyone from anywhere, because the opposite is already present. Everything necessary to the situation is there, so that everything there is necessary. Each dream has its own fulcrum and balance, compensates itself, is complete as it is.

Now this is the underworld perspective. It takes the image as all there is—everything else has vanished and cannot be introduced into the underworld until it becomes like the underworld. We cannot see the soul until we experience it, and we cannot understand the dream until we enter it.

Becoming the same as what we are dealing with is the homeopathic mode of healing. It requires the feeling for likeness, a sense of kinship with what is taking place. The experience is like modes 4 and 3, identity and conjunction: because we feel the same as what is happening, we can join with it, which then leads to self-regulation, and finally to conversion out of oppositionalism altogether. For the only way to "overcome the opposites" would be to leave the construct itself. There is no need to remain in an oppositional universe when approaching the dream or any psychic phenomenon. As Freud said, the unconscious knows no negation. All sorts of what would be incompatibilities from the dayworld view exist side-by-side and easily convert one into another. Images do not oppose each other. They are not set up in polarities or even in pairs. Life and death, upperworld and underworld, and bridges too, are all *eidola.* We may dissolve our constructs in the dream, and the dream opposes itself to nothing and asks for no compensation, but, like each figure in the underworld, like Sisyphus, or Ixion turning on his wheel, each dream is working at the soul's fate in its own style.

Within the underworld perspective, the world does not fall into duality, needing balancing and bridges. Not only are Hades and Pluto one, and Hades and Zeus, and Hades and Dionysos, and Hades and Poseidon brothers, not only do Hades and Hermes share the same hat and Hades and Persephone the same kingdom, but the chthonic aspect in any archetypal pattern faces it away from external relations between things and the need for dyadic dialectics, turning it instead toward internal relations within things and imagistic explications.

The dream is no more a compensation than is Hades a region balanced by another one. Commentators on Greek thought emphasize the intermixing of cosmoi and the absence of dualism. The Greek world is imagistic, polytheistic. Dualism is a consequent of monism and appears most strongly in monistic fantasies, such as our Judeo-Christian tradition with its separation of upper and lower waters of heaven and hell. My own contrasts of 'upper' and 'under' reflect this cosmology, in which all of us are stuck, more than they do the polytheistic Greek world that I am trying to evoke. But then we can be only where our tradition has deposited us, and speak from there.

Dreams themselves do not speak that way. They are homeopathic by nature. They present in a single image what we see in the language of opposites. In dreams of medically terminal patients, those upon whom the physician has prophesied death, the psyche seems to refuse breaking itself apart into opposites of life and death.[14] It makes no distinction between killing and curing, poison and medicine, dying and giving birth. It does not recognize the dayworld question: is the patient getting better or getting worse, where worse means only death. As the psyche moves toward the underworld—which is a perspective and *not* necessarily actual death—there develops an ever stronger feeling for sameness, an identity of opposites, where the cure is the disease, the healing is a deeper wounding, and the newborn infant is death. One cannot distinguish here from there. There is only the image.

This takes us to the question raised at the beginning: for what sort of mind wrestling with what sort of issue is the ideology of oppositionalism so useful? The apparent answer is the heroic ego, who divides so he can conquer. Antithetical thinking, found by Alfred Adler to be a neurotic habit of mind, belongs to the will to power and the masculine protest.[15] These descriptions apply as well to the heroic ego as we have been imagining him.

Lest the hero become too easy a scapegoat, only to return from the badlands where I am repressing him and come riding later into the reader's mind with a band of cohorts each packing strong justifications and telling arguments in defense of their revengeful leader, we have to pardon his erroneous ways. They are in service of a principle beyond the will to power. This is the *principle of distinctions.* Although the underworld viewpoint may not divide 'here' from 'there,' living as it does wholly in images, it has another viewpoint that wants to clarify. It does this by means of contrasts—the sharper, the clearer; so it limns light against dark in pairs.

Oppositionalism offers the simplest mode of abstract distinction. It is attractive for this very reason. Something both simple and abstract so often seems like the base of all things, whether a monist deity, Pythagorean numbers, Kantian categories, or an elegant mathematical theorem.

The first vice of its virtue is that oppositionalism can abstract only what is simple, and it simplifies whatever it abstracts. For instance, when Zeus and Hades are brought into opposition as "upper" and "under," we have neglected all their imagistic complexities except for the simplest one of spatial location, and we have simplified even this spatial location to a vertical axis of "above" versus "below." This kind of simplified abstraction, even with diagrams, has become a permanent symptom of analytical psychology, owing to its base in oppositionalism. What is left out in this mode of making distinctions are the actual personalities of Zeus and Hades, and what is left over for the individual in analytical psychology to deal with are the concrete complexities of his particular images that do not come in neat pairs.

Oppositionalism distinguishes by drawing to extremes. These extremes must touch, because they need each other for the distinction to become apparent. Thus, opposites are held together, not by a mystical law of all things, but by an epistemological necessity, a necessity which derives from an archetypal perspective that requires clear distinctions.

This result suggests that both the romantic, metaphysical view and the Scholastic, epistemological view, to group them as such, are founded in and expressions of a perspective that must see clearly, so as to know most encompassingly, so as to order and use. Have we not come back to the solar hero and his daylight desire to master phenomena?

For this perspective, "overcoming the opposites" is a transcending, mystical experience. For it to abandon thinking in opposites is to lose consciousness, whose very definition (by this perspective) is the clarifying mode of seeing, knowing, and ordering. Such a loss feels like an ontological shaking of the foundations, because it means also losing the belief that being is finally accountable in terms of simple abstract pairs in mystical tension. This is a favorite root metaphor in many philosophies. This notion of being makes it accessible to the logical understanding of a clear mind. Again we see that what seem to be the most sovereign ontological positions have clay feet. Philosophies cannot be cut free of the arche-typal fantasies that they reflect and that are the base of their conviction.

What is lost more seriously in oppositionalism is the phe-nomenal world that is mastered by it. When *distinction* is not distinguished from *clarity*—Descartes made them inter-changeable—we can have no underworld, no depth and shad-ing, except as utter darkness in compensation. The best dis-tinctions are the clearest, and the clearest are, of course, contradictions. Then metaphorical ambiguity can only mean dim-witted obscurity, for twilight has disappeared and psyche too, as it all but did for Descartes.

Fortunately, the underworld perspective offers another, a psychological, mode of distinction, where sharp sight means *insight* into the thing at hand (not in comparison with some-thing else) and where clarity means *precision* (of internal rela-tions within images, not logical relations between them). A psychic approach to distinction works at the particularization of an event, a dream say, by means of imagistic resemblances, in search of what the dream is "like." When we make these moves for distinguishing a dream, we are always moving it deeper into what is actually there and what it feels like, sounds like, looks like. We have no need for pairs and their tensions, no recourse to enantiodromia, compensation, the lot.

The perspective I have just sketched and called *psychic* imagines opposites to be one way of noticing similarities; they are a special case of "likeness." Tarde, Coleridge, Ogden, and Jung implied that only *similars can be opposites*. Only those pairs having something material, essential in common can be sensibly opposed. A turkey cannot be opposed to a theorem, unless we can discover in what way they are like each other. Our psychological view is able to save the phenom-enon of opposites by regarding opposition as an *extreme meta-phor*, a radical way of saying one thing as though it were two violently differing things in sharp war with itself (Heraclitus again), which the valiant ego must imagine literally and meet as a challenge.

Enough. A last way out of oppositionalism is the best: stop fantasying in its terms, so as to see and see into each thing for what it is. This way out is also the way into the underworld of images.

CHRISTIANISM

A third reason for our difficulty with the underworld is our Western Christian perspective. Between us and the underworld stands the figure of Christ as he was presented by the early Church Fathers. "But it was for this purpose, say they, that Christ descended into hell, that we ourselves might not have to descend thither."[16] Later, Luther said: "Christ's resurrection is our resurrection."[17] As the heart grows in faith in Christ, "It weakens death from day to day and deprives him of his strength, until he is submerged entirely and disappears. . . . Through Him . . . we will bury death also physically and do away with him entirely, so that nothing will be seen or known of him any longer." [18]

Let us compare: Orpheus and Dionysos went down to redeem close personal loves: Orpheus, Eurydice; Dionysos, his mother Semele. Hercules had tasks to fulfull. Aeneas and Ulysses made their descents to learn: there they gained counsel from the 'father,' Anchises and Teiresias. Dionysos, in Aristophanes' *Frogs,* went down another time in search of poetry to save the city. But Christ's mission to the underworld was to annul it through his resurrected victory over death. Because of his mission, all Christians were forever exempted from the descent. Lazarus becomes the paradigm for all humankind. We shall all rise. The eternal life is not in the underworld but in its destruction. As Paul says in I Cor. 15:55, freely quoting from the prophet Hosea (Hos. 13:14):

"O Thanatos, where is they sting? O Hades, where is thy victory?"[19]

"The word victory appears only three times in Paul's letters, all of them in this one paragraph," announcing with trumpets the Christian mystery—the eradication of death.[20] In these trumpets and this destruction are we not again meeting Victory (nike, nikos), child of Styx, still infused with his mother's hatred? The conquest of Hades summons ugly imagery—echoes of Hosea, the sting of scorpions, serpents, hornets, and infernal locusts,[21] and the goads that earlier mythologems gave to Hekate. The strong language evidently indicates an equally strong mission in early Christianism to wipe out a fundamental bastion of contemporary polytheism, the Halls of Hades.

Sleep, too, stands in the way of Paul's annunciation, for he opposes sleep to transformation. "We shall not all sleep, but we shall all be changed" (I Cor. 15:51). As we know, sleep and death are twin brothers; to sleep is to enter death's kingdom, perchance to dream, and to be filled by psyche. Rather than this, the dead shall be raised "in the twinkling of an eye." To change is not to sleep, and to sleep is not to change. Christianism's way of redemption does not pass through sleep. This means for psychology that what goes on in sleep and dreams should not be looked at with a Christian view toward redemptive change.

Let us try quite carefully to understand what kind of transformation Paul is proclaiming. The word he chooses for this move is allagēsometha, "translation," which also has connotations of barter and exchange. It is not just moving from this place or condition to that; it is giving up or putting off this, so as to gain that. According to some commentators on this passage, "a radical translation from psychikon to pneumatikon must take place."[22] The change is one of "spiritualizing soulishness."[23] To rise and to meet the Lord in the air (I Thess. 4:17), we must become pneumatic, spiritualized.

The victory over sleep and death is part of Christianism's larger mission that exchanges soul for spirit.

The ascension requires that we leave not only our blood behind, like the *thymos* which did not belong in the underworld and whose desires cost soul. Paul goes Heraclitus one better—or worse, because the Christian ascensional mystery exchanges *psyche* for *pneuma*. We pay for spirit with our souls.[24] Christianism's defeat of the underworld is also a loss of soul.

Christ's conquest was very vividly imagined by early Christianism. Second Timothy 1:10, the Epistle of Barnabas, and Justin Martyr considered the victory over death to have already been achieved by Christ's own resurrection.[25] The underworld would be wiped out not at the end of time; it had already been destroyed. Christ's dying and resurrection was absorbed by the classical mythologem of the *nekyia,* now not a journey, but a *descensuskampf,* for Christ harrows Hell, and in one version, forces Thanatos to hide behind his own door. Christ was thus greater than the greatest of Man-Gods, Hercules, who might have driven Hades from his Throne but had not, like Christ, actually wiped out the entire kingdom, including death itself.[26]

One effect of this battle with the underworld was the Satanizing of Thanatos. The black figure with wings, indistinct, and even at times gentle in pagan descriptions, became "the last enemy" (I Cor. 15:26) and the personification of the principle of evil. The underworld became thoroughly moralized; death became equated with sin. As is so often the psychological rule, the sin that one commits is attributed to that which one commits it upon. Projection. The moral justification for destroying an enemy is that the enemy is destructive.

The Christian image of Hell was thus a projection of a hellish image in Christianism. It must have been in raging despair over the bad exchange it had made. It had lost soul, depth, underworld, and the personifications of the imagination in exchange for idealized spiritualizations in high heaven.

Only in one way—by losing Christ—could the underworld reappear and then as perdition, damnation, and terror. This terror led to a whole new problem: the underworld as the devil's realm. To fear the devil (and what other reaction is possible in view of this intolerable image?) indicated his nearness, which also indicated one was in danger of losing Christ. So the devil was established by the fear. The devil image still haunts in our fears of the unconscious and the latent psychosis that supposedly lurks there, and we still turn to methods of Christianism—moralizing, kind feelings, communal sharing, and childlike naïveté—as propitiations against our fear, instead of the classical descent into it, the *nekyia* into imagination.

The underworld that did sometimes reappear, at least in the vision of John, still retained associations with the static fixtures of classical myths. It is implied (Rev. 22:11) that in the hereafter the evildoer still does evil and the filthy still are filthy, that only Christ saves from these damned repetitious fates. He who was with Christ was saved; he who was not was lost to the underworld. Christianism, in a two-sided masterstroke, both did away with the underworld and horrified it as the perpetual alternative to the Christian path. Christianism or underworld: one had to choose, and who would choose the horror?

Dreams that have their home in the underworld must, too, become anti-Christian. And indeed they do play a minor role in the New Testament,[27] just as the word *psyche* gives way to *pneuma*.[28] The verb *to dream* does not appear in the New Testament, and *dream* appears just three times, only in Matthew. Dreams could only be revelations of the nightworld, messages of temptation from Satan's tribe of daemons. Or, at best, they might be taken pneumatically, as messages of the spirit within the context of the upperworld. The Hebrew world had Sheol, and dreams were heard; but

when a dream comes to Pilate's wife, a dream that even
bore upon Christ's own fate, it was not listened to (Matt.
27:19), for this is now the New Testament. Christianism and
the underworld fell into opposition—material, functional, and
logical, and we are left in a condition where Christian consciousness and psychological soul-making through attention
to dreams have been forced into contradicition.

It is in terms of this opposition that we may reconsider
Jung's unremitting vexation with the figure of Christ. Jung's
preoccupation with this image has been taken up biographi-
cally, theologically, and alchemically, but it seems necessary
to imagine this prolonged discomfort of Jung, the psychologist, also archetypally. Jung sensed the inherent opposition
between Christianism and the underworld and attempted to
darken the figure of Christ with Hermes-Mercurius. He did
not go as far as Hades, but he did place Hermes-Mercurius
as archetype of the unconscious in opposition to Christ as
archetype of the upperworld's consciousness (*CW* 13:§ 299).
His choice of Hermes-Mercurius as the darkener, as the
psychopomp to the underworld, echoes the Homeric hymn
to Hermes, where this God is "the only recognized messenger
to Hades," as he is Bringer of Dreams.[29]

Jung's attempt to darken the Christ figure must be understood in terms of soul-making, in terms of a recognition that
only through reestablishing the underworld, which it was
Christ's mission to void, could the soul-making of descent
and deepening towards death, so basic to the work of psychotherapy, happen at all. I understand Jung's struggle as
one between two archetypal obligations: Christianism that
denies the underworld, and soul-making that inevitably goes
there.

Aniela Jaffé, whose sympathetic and scholarly understanding of Jung's ideas is unsurpassed among his followers, has
written that the "psychological path of individuation is ultimately a preparation for death."[30] If this is the ultimate intent

of Jung's fundamental therapeutic principle, then the soul's process of individuation moves toward the underworld. Then every resurrection fantasy of theology may be a defense against death, every rebirth fantasy in psychology may be a defense against depth, and every dream interpretation that translates images into daily life and its concerns, a defense against soul.

5

DREAM

DREAM ROMANTICS

We begin by looking back. First in Freud and then in myth, we saw that the dream belongs to the underworld, but ever since Freud, interpretation of the dream has meant translation into the upperworld. Depth analysis, despite its name, moves dreams toward daylight. Now if we refuse dream interpretation in the usual analytical sense, then what alternatives are there for working with dreams?

There is one we shall refuse straight off. I mean the romantic notion that drifting through images on the bark of sleep is enough, calling like Keats:

> O Magic sleep! O comfortable bird,
> That broodest o'er the troubled sea of the mind
> Till it is hushed and smooth! O unconfined
> Restraint! imprisoned liberty! great key
> To golden palaces, strange minstrelsy,
> Fountains grotesque, new trees, bespangled caves

Echoing grottoes, full of tumbling waves!
And moonlight; ay, to all the magic world
Of silvery enchantment!

[*Endymion,* ll. 453–61]

Let us not believe that the romantics are all dead. There are some with us still—and, of all places, in the laboratories of sleep research, where we find again the romantic trust and delight in the nightworld, for some REM-sleep researchers claim that dreaming per se is beneficial, whether dreams are remembered or not, worked on or simply let to hush and smooth the troubled mind. It is enough to dream; to have dreaming interrupted or prevented occasions general psychic disturbance, so they say.

Alfred Ziegler, who works in similar laboratories with a dissimilar attitude, has shown that dreams cannot justify the optimistic philosophy and euphemistic conclusions of his co-researchers, because *dreams are preponderantly unpleasant.*[1] Even in the ideal conditions of the sleep laboratory, where we "return to nature" in the most romantic sense of descent into the private cave of our own souls, protected, warmed, and delivered over in silence to what nature offers us, far more dreams are unpleasant than pleasant. Ziegler raises the 'unromantic' question: perhaps nature means "to harm us," even "finally to kill us"; and there is plenty of evidence of pathology during dreaming (REM sleep), including heightened blood pressure and nighttime heart attacks. Ziegler's angle of approach is physiological, his thought biological, but the myth informing his attitude is classical. He too is returning the dream to its background in the chthonic underworld of Hades.

A second alternative is so close to the romantic position that it too is unsatisfactory. This one comes from Jung, although he himself did not hold to it literally. Jung said: "the dream is its own interpretation" (*CW* 11:§ 41), and sometimes the most we can do is "to dream the myth onwards" (*CW* 9,i:§ 271). To take Jung at his word here would not admit enough the work that is in the dream nor the demand on the understanding that the dream presents.

The ancient art of the dream interpreter is not only a defense against dreams but has arisen, as has all hermeneutics of what we today call "symbolic material," hand in hand with the dream. Both are gifts of Hermes: the work of the mystery and the work on the mystery. For dreams are not only "natural phenomena" (*CW* 17:§ 189); they are above all *imaginative products*. They are elaborations, linguistic and imagistic complexities, attesting to what Freud called "dreamwork" *(Traumarbeit)*. Even the dumbest dream can astound us with its art, the range of its reference, the play of its fancy, the selection of its detail. If we follow our own principle of likeness, then our response to the dream must go beyond the natural appreciation of dreaming it onwards. We shall as well have to respond with critical, imaginative appreciation, with a work that resembles its work.

There is still a third alternative: carrying dreams on into waking life, or what are called *waking dreams*. Let us take this dream: "I am in a doctor's waiting room. He hands me a baby with dirty diapers and says, change it." Rather than interpret the dream in the old sense or letting it float through the associative mind in the romantic sense, we may get back into the dream. In this case, we return to the waiting room, feeling the feelings of the "me," the doctor, the baby, the dirty diapers, and even the room itself. We enter into and become all parts of the dream.

This alternative does not truly move beyond feelings, and so it too becomes another romantic variety. Becoming a doctor, a diaper, a room is not what the dream said in its actual imagery. This is clear and distinctly stated: "I" am handed a baby by a doctor and told by him to change it. The doctor wants the baby "changed"—that conundrum is given me by the dream-doctor. To turn me into that baby, or a doctor, or a waiting room, encourages my fantasying to idle and associate, thereby bloating the image beyond its precise limits. Moreover, the identification with all the other parts obviates the nasty challenge handed the dream-ego: to take hold of a beshitted baby and "change" it. For all its value in teaching one "what it feels like" to be a dirty diaper and be shat on, to be a doctor and give clean-up orders, to be a waiting room and provide space for others who are ill, empathetic identification with all the figures in a dream finally returns the dream to the waking-ego, who romantically absorbs the dream through his feelings. This engorges the ego, who swallows his own dream by becoming its images, instead of working on his reactions within them. Therapeutically, the work done is for the sake of the waking ego, ego psychology. The dream still serves the dayworld, and so this method is appropriately called a *waking dream*.[2]

DREAM-EGO

A fourth course, and the one that shall be ours, takes its direction from Freud's term *dream-work*. Freud uses this term for a series of peculiar mental operations that go on in the night: condensation, displacement, regression, archaisation, symbolization, overdetermination, reversal, distortion (*IL*, p. xi; *ID*, p. vi). Of course these words are all dayworld concepts. That we look at the dream in these terms indicates that already a translation has taken place from nightworld activities into the language of daylight. What goes on in dreams has already received a pejorative description. The work of the dream is called regression, displacement, distortion, and the like.

Even worse, later Freudians, such as Róheim, then take these concepts so literally that they state the basic work of

all dreams is to regress and displace a person through symbol-
izations into the maternal vagina and archaic uterine waters
of fetal sleep.[3] The subtle dreamwork of the night has been
captured by the gross and undifferentiated concepts of the
dayworld and made to serve its monocular "basic view."
Dreams become distorted and condensed, as the theory states.

So, if our therapeutic job is to walk the ego back over
the bridge of the dream, to teach the dreamer how to dream,
we cannot use these terms for its work. We must reverse
our usual procedure of translating the dream into ego-lan-
guage and instead translate the ego into dream-language. This
means doing a dream-work on the ego, making a metaphor
of it, seeing through its "reality." Let us then suspend an
entire series of ego-operations, the ego-work, the modes by
means of which the ego has been approaching the dream
and performing its translations.[4] These are *causalism* (seeing
dream sequences in causal connections); *naturalism* (assuming dream events should accord with the upperworld of nature; *moralism* (seeing moral positions in the underworld and
the dream as compensatory expression of self-regulatory conscience); *personalism* (believing the realm of the soul to be
concerned mainly with personal life); *temporalism* (connecting dream events with the past or the future, either as recapitu-
lations of what happened or foretellings of what is to come);
voluntarism (seeing the dream in terms of action which requires a response in actions—"dreams tell us what to do");
humanism (that the dream is primarily a reflection of and
message for human affairs); *positivism* (reading the dream
as a positing, a positional statement, to which positive and
negative judgments can be applied); *literalism* (taking any
dream or aspect of any dream with singleness of meaning,
thus forgetting that every bit of the dream, including the
dream-"I", is a metaphorical image).

As the ego sees a set of pejorative factors at work in the
dream (regression, distortion, displacement), so the under-

world perspective sees a set of pejorative attitudes (humanism, personalism, literalism) at work in the ego. It is these attitudes which must first be suspended before we can approach the dream in an altogether new style.

Take, for example, the *Tagesreste,* the "day-residues," which according to Freud constitute our dream imagery. We no longer take them at face value, referring back to real events in a literal world of the day. Instead we imagine that the dream is digesting certain bits and pieces of the day, converting its facts into images. The dream is less a comment on the day than a digestive process of it, a breakdown and assimilation of the dayworld within the labyrinthine tracts of the psyche. The dream-work cooks life events into psychic substance by means of imaginative modes—symbolization, condensation, archaisation. This work takes matters out of life and makes them into soul, at the same time feeding soul each night with new material. It is like the worldwide practice, especially Egyptian, of putting objects from life into the tombs of the dead. Their whole world was transferred with them. They had to have immense supplies, for psychic life is an unending process, needing ample materials.

The right work with dreams aids this transferring or dying process that goes on anyway in the dream itself. It is a work that parallels what the dream is already doing. Interpretation, like dreaming, becomes a dying to the dayworld by ruminating it from literal realities into metaphorical realities. The more I dream of my mother and father, brother and sister, son and daughter, the less these actual persons are as I perceive them in my naive and literal naturalism and the more they become psychic inhabitants of the underworld. As they rise into the vision of my nights and I mull and digest their comings and goings, the family becomes a *familiaris,* internal accompaniments, no longer quite the literal people I engage with daily. Gradually the family moves from being the actual persons I must resist and contend with, to living ancestors, ghosts or shades, whose traits course within my psychic blood giving me support through their presence in my dreams. My family home shifts its ground from *gē* to *chthōn*.

How long we go on dreaming those old family scenes! There is mother scolding, her eyes framed in glasses, father's back turned, a long-dead brother still in the other bed. Why these eternal returns to the same figures? What does the psyche want? What is it doing bringing us back former loves as present agonies; night upon night, faces we kissed goodbye come back asking still for something more. Usually we think these repetitions and perseverations mean a complex has not been resolved; but what does that explanation really say?

Perhaps there is a work going on in the dreams, a prolonged cooking of obdurate residues that dissolve the all-too-solid flesh of remembered persons into their *simulacra,* shades of themselves, so that they may depart, freed of our attachments, and we may live in their presence without being oppressed by their life. These figures are more than complexes to be resolved; they are also emotional substances going through the work of soul-making.

THE SUBJECTIVE LEVEL

These reflections require that we turn again to the persons in dreams (see Ch. 3). We need to reexamine the notion of the subjective level of interpretation, as Jung called it, and as it has been since applied in therapies since Jung, especially Gestalt.

Freud and Jung both generally assume all figures and landscapes of dreams as interior psychic possibilities. Dream events belong to one's depth; this is the starting point of all depth psychology, a field that began with Freud's great volume on dreams. There he says (*ID,* p. 299): "every dream treats of one's own person." Jung worked out two levels of interpretation, which we have already discussed, but let us remember too that "objective" and "subjective" are levels of interpretation, not of the dream. The dream itself is wholly subjective. What walks through my dreams is not actual, other persons or even their soul traits mirrored in me (ikons or *simulacra* of them), but the deep, subjective psyche in its personified guises. A dream presents "me," subjected to "my" subjectivity. I am merely one subject among several in a dream. In sleep, I am thoroughly immersed in the dream. Only on waking do I reverse this fact and believe the dream is in me. At night the dream has me, but in the morning I say, I had a dream. A true subjective level of interpretation would have to keep me subjected to the dream.

Gestalt technique seems to attempt this by means of role identification. Yes, it says, you are indeed only one subject among several in a dream, so subject yourself to them. Let them enter you; become them; identify. Let us look at this method.

The technique of role identification means fusion with, mimesis of, and thus loss of, the image. It is no longer distinct from me. It and I have joined in feeling. We have merged in the same Gestalt, as in the example above (p. 93).

Next, when I take a dream image as a psychic potential—my older brother as my capacity to carry problems (p. 59)—and enter into his image and incorporate it with my feelings, I am performing more than a role. I am performing a reductive operation; I am reducing the *eidolon,* in which there is something archetypal, to a trait that can become part of my wholeness. This is indeed "growth"; but what grows is the ego, whose personality enlarges at the expense of the dream persons that it has become.

In this subtle way, Gestalt dream-work, following from Jung's subjective level of interpretation, can expand my person to take in the persons of the dream and eventually the Gods, who are in those dream persons. Gestalt is a *humanistic* psychology, that is, it affords a psychological technique with which humanism can wipe out the last trace of its ancient enemy, the Gods, from their last retreat in the soul.[5] Ever since Protagoras, all modes of humanism have tried to maintain man in the center as the measure of all things. Now, by means of "subjective interpretation" or "Gestalt technique," the first and immediate experience of the mythic, what happens in dreams, can be put into the human being as traits and parts of his nature. So, this mode of dream interpretation becomes just one more modern way of inflating the ego. The ideas of wholeness and creative growth cover the old *hubris* of the hero, and the path of integration is his old heroic journey in which he meets all the freaks of nature that are also divine forms of the imagination. As he proceeds from figure to figure, station to station, they disappear. Where have they gone when they are overcome and integrated, but into his own personality, divinizing man into the apotheosis of a gigantic freak himself.

You will recall that in the section "Dream Persons" in Chapter 3, I quoted passages from Jung and Dodds that led me to say: "In dreams we are visited by the *daimones*, nymphs, heroes and Gods, shaped like our friends of last evening." How can we now more precisely formulate the relation between the archetypal persons (1), coming through the figures of my friends (2), and my own personality traits and potentials (3)? To take the friends only on the subjective level, as personal potentialities, loses the underworld. But then, why don't the shades and Gods come in their own shapes; why do they bother with the dream-incarnations, my family and friends and odd strangers? These dream-persons must somehow be necessary.

They are necessary for soul-making. They are necessary for the work of seeing through, of de-literalizing. Without my friends of last evening, a dream would be a direct communication with spirits in a numinous vision. A dream is not a vision, however, as the psyche is not the spirit. The dream brings in the vale of the world, those banalities and trivialities and beautiful complexities like my friends, which are necessary for what dreams do in the soul. The friends are figures of this in-between realm that once was called the *metaxy*. They are neither only human nor only divine, neither subjective nor objective, neither personal nor archetypal—but both. The persons with whom I had dinner and who return in my dream embody *both*, my traits and actions and divine traits and actions. (The "objective level" of their traits and actions, of the actual dinner companions, has already been dealt with above. We are not, as we said there, dreaming of *them*. They are not *in* our dream.)

Because these friends embody *both*, they cannot be resolved by a one-sided interpretation, by a personalistic reduction into me or by an archetypal reversion *(epistrophe)* to spirits, without losing the in-between world of soul. So, after all, it seems that the mode of psychological connection with the *daimones*, nymphs, heroes, and Gods is by means of the "subjective level," but only if we extend subjective to mean impersonal, to include persons that are not mine, any more than my friends are mine.

The subjectivizing move is fundamental in depth psychology. It is usually called *taking back projections*. So, of course, we make this move with dreams too. By this I mean: by taking these dinner companions inwardly and by searching for the traits we have in common and the feelings they evoke— she is so passive, he so poisonous, the other such a wonderful listener—I am taking them in. I am seeing myself mirrored in them, them mirrored in me. I am reflecting on the shadows we share. This is an underworld procedure. Taking them in, however, is not to integrate them into my personal subject and so have done with them. Rather, there is an archetypal sense that now begins to emerge from "She-who-is-Passive," "He-who-is-so-Poisonous," and from the "Other-who-wonderfully-Listens." In the one figuration of my friend are my subjective personal traits and potentials and the archetypal personae who are the deeper potentials within each of our subjectivities. These personae lead us out of the subjective as it is usually conceived.

There is still one further consideration about the subjective level that I think brings down its whole structure. As long as dream persons are personal parts of the dreamer, we must amplify with mythical parallels in order to get the dream out of personal subjectivity. Jung's method of amplification, which deliberately raises dream images to mythic proportions, is a necessary consequent of his subjective level of interpretation. Now, here is the rub: how amplify that good ol' boy, front and center? We may find him doing all sorts of things that persons do in fairy tales and myths; that is, his behavior and accoutrements may be thoroughly amplified into archetypal dimensions, but who is he himself? Do we not take this dream-ego as the dreamer? The dream-ego is the rock on which the subjective level founders.

When an interpretation addresses the dreamer in terms of what the ego is doing in the dream or addresses the dream-ego's behavior in terms of the dreamer's life, the ego in the dream is being treated on the objective level, as the actual figure of daily life. I am being held accountable for what the "I" in the dream is doing. The distinction disappears between the dayworld dreamer and his nightworld dreaming. Here precisely is the inconsistency in most dream interpretation: all figures are taken on the subjective level, but the ego remains on the objective level. Although the interpreter may recognize that my car in my dream is not my actual car but images my "motoric driving," my "wheels," and that my sister in my dream is not my sister but the way her image affects my soul, still the "I" in the dream remains the I sitting in the client's chair of the consulting room. The "I" remains literal and intact, never truly resolved into its own image.

So, to reach the fully subjective, a dream-worker must reach into the last pocket of objectivity, the dream-ego, its behaviors and its feelings, keeping them within the image. The job becomes one of subjecting the ego to the dream, dissolving it in the dream, by showing that everything done and felt and said by the ego reflects its *situation in the image,* i.e., that this ego is wholly imaginal. Not an easy job, for the ego is archetypally an upperworld phenomenon, strong in its heroic attitudes until, by learning how to dream, it becomes an imaginal ego.

An imaginal ego is at home in the dark, moving among images as one of them. Often there are inklings of this ego in those dreams where we are quite comfortable with absurdities and horrors that would shock the daylight out of waking consciousness. The imaginal ego realizes that the images are not his own and that even his ego-body and ego-feeling and ego-action in a dream belong to the dream-image. So the first move in teaching ego how to dream is to teach it about itself, that it too is an image.

An imaginal ego is further built by voiding its old ground, the attitudes mentioned above—moralism, personalism, naturalism, literalism—deriving from the corporal perspective. The old heroic ego loses its stuffing and returns to a two-dimensional shade. Then it is able to reflect its deeds metaphorically. Then it may realize that the ego in the dream is also a wholly subjective figure, or shade, who is now voided of the I who lay himself down to sleep. Ego-behavior in the dream reflects the pattern of the image and the relations within the image, rather than the patterns and relations of the dayworld.

Admittedly, the dream-ego and the waking-ego have a special "twin" relationship; they are shadows of each other, as Hades is the brother of Zeus. But the "I" in the dream is no secret stage director (Schopenhauer) who wrote the play he acts in, no self-portrait photographer taking his own snapshot from below, nor are the wants fulfilled in a dream the ego's wishes. The dream is not "mine," but the psyche's, and the dream-ego merely plays one of the roles in the theatre, subjected to what the "others" want, subject to the necessities staged by the dream.

That the dream is like a shadow play, a mask, further connects it with the underworld. One of death's most ancient visibilities was in the shape of a masked dancer.[6] Again, what is hard to realize is that *all* the persons, *including myself,* may be taken as masks, playing our death roles. The Dionysian aspect of Hades does indeed make the dream akin to drama, as Jung said. Sometimes the dream puts this explicitly: we are at and in a movie, an opera, in the staginess of an historical novel, a pageant. In the drama of our dreams you and I, even if we are in the audience, are in the theater, actors all of us, dream-persons all of us, wearing the mask appropriate for the character we must play in the way we must play it.

This is hard to grasp. Something still holds on, even in the dream, to the upperworld "I." All right—the others are not the same persons as life; but at least I am I. Am I a mask embodying an archetypal numen, as I argue in a dream with the gas station attendant who is overfilling my tank, as I take my clothes to the dry cleaners? Surely when I have an orgasm in a "wet dream," it is the same I who awakens in the wet bed. If we follow Jung (see p. 60), however, and "reach down, or up, to quite other levels than so-called common sense would suspect," then why make exceptions about kinds of dreams or kinds of persons in dreams? We are obliged to assert that all dreams have their home in the underworld and all their persons are shades. We must search for the numen in the dream-ego, too. The "I" who wakens and remembers is left with traces of all sorts, not only wet ones, of the play he has been in and the role he has played, but the remembering I goes on in a different place, maybe in a quite different person. Just as the dream releases the shade of my brother and father from their actual embodiments, so it releases the dream-ego from having to embody the waking-ego and act in its name. Again, in dreams all persons, including myself, are dead to their lives, shadows of what they are elsewhere. Even their orgasms are in the land of the dead.[7]

KINDS OF SOUL

We are trying here in our own way and by means of the dream to restore a view of the soul that is still widespread among so-called primitive peoples. (These are sometimes called pretechnological, or animistic, or fourth-world, and the like. We can also regard them as having escaped the doctrines of soul, person, and ego that come with the monistic psychology of invading cultures.)[8]

According to a Scandinavian school of ethnological research on soul (Arbman, Paulson, Hultkrantz), there is a world-wide experience of two kinds of souls, documented not only in the higher cultures of Homeric Greece, Ancient Egypt (Ka and Ba), China (hun and p'o), but continues to be found in this century among peoples who stretch across the great Asian land mass, from the Lapps on the Atlantic to Siberians facing Alaska, and then among American Indians as well.[9] Ankermann shows similar experiences among Africans.[10]

This "dual pluralism" of soul, as Paulson calls it, refers on the one hand to a *life-soul* that is multiple, having various associations with body parts and emotions, and so is also called "body-soul" "breath-soul," and "ego-soul."[11] On the other hand, there is a *free-soul* or *psyche-soul* (Arbman's term), which is equivalent with and manifests as a "shadow-soul," "ghost-soul," "death-soul," "image-soul" (Ankermann), and "dream-soul." In Arbman's words, the "body-soul or -souls and the psyche-soul are independent of each other, have different natures and origins, as well as different tasks and spheres of activity."[12] The psyche-soul "appears only outside the body" and, limited to this form of existence, "it is out of play in waking, conscious, and active states of the person," says Paulson.[13] During these waking conditions, the psyche-soul is fully passive and no longer represents the personality as it does during dreams, visions, and shamanistic trances. The relations of this free-soul or psyche-soul with a person's death and the dead, one's illnesses and treatment, the shadows and ghosts, one's name and likeness—all these make it a highly relevant and specific concept for what we are here speaking of as persons of the dream and especially for the dream-ego.

What we have been articulating all through this essay as "dream-ego" and "imaginal ego" refers to the psyche-soul of primitive experience. The other perspective, waking-consciousness in the daylight world, is what this school of ethnology describes as life-soul, body-soul, ego-soul. The hyphen in all these terms keeps us aware that *the ego too is a soul.* How different psychology might look were we to keep the term ego always hyphenated with soul! This ego-soul as body-soul can easily be related to Freud's muscular notion of ego and my frequent metaphor of hero and Hercules. (My contrast further on in this chapter between the body-perspective of Hercules on the one hand and, on the other, the image- and death-perspective of Narcissus can also be compared with the ethnological evidence.)

Compared only! I would not want the ethnological research to be taken as universal evidence for my thesis. Depth psychology has been this route: we have already been sidetracked twice by the universal-evidence way of establishing a root metaphor. The Freudians used ethnology to show the universality of their Oedipus complex, and the Jungians used it again to show the universality of their mandala pattern of four-foldedness. We may not go this route, even if it affords great security; after all, whose life-soul would not breathe sweet ease in the support of firm and positive evidence gathered by serious independent researches from strange quarters of the globe where the simple folk had never heard a word of contemporary psychology (beyond what's talked by the funny people in the mission station). No, we have to stay within depth psychology. The soul is the only ground of our field. Although this important evidence all has to do with soul, it is presented in the objective, positive language of daylight consciousness. Thus it cannot provide the foundation for a psychology of the underworld. We have to stay with the dream-soul and look at things its way. Then we can take the research, not in the literal manner of empirical support but as a comparison, a likeness, another way of saying what we are saying, a most helpful story.

The grounding of my dream theory in underworld mythologems is also "nothing more" than a helpful story, but with an important difference. Mythical images are not firm evidence for anything positive. They cannot carry systematic structures on their backs. They don't stand still long enough, and they are too shady, as if to say they are thoroughly nightworld phenomena, even should their content show celestial beings in a solar empyrean. As nightworld phenomena, mythical images offer depth and background, a psychic dimension that rather voids a positive statement than confirms it. The support they might contribute to any positive reality is its background in fantasy.

We should observe here that the two-soul theory and our own account do not altogether coincide. The two-soul theory seems to draw a hard-and-fast line between psyche and life, and I have frequently been drawing that same line. A convergence, however, may be taking place in the dream, for there the dayworld seems to go through a process that transfers events out of life and educates the dreamer into death. This is not to call the dream a bridge, but it is to say that there is an operation, which we call dreaming, that makes the heroic ego a more subtle body, enabling it to become a free soul. From one vantage point it seems as if dreaming releases the free or psyche-soul from its misapprehension that it belongs to life. From another position it seems as if dreaming works at moving the ego- or body-soul into a deeper, more psychic dimension. Whichever way we choose to phrase it, the dream is that most near and regular place where we can experience the subtle play between kinds of soul.

Public performance on a stage, perhaps because it puts us into the underworld of theatre, also constellates the curious interplay between life-soul and image-soul. The almost depersonalization experience of stage fright makes one feel deserted by one's soul. All that one memorized and trained for has suddenly vanished. It is as if another soul must play the role, and this moment of going on stage is like a *rite de passage*, a transition into death.

Because the dayworld-ego refers to the objective level, its shade, the dream-ego, is generally out of place in the underworld. It goes on reacting with attitudes learned above. In dreams, we run from pursuers, resist being cheated, abuse animals, escape toward the light, fear the grotesque, and suspect the strange. Again and again, we find "reasons" for leaving the shadows. (By *shadow* here I do not mean the moral confrontations that Jung emphasized by this word; I mean the other main figures in a dream, whom the dream-ego misunderstands, resists, and who could be its mercurial teachers.)

Usually a good deal of dream analysis is required before the dream-ego begins to behave in dreams as a familiar of the underworld, keeping its laws, which differ from those of the upperworld. In dreams, nothing may be taken naturally, nothing may be referred back above—there is no return upward. There are no good or bad prospects of dreams, because hope is a foreign category irrelevant in the underworld, where every dream is anyway a self-satisfied wish. Nothing can be understood in terms of compensation, which only reflects the dream back up to the dayworld, as if the dreamworld had no autonomous intention of its own and were merely in harness to a dayworld for the sake of the dayworld's idea of balance.

The interpreter's role is to help the ego-shade adjust to his underworld milieu. The interpreter is a guiding Virgil, or a Teiresias, or a Charon;[14] he is not a Hercules or an Orpheus. His work is in service of Hermes *chthonios* or Hermes *psychopompos,* corresponding to the one way direction downward. Hermes takes souls down; the hero standing behind the ego tries to bring them back up again.

Therefore, the movement from the subjective interpretation back into the dayworld in answer to such questions as "what does this mean in my daily life?", "what should I do?", "how does this affect my relationship with these people whose images appeared in my dream?" and thus reading the dream for communications about the dayworld, is to approach the dream through the hero myth and not through the perspective of the underworld. Even the mantic approach to interpretation, which reads dreams as containing "messages from the unconscious self" that has an eternal knowledge, ultimately returns the dream to the dayworld's ego. For whom is the message; who wants to know it; who will carry it out—none other than Old Ego. In brief: a dream tells you where you are, not what to do; or, by placing you where you are, it tells you what you are doing.

If only we could remember the affinity of sleep with death, we might not try to recall each dream to life and apply it there. Essential in older traditions, including the "primitive" ones, is the idea that the soul separates from the body during sleep. It "wanders" then, a "wandering" which means that its logic does not proceed in linear contiguous steps and its attention is not fixed on the aims of the day. Plotinus (*Enn.* 2. 2, 2) associated the mode of straight and aimed movement with the body (-soul) rather than with the psyche (-soul). In sleep, the soul moves differently, rather in the style of *phantasia*, which Greek thought often connected with "wandering"; or, according to Plato in the *Timaeus*, wandering could mean being moved by necessities in the soul that are not subject to reason. No wonder that dreams have always been considered mysteries or even madness.

The belief that the soul wanders away from body in sleep is another way of stating that dreams leave the body-soul's literalistic and naturalistic perspective. If so, then to grasp at dreams with body techniques and apply their images directly to the relation of bodies is to miss their wandering. Therapies that go at dreams in terms of body-language, body-ego, and physical life are attempting to force the free soul into perspectives that sleep allows it to leave. The key here is indirection: if the soul wanders from the body in sleep, then our way of letting the soul return to concrete life must follow the same wandering course, an indirect meandering, a reflective puzzling, a method that never translates the madness but speaks with it in its dream language.

The Ba-soul "enjoys limitless freedom of movement" (*Ba*, p. 98). It must have power over its legs and feet and act with its own arms and hands, which were a New Kingdom depiction of the underworld soul (*Ba*, p. 76). The soul stands on its own feet, has its own limbs, and handles things in its own fashion. The soul moves by means of its soul-body. Madness begins when we attempt to force its legs into ours and turn its hands directly to our dayworld tasks. This is rightly called "acting out." Loss of the subtle movements of the Ba-body in the gross muscular body is a Herculean madness.

HERCULES IN THE HOUSE OF HADES

Hercules had to go mad, literally, in order to understand the underside of things, maybe because his journey to Hades was a mess. When imagining Hercules in the House of Hades (Euripedes, *Alcestis* 846–54; Homer *Il.* 5. 397, *Od.* 11. 601; Apollodorus 2. 5, 12)—his aggressiveness in drawing his sword, aiming his arrow, wounding Hades in the shoulder, slaughtering cattle, wrestling the herdsman, choking and chaining Cerberos—we are presented with the imaginal paradigm of the life instinct, as Freud called it, within the realm of the death instinct (*EI,* p. 59). This fusion is precisely, according to Freud, the origin of aggressivity (*BPP,* p. 73f.; *CP* 2: 260). Rather than die to metaphor, we kill literally; refusing the need to die, we attack death itself. Our civilization, with its heroic monuments, tributes to victory over death, ennobles the Herculean ego, who does not know how to behave in the underworld.

Hercules differs from the other heroes, who, as Kerényi says, "were tragically connected with death."[15] The *heroic ego,* as I am using the term all through this book, should be more appropriately differentiated as the "Herculean ego," for only he of them all is an enemy of death. Yet there is justification for my term because the hero then, in a living world of Gods, and the heroic today are two very different cases, although the second arises from the first. Then he was half-man and half-God, but when the Gods are dead the hero becomes all too human. The divine portion is assumed wholly by the human, and we are left with the founding figure of humanism and its worship of man.

Then, the hero was actually an underworld figure, known only in his *tumulus* or burial mound, which attached him to a definite place, so that the cult of the hero was a *reminiscence* of imaginative struggles, a memorial mode of

being founded and located and carried through the vicissitudes of life. Even the term *heros* has been considered "chthonian" by some scholars, denoting a power of the lower world
and hence the "common use of the word in later Greek for
a deceased person."[16] The sacrificial act to the hero was
gloomy and different in detail from the *thysia* allotted to
the high Gods, but the same low altar or hearth, the same
rites, the same kind of bloodtrench that funneled the flow
underground was common to the cult of heroes and of the
dead. The victim was held over the trench, head down.[17]

Today, cut off from this psychic background, the heroic
becomes the psychopathic: an exaltation of activity for its
own sake. The locus of its cult is not the burial mound on
which the city and its deeds are founded, but in the human
body itself, the humanistic ego. Even should this ego be enno-
bled by the mission of solar hero or culture hero on the
high plane of good works, without the other half of the hero—
the Gods and death—and without the psychic trailing that
holds each to his depth like the chthonic snake-form they
each formerly had, "the legends of heroes become tales of
warlike men."[18] In Macedonia, Hercules himself was called
aretos, "the warlike."[19] Here precisely is the cause of my
passion and the ground of my attack on the heroic ego. The
archetypal hero continues, for the Gods of which he is half-
composed do not die. All the Gods are within, as Zimmer
said and Jung discovered in the complexes of his patients.
The hero still exists in his burial mound, now the human
ego-complex. This is the fixed locus where we worship and
from whence comes the ego's strength. Ego psychology is
the contemporary form of the hero cult. In the end, Hercules
goes up in fire. Are the legends of the ego that we now call
psychology developing into what will become tales of warlike
men? Will ego psychology lead us into war and fire?

There remains a question in mythology whether or not
Hercules was ever initiated into the Greater Eleusinian mys-

teries, which would have meant a change in consciousness from dayworld's life to nightworld's death.[20] This initiation was a central question in the Hercules myth; the other heroes were not enemies of death. From the actions of Hercules in the underworld, however, it would appear that the initiation, if it ever took place, never took effect. For us this means that our heroic ego is uninitiated and that our nightly descent into dreaming is a mode of initiation. This means a radical reversal of theory. The dream is not compensation but initiation. It does not complete ego-consciousness, but voids it.

So it matters very much the way we descend. Ulysses and Aeneas, as we pointed out above, go down to *learn* from the underworld which re-visions their life in the upperworld. Hercules, however, goes down to *take,* and he continues with the muscular reactions of the upperworld, *testing* each phantom for its reality, e.g., at the vision of the *Gorgoneion,* he drew his sword, and Hermes had to inform him that it was an image. The shades themselves had fled on his arrival, like dreams that disappear from the daylight mind. Freud says (*TD,* p. 149), "We shall place the testing of reality as one of the great institutions of the ego." He explains (*CP* 4:148) this testing as if he had just been reading the story of Hercules in Hades. "A perception which is made to disappear by motor activity is recognized as external, as reality; where such activity makes no difference, the perception originates within the subject . . . it is not real." In the same paragraph, we learn that this testing procedure between outer and real and subjective and not real relates to the "actions of the muscles." A consciousness that works in this mode defines reality only as that which responds to muscle power; subjective imagination is simply not real. Since it is there and bothersome nonetheless, Freud says, the individual has to "*project,* i.e., to transfer outwards, all that becomes troublesome to him from within."

In another place, Freud refashions Hercules in psychological terms, writing (*CP* 4:62): "Let us imagine ourselves in the position of an almost entirely helpless living organism as yet unorientated in the world and with stimuli impinging . . . [Hercules in the underworld]. This organism [Hercules] will soon become capable of making a first discrimination and a first orientation. On the one hand, it will detect certain stimuli which can be avoided by the action of the muscles— these it ascribes to an outside world; on the other hand, it will also be aware of stimuli against which such action is of no avail [the Gorgon's head] and whose urgency is in no way diminished by it—these stimuli are the tokens of an inner world. . . . the living organism [Hercules] will thus have found in the efficacy of its muscular activity a means for discriminating between 'outer' and 'inner'."

"It is not meet to act and speak like men asleep," said Heraclitus (frg. 73, Burnet).[21] Perhaps in nightlife it is not meet to act and speak like men awake. The distinction must be kept, but Hercules cannot see the difference, because he seems unable to imagine (he has already slain the imaginary beasts, the animal powers of imagination, and washed away the shit of the animals' home where imagination breeds in putrefaction).

The villain in the underworld is the heroic ego, not Hades. It is the ego who does the damage, an observation already noted by the romantic Steffens long ago: "It is the waking-consciousness in the dream that narrows and opposes the true inner dream, the deep reflection of the soul on the hidden richness of its interior existence, just as the dream disturbs waking-consciousness during the day."[22]

We can discover the hero in ourselves when in a dream the ego acts aggressively toward what it suspects, what is unfamiliar, and what is autonomous (animals). Also, heightened activity gives us away—rushing, change of scene, leaving for the next task, and speeding through space in chariots of locomotion. Myths say we may not use the sword in the underworld; we may only struggle with the shades in close embrace or throw stones. Hades never takes an active part in the Homeric imagination.[23] He receives the souls that come down. Mildness, says Kerényi, is his characteristic trait.[24] Later, in fourth-century Attica, scenes of the cult of souls of the dead show piety and intimacy, and "the blood of the sacrificial animals is never spilt."[25]

Let's not underestimate Hercules' propensity to violence. When he gets to Hades, he wants to feed the shades the blood they ask for. He wants to restore their thymos and release them from psyche into action, the nature of which is revealed by his own actions (slaughtering the cattle). The cult of Hercules was anyway involved with blood. The main reason against his Eleusinian initiation was the extent of the blood on his polluted hands, says Kerényi,[26] and Farnell[27] says that, "As a most virile hero-god he preferred the blood-sacrifice of the male animal, especially the ox or bull, the swine and ram. . . . he might be satisfied with an offering of cocks, for the cock is a fighting bird." Lucian says, "the god is an eater of beef."[28]

Perhaps the psychologies that focus upon action therapy, from EST, pillow punching, and couples shouting to the step-by-step disciplining of the muscles in behavior therapy and the muscles work of tough Rolf and gentle Reich, as well as the Oriental schools of trained violence, are each modes of coming to terms with Strong Hercules, Warlike Hercules. These are ego therapies, but if that is where the disease lies, then let's go to the pathologized place. But only when we have a deeper aim, a link outside the ego to the dream, as the hero links with the Gods and death, are we truly moving the ego-complex. Otherwise therapy becomes but one more accomplishment of the beefeater, a new hold he learns to get on life, again image lost in behavior.

The initiation of the heroic ego—learning the metaphorical understanding of the dream—is not only a "psychological problem," only for the sophistication of the therapy session. It is cultural, and it is vast and crucial. The culture-hero Hercules as well as all our mini-herculean egos mimetic to that Man-God, is a killer among images. The image makes it mad, or rather evokes its madness, because heroic sanity insists on a reality that it can grapple with, aim an arrow at, or bash with a club.[29] Real equals corporeal. So it attacks the image, driving death from his throne, as if recognition of the image implies death for ego. The heroic ego literalizes the imaginal. Because it lacks the metaphorical understanding that comes with image-work, it makes wrong moves, and these violently.

Hercules in Hades shows us that iconoclasm is the first move of murder. Of course our culture must have the constraint of the Sixth Commandment (forbidding killing), for the murderous possibility is already entailed in the Second (forbidding imaging). If we do not recognize the divine power in images, then what can restrain the ego's literalism but moral prohibitions? Without metaphorical understanding, everything is only what it is and must be met on the simplest, most direct level. Everything then is a call to action, and the hero is there to realize himself in a reality that serves his literal notion of it. A view of reality that does not recognize other views is of course delusional. In the heroic ego's case, the delusion is self-divinization, the perspective of the human ego as the superior, indeed the only, actuality. The rest is not real.

Without imaginal understanding, we may expect killing, as if our culture cannot ever take down the wild Western ego until it has restored the ancient sense of image and recovered the imaginal from the broken shards of reformational literalism. Now there is nothing between earth-man and heavenly God, body-ego and abstract Self, or between hard fact and sheer fantasy. Into that nothing-between that open country of As-If, the *metaxy* where the psyche's imagination configurates its fictions, stalks ego with his weapons and his bible, confronting images as demons or hallucinations, creating out of what he calls the wilderness of the unconscious his egocentric civilization and a psychology for it without soul.

Yes, now we worry about the relation between violence on the television screen and violence in the streets, but the grounds for this confusion between image and act, and particularly the violence of the act when imaging is forsaken, is bedrock to our tradition. The first murder was divine and of the image, and its consequent took place in the first human act upon release from Eden—a murder (as we are created in the image of the divine, we can do only what the Gods imagine for us in their behavior). This confusion between imaging action on the screen and acting action on the street is further sanctified by Saint Matthew (5:29), whose Gospel denies distinction between the adulterous image in the heart and its act in the flesh. Imaging *must* be forbidden when it is taken literally, as no different from action. *Taking images literally,* with the same kind of realism as the ego uses in the daylight world—this is the heroic error, a mistake of Herculean proportions, given further Judeo-Christian blessing through warnings against demons, dreams, ikons, and all forms of the soul's imagining.

Each morning we repeat our Western history, slaying our brother, the dream, by killing its images with interpretative concepts that explain the dream to the ego. Ego, over black coffee (a ritual of sympathetic magic), chases the shadows of the night and reinforces his dominion. No one sees the mark of Cain where his third eye could be.

For us the golden rule in touching any dream is keeping it alive. Dream-work is conservation. We have to set aside what we naturally and usually do: projecting the dream into the future, reducing the dream to the past, extracting from the dream a message. These moves lose the dream in exchange for what we get from it. Conservation implies holding on to what is and even assuming that what is is right. This suggests that everything in the dream is right, except the ego. Everything in the dream is doing what it must, following psychic necessity along the wandering course of its purposes, except the ego. The river must be dry, the bridge so high, the tree uprooted, the dog run over, the party conceal a poisoner, the dentist demand complete extraction—only the ego's behavior comes under suspicion. It tends to do the wrong thing and make the wrong appraisals, because it has just come from somewhere else and cannot see in the dark.

Like Hermes with Hercules, we take the dream-ego as an apprentice, learning to familiarize itself with the underworld by learning how to dream and learning how to die. It would still cling to the physical, to the *shtula* (Hindu)[30] or *molk* (Iranian)[31] aspect, reacting literally to what is visible as if it were corporeal. It does not yet have the *suksma* or *malakût* vision of metaphor and cannot see through the other figures until it has learned to let them see through itself. Again, in the language of Heraclitus (frg. 21, Kirk): "what we see when asleep is sleep."[32] We do not see the waking world in sleep; we see Hypnos. Dreaming is the mode by which the ego learns to "see sleep." The first task of interpretation is to protect that sleep, where protection means *seeing* in the sleep, waking the dream-ego within its dream.

DREAM-WORK

Let us look again at the work going on during sleep. What is the relation between work and sleep, and what kind of work happens in sleep? What does it mean to insist that a dream is a piece of work?

Freud considered the dream-work to be "the most important part of the dream" (*NIL,* p. 17), and a recent survey among Jungian analysts shows the overwhelming majority of them take the dream as the main instrument of their work.[33] The work of dreams and the work on dreams is essential to depth psychology. What is this work, and why do it?

First, we should dissociate "work" from Herculean labor and return the idea of work to the example of the dream, where work is an imaginative activity, a work of imagination such as takes place in painters and writers. Not all work is done by the ego in terms of its reality principle. There is work done by the imagination in terms of its reality, where joy and fantasy also take part. Here Bachelard and Jung are better guides than Freud and Marx, for work as an imaginative activity takes on an alchemical signification beyond the moral duties of senex consciousness. Then the psyche is always at work, churning and fermenting, without forethought of its product, and there is no profit from dreams. As long as we approach the dream to exploit it for our consciousness, to gain information from it, we are turning its workings into the economics of work. This is capitalism of the ego, now acting as a captain of industry, who by increasing his information flow is at the same time estranging himself both from the source of his raw material (nature) and his workers (imagination). Result: the usual illnesses of those at the top. Simply 'working' on your dreams to get information from them is no life insurance.

In the imagination, there is no separation between work and play, reality and pleasure. This means we may leave behind the notion of man as a playing animal *(homo ludens)* and recent philosophies of play, which ennoble the child and the puer, as the new Gods of the times. These philosophies are themselves rebellious residues from the high days of Protestantism and its work ethic. They still live off the contrast between work and play, between which and embracing both is imagination. In that middle ground, there is no separation between dream-work and the play of fancy.

The dream-work is done by the complexes, as Jung pointed out already in 1906, when he showed the relation between complex and dream figures (*CW* 2:§ 944; cf. *CW* 8:§ 202). These complexes are "the little people" (*CW* 8:§ 209), who act like the dactyls, doing the fingerwork in the primal clay of the imagination. They are the gnomes who work at night, the underworld smiths and labyrinth makers, the artisan craftsmen who cannot cease from shaping, or, in Jung's language, the continual activity of psychic fantasy that makes what we call reality (*CW* 6:§§ 78, 743). Dreams are made by the persons in them, the personified complexes within each of us; these persons come out most freely in the night. To understand a dream, we must examine carefully what these persons have wrought and how their interrelations have collaborated into what we call a *dream*. The dream is the work of fantasy figures, who craft the psyche when our eyes are closed. There is a forming going on at night, for "sleepers are workers" said Heraclitus (frg. 75, Wheelwright), "and collaborators in what goes on in the universe."

It is this dream-work, as Freud said, that protects sleep, the dream's only true purpose. This sleep, I believe, is not the biological sleep that Freud meant but rather the poetic sleep that the romantics meant. I believe that Freud, too, implied this romantic poetic sleep, for he sees in sleep a return to primary narcissism (*TD*, p. 138), another term taken from myth and one of the favorite mythologems of poetic consciousness. Is Narcissus the patron saint of imagination? His love was wholly given to and fulfilled by the reflected image that took him to the underworld.

NARCISSUS AND THE DREAM

By means of narcissism and Narcissus, we may try another approach to what Freud said was the most hotly disputed point of his entire dream theory: the overall explanation that "all dreams are wish-fulfilments" (*NIL*, p. 41). The Jungian critique of Freud's hypothesis has concentrated upon the wish and neglected the fulfilment. The Jungian critique has said, dreams are not wishes, for quite patently I dream all sorts of things far from what I ever might wish, but it has not inquired more deeply into the nature of dreams as fulfilments. So let us ask, "if the content of a dream is the representation of a fulfilled wish" (*OD*, p. 61), then precisely what fulfills the instinctual wish? The dream-work itself can be our only answer: *the images made in dreams fulfill the desire of instinct.* Narcissus' desire was fulfilled by the image of the body experienced in reflection. It wanted nothing else.[34]

To take hold of the radicality of this conclusion, we need to recall Freudian theory. At night in sleep when control is relaxed, the seething cauldron of the id with its libidinal desires would boil up and scald us with polymorphous perverse sexual wishes were there not some psychic censoring mechanism that allowed us to sleep. This mechanism, which turns the sexual urges into acceptable disguises, is the dream-work. All its complicated labor is the transfiguration of latent sexual wishes into manifest imagery. This imagery partly allows the id to let off steam and partly keeps us lulled from what is truly (sexually) going on. Thus, the dream-work is so important because it gratifies *both* the sexual instinct *and* the instinct to sleep. The dream-work, in short, fulfills instinctual demands.

Here we are closer to Jung than we might at first believe. Jung took archetypal images to be representations of instincts, as their other side. An image completes instinct by guiding it to its goals or, in Freud's word, fulfills it. Thus, for both Freud and Jung the work that goes on in sleep fulfills an instinctual or archetypal need. This gratification does not occur through what the dream means, by the noetic signification of the dream, for dreams are astoundingly un-understandable. As Freud said, they are not communications. Nor are the wishes satisfied by the internal emotions and actions in dreams, as if our desires are fulfilled by instinctual dreams of fighting, copulating, eating, fleeing, and the like. Such dreams occur not that often and one awakens not that often from them with a satisfied feeling of fulfilment. No, the fulfilment that the dream brings is narcissistic, satisfactory to Narcissus. In some amazing way, instinct is satisfied in the night-world by its own images, images of itself, as if it were enough for the psyche to see its own reflection by means of images, as if it were enough to imagine in poetic form its physical body and needs, its love, and its own self.

Freud's theory seems so scientifically biological that we tend to miss its romanticism. Narcissus, as Freud himself indicates, is the giveaway. After all, blood-and-gland instinct demands fulfilment in its own kind. Yet Freud maintains that the entire process of satisfying instinctual wishes is internal, wholly psychic or narcissistic. No external event is needed, no fight, flight, food, foreplay, or any other "f." The instinctual craving is gratified solely by the image, and the psyche sleeps in peace. Dreaming becomes a superinstinct: it satisfies both other instinctual cravings, including the need to sleep, as well as narcissistically satisfying its own demand for images.

We can put Freud's theory into the language of Plato's *Cratylus* (403–04): "What keeps souls in the underworld?," asks Socrates. ("What keeps the psyche asleep?," asks Freud.) Answer: Desire (Wishes); the soul wishes to stay there, for it finds satisfaction there. What satisfies the desire? (What fulfills the wishes?) Answer: the benefactory intelligence of Hades (404a), "his knowledge of all noble things" from which his name itself derives *(eidenai).* That is, Hades has a hidden connection with *eidos* and *eidolon,* the archetypal intelligence given in images. Hence, what fulfills our deepest wish is Hades, in whose dreams is the intelligence of archetypal ideas; and we must sleep in order to see these ideas. It is these images, these visible ideas, that fulfill the desire of the soul, feeding it with intelligence as it sinks into the night, or as the romantic von Baader put it: "Images do the soul good! They are its true food."[35]

The best food are the images of myth. This premise, that the psyche, and psychology, is best satisfied by myth, we find first of all in Freud's style of using old myths and rewriting them into new myths. We find the same premise theoretically expressed by Jung and, of course, before either of them, by the romantics. They especially recognized the analogies between myth and dream. Already von Schubert (1814) drew precise parallels between the symbolic imagery of the dream and that of the Dionysos cult and the Eleusinian mysteries.[36]

Although the dream itself is unconcerned with waking-life (*CP* 5:150), the dream-work, as a satisfaction of instinct, will have its effect upon waking-life, even if indirectly and without benefit of the connections to life made by ego-counseling based on dreams. How do such effects come about, if not by direct advice extracted from the dream?

From the comparison of dreams with myth, healing cult, and religious mysteries, we can understand that changes take place in participants even without direct interpretative intervention. It is not what is said about the dream after the dream, but the experience of the dream after the dream. A dream compared with a mystery suggests that the dream is effective as long as it remains alive. The healing cults of Asclepius depended upon dreaming, but not upon dream interpretation. This implies to me that dreams can be killed by interpreters, so that the direct application of the dream as a message for the ego is probably less effective in actually changing consciousness and affecting life than is the dream still kept alive as an enigmatic image. It is better to keep the dream's black dog before your inner sense all day than to "know" its meaning (sexual impulses, mother complex, devilish aggression, guardian, or what have you). A living dog is better than one stuffed with concepts or substituted by an interpretation.

For a dream image to work in life it must, like a mystery, be experienced as fully real. Interpretation arises when we have lost touch with the images, when their reality is derivative, so that this reality must be recovered through conceptual translation. Then we try to replace its intelligence with ours instead of speaking to its intelligence with ours. Images, by satisfying instinct, will in themselves alter the way we live, just as will the satisfaction of any other instinctual requirement. Before an interpretation ever begins, the dream is already working upon consciousness and its dayworld by digesting the day residues into soul-stuff and by placing one's actions and relations into its dream fantasy, making them part of a dream narrative, weaving the dayworld into another story. Only such changes that are changes in soul can affect the psychic aspect of one's actions and relations. Other changes, those attempted through the conscious correction of the ego's course, are attempts of the will. They are labors of Hercules, rather than reflections of Narcissus. These direct interpretations into life only cast a new shadow in the underworld, a new move requiring compensation, a further expiative correction.

THE DREAM'S DUPLICITY

Direct translations betray the dream also in another way: they falsify its ambiguity by deriving a message from it. Now, what about this ambiguity of dreams upon which all writers on the subject love to dwell? First of all, dreams are usually not at all ambiguous in their visible actuality. The images come in sure shapes: the snake was silvery and enormous and right on the bedroom carpet; the policeman was crouching by the barrier on the left with a shield in front of his body; I opened the door and there was Groucho Marx. I feel rage, or fear, or sweeping desire as I touch soft skin, and I hear distinct voices stating ideas, snatches of complex music, or read whole phrases sharp as print on this page.

So we must distinguish between the concrete definiteness of most dream imagery and the feelings of vagueness about it, the murky slipperiness, its elusive character and inherent ambivalence when the dream is fished into daylight. Is it the transition to light that gives the dream its shadowy quality? We all know how much an art it is, not to dream, but to recall it.

Yet there are vague dreams. Let us take vagueness as a valid phenomenon. Opaqueness, elusiveness, equivocation, indefiniteness then must be part of the dream's shape. These characteristics belong to the image and are not merely the "fault" of daylight consciousness, owing to its stubby grasp of the nightworld.

Vagueness puts a dream in the cloudy region, a mixture of water and air—opaqueness, a mixture of water and earth. The elusive, quick-flitting dreams are accurate presentations of mercurial fire, just as those long convoluted dreams that seem to lead nowhere are like labyrinths winding through the earth. *The way in which a dream comes already is part of its statement,* expressing an elemental condition. Dreams come in styles; we might say, in literary genres. These genres reflect not merely a typological difference in dreamers or merely a tendency toward one or another psychopathology, as if depressives dream laconically, hysterics effusively, schizos bizarrely.[37] We need to recognize the multiplicity of genres of imaginative products and that dream-work, like any work of *poesis* (the making of images in words), is shaped not only by its content but also by its manner of presentation.

Literary reflection of this sort might save analysts from one of our errors. How often we use the criteria of one element, or one season (Northrop Frye), for condemning products of another. Why shouldn't there be dreams of ice, of houses burning, of walls giving way to rising waters? Must flying be an inflation and drowning a danger—or have we forgot that Perseus, Icarus, Bellerophon all must go through the air in order to imagine their way to their aims and that only by dissolution in water is the old king in alchemy changed and Hermaphroditus created? And these elemental and seasonal contents may also appear in the lapidary coldness of the dream's wording, or its blaze, or its humorous moisture and swollen hyperbole. Too often we analysts suspect 'latent psychosis' when a dream does not match the expectations of style that we impose on the material.[38]

Melodramatic pathetic dreams with everyone changing sex and identity, dying and returning, is a style of watery imagining, just as there is an imagination of fire, sudden, flashing out, gone. Slow dreams in which all things seem to flower in warmth (such as women may have in pregnancy) do not imply that healing is occurring or individuation taking place. These are dreams in the genre of summer, of a season only. The style may be read as a rhetoric belonging archetypally to the particular images of that particular dream, rather than as part of a general process that sets up expectations, that only mislead us in regard to the dream material that follows.

If we speak of dreams as material (and in the next section we shall be doing so in more detail), we must take into account Bachelard's studies of the elements of imagination. His poetics of matter help us see that the style of a dream expresses an element—fire, air, water, earth. We learn through him that style or genre is dream content of the most elemental sort. In each of these elements, there are many meanings. Fire is as much a combustive violence as it is light and warmth and meditative reflection; it protects, it quickens with life, and it purifies for death. The elements of imagination, unlike the elements of science, are necessarily polyvalent.

The ambiguity of the dream lies in the essential nature of the imagination that, like a flowing river (cf. Heraclitus frgs. 12, 49, 91), *must move.*[39] The essence of psyche is the principle of motion; Aristotle too saw that. Any image that can "stand" for a psychic meaning at once brings psychic flow to a standstill. Such are the signs which Jung derides, images that signify nothing imaginative. A dream, to remain a dream (and not a sign or a message or a prophecy), can therefore have no one interpretation, one meaning, one value. "In the realm of the imagination there is no value without polyvalence," says Bachelard.[40] The ambiguity of dreams lies in their multiplicity of meanings, their inner polytheism, the fact that they have in each scene, figure, image "an inherent tension of opposites," as Jung would say. The tension is more than that, however, it is the tension of multiple likenesses, endless possibilities, for the dream is soul itself, and soul, said Heraclitus, is endless.

The image may be sharp, but the meaning many-edged. For instance, in a dream I am running and being pursued. Does this mean: I am running because I am pursued or I am pursued because I am running? Or does it mean: to run is to feel pursuit; when I run it is like a pursuit? Another image: I drive and the car goes off the road, says the dream in its sure shape. Does this mean: that my driving goes off; or that even when I drive, the car goes off autonomously; or that I drive the car deliberately, but unconsciously, off the road? What are the relations between my "drive" and "going off the road"?

Duplicity or multiplicity is not in the precise image but in its significance. Yet, this potential for multiple meaning must lie in the image itself, despite its sharpness. In fact, duplicity is a basic law of imagination, says Bachelard:

> a matter to which the imagination cannot give a twofold life cannot play the psychological role of a fundamental substance. A matter which does not elicit a psychological ambivalence cannot find its *poetic double* which allows endless transpositions. It is necessary then to have a *double participation*—participation of desire and fear, participation of good and evil, peaceful participation of black and white—for the material element to involve the entire soul.[41]

Bachelard's phrase "black and white" goes all the way
back to the description of classical images by Philostratus
(born c. 191 A.D.). In his book, which presents succinct images
for basic ideas, themes, and figures, the God of dreams was
a standing person "in a relaxed attitude, wearing a white
garment over a black one."[42]

Here we have the problem of dream duplicity presented
in fantasy form. We see the two aspects: one over, one under;
one white, the other black. The dream itself is indolently
relaxed about its dressing, as if it says, "It is not I who am
loaded with tension. I can stand all this with ease. It's my
natural get-up, the way I like to come on. It's your problem,
analysts and interpreters, that you have to speak of me as
an innate duality, polarity, and tension." So interpreters call
the black-and-white aspects or the over-and-under garments
positive and negative, subjective and objective levels, latent
and manifest, masculine and feminine, gē and *chthōn,* horn
and ivory, life and death. And they declare the task to be
one of translating black into white, or the reversion of white
into the concealed black, or uniting the opposites that are
in compensation. Do what we will, the dream presents itself
in the robes of duplicity, stating simply that an ambiguity
of significance is its habitual presentation. If dreams are the
teachers of the waking-ego, this *duplicity is the essential in-
struction they impart.* The duplicity, however, is less that of
logical paradox than of ironic humor; the hermeneutic, not
of oppositions, but of jokes. Little wonder one once asked
Hermes for a dream.

DREAMS, THE WORK OF DEATH

Let us imagine the dream-work to be an activity, less of
a censor than of a *bricoleur.*[43] Censors suggest morals, or
they implicate us in spies, codes, and detection. But the dream
bricoleur is a handyman, who takes the bits of junk left over
from the day and potters about with them, tacking residual

things together into a collage. While the fingers that form a dream destroy the original sense of these residues, at the same time they shape them into a new sense within a new context. If the dream expresses the id, as Freud said, then it serves its two principles, love and death. Death is the scrap dealer, stripping the world for spare parts, separating, destroying connections (*EI*, p. 53), which love—continuing Freud's original metaphor—fuses into new unities. The imagination at night takes events out of life, and the *bricoleur* in the service of the death instinct scavenges and forages for day residues, removing more and more empirical trash of the personal world out of life and into psyche for the sake of its love.

Imagination works by deforming and forming at one and the same moment. Bachelard has spoken of the *deformative activity of the imagination*, as if the formal cause at work in the imagination is the principle of deformation, or "pathologizing" the image.[44] The pathologized or deformed image is fundamental to alchemy and to the art of memory (*MA*, p. 190 f.), both of which present complex methods of soul making. It is the pathologized image in the dream, the bizarre, peculiar, sick or wounded figure—the disruptive element— to which we must look for the key to the dream-work. Here is where the formal cause of the dream is best doing its deformational work, striking its type into the plasticity of the imagination.

Something—is it the psyche itself?—seems to want and yet resist being twisted into shapes that are unnatural. On the one hand, Freud imagined the psyche at its most infantile level to be perverse: the original instinctual child is naturally twisted. On the other hand, something else in us, and equally deep, wants "nothing to extreme," wants to remain in the fantasy of natural balance and harmony.

Alchemy resolved this dilemma by conceiving its deformational work to be an *opus contra naturam*, a work against nature but yet in the service of a wider nature that is animated or ensouled. Alchemical work had to deform nature in order to serve nature. It had to hurt (boil, sever, skin, desiccate, putrefy, suffocate, drown, etc.) natural nature in order to free animated nature. As soon as psyche enters into consideration, the only-natural is not enough. Soul-making is like any other imaginative activity. It requires crafting, just as does politics, agriculture, the arts, love relations, war, or the winning of any natural resource. What is given won't get us through; something must be made of it. There is evidently in the soul something that wrests it out of the only natural: we experience this twist as perversion or as the torment and torture of pathologizing and are then forced to grope our way through the twisted and tortuous labyrinth of soul-making.[45] Analysis is the scrutiny of these twists and turns in our nature, which we call complexes, and it aims towards a *lysis,* a way out. We suppose the pathologizings brought by our complexes to come from historical forces, but why not from character itself, the nature we are born with? Is not the natural person from the beginning a complexity? And are not the Gods who clothe themselves in our complexes and speak through them also from the beginning complicated figures of extreme inner tension?

So when the Renaissance image makers placed the key to the kingdom in the hand of Hades-Pluto, they were saying that the key to initiatory mysteries, all hidden events in the soul, is in the hand of the God who takes things out of nature and into psyche through deformation.[46] Destruction, cruelty, wounding, failure, rape of the natural, even all unnatural events in dreams, may be approached through this dark light.

The vital and mobile new images that Bachelard insists are necessary for the imagination leads him to seek for the image that is not established, not static in its signification. He asks: "How do we pull it loose from the too stable bedrock of our familiar memories?"[47] How tear it free from what it already means to us? We may answer: through the shock of deformation, especially the pathologized deformation which restores to an image its capacity to perturb the soul to excess that, by bringing an image close to death, concurrently makes it live again. For it is the shocking dream of which the nightmare is paradigm that we remember most, that most stirs the soul's *memoria.*[48]

The work on dreams follows the work of dreams. We work on the dream, not to unravel it as Freud said, to undo the dream-work's undoing, but to respond to its work with the likeness of our work, all the while aiming to speak like the dream, imagine like the dream. Work on dreams does not forego analysis, but the analysis is in service of another archetypal principle and carried out in another attitude than the usual one. Analysis of course means making separations and differentiations. A dream is pulled apart, even violated, and this is indeed the necessary destructive work of intellect and of discriminating feeling. But now, the archetype served by a dream analysis is not only making conscious where consciousness means sunlight; we may place this destructive analytical work now in connection with Hades, who would take the life out of all our natural assumptions, all our futuristic previews, or with the *bricoleur* and his Hermetic sleight-of-hand that steals what we want to hold fast.

Analytical tearing apart is one thing, and conceptual interpretation another. We can have analysis without interpretation. Interpretation turns the dream into its meaning. Dream is replaced with translation. But dissection cuts into the flesh and bone of the image, examining the tissue of its internal connections, and moves around among its bits, though the body of the dream is still on the table. We haven't asked what does it mean, but who and what and how it is.

We may also understand our resistance to dreaming as a resistance in our "natural" nature to Hades. We "can't re-

member," go vague, forget to jot it down, or scribble it beyond
deciphering, and excuse ourselves by pointing to the obvious
slipperiness of dreams. Yet if each dream is a step into the
underworld, then remembering a dream is a recollection of
death and opens a frightening crevice under our feet. The
other alternative—loving one's dreams, not being able to wait
for the next one, such as we find in enthusiastic *puer* psychology, shows to what extent this archetype is in love with easeful
death and blind to what is below.

Again, a duplicity. This time the experience is fear and
desire. Like Persephone, we are both repelled and attracted,
sometimes seizing only half the experience, struggling like
her against being carried down by the dream, other times
in its embrace and ruling from its throne. Beyond Hades as
destroyer and lover, however, there is Hades of incomparable
intelligence. Work with dreams is to get at this hidden intelligence, to communicate with the God in the dream. Because
the dream is both black and white, its intelligence is neither
altogether obscure nor altogether clear.

Heraclitus (frg. 93) observed as much in a similar context:
"The Lord whose is the oracle in Delphi neither speaks out
nor conceals, but gives a sign." "The saying seems to be an
image (metaphor)," says Marcovich in his comment, "its implication might be the following: 'As Apollo neither speaks
out all nor conceals all, but shows forth a part of the truth,
so also *Logos* inside the things is neither inaccesible to human
knowledge nor self-evident, but requires an intellectual *effort*
from men,' i.e., *insight* or faculty to interpret correctly the
signs emitted by Logos. . . ."[49]

This intellectual and imaginative effort is the waking-ego's
contribution to the dream-work. We might call this effort
our Western version of *ta'wil*.[50] It is an effort of intelligence
that leads us into the dream, the effort of following its imaginatively deformative leads, where exegesis is exitus, leading
life out of life, where dream interpretation is not a life science

but a death science, like a philosophizing which too was once considered to be a leading of life towards death.

The *ta'wil* that leads a dream "back" to its archetypal ground, to its background, leads it both "in" to soul and "out" of life;[51] yet this discovery of the archetypal background gives a sense of primordiality, of beginning at the beginning; it gives, in Bachelard's words, "a mad surge of life." "As I see them, archetypes are reserves of enthusiasm which help us believe in the world, to love the world, to create our world."[52] We move from a dream to this joyfulness in the world not directly, dream to world, but indirectly, dream to archetype to world, and the first step, *ta'wil*, is an exitus out of world.

Our dream-work takes the term *depth psychology* to its logical and most serious consequences. The dream has led us back from Jung to Freud and then to a romantic tradition before Freud that can be expressed by the following fragment of Heraclitus, whom we have been continually referring to as the originator of the depth metaphor for the soul and as the first psychologist in the Western tradition. It was Heraclitus, as we pointed out earlier, who took as *archon*, or root principle of all things, not air or water, atoms or numbers, strife or love, but soul.[53]

> When we are alive our souls are dead and buried in us,
> but when we die, our souls come to life again and live.
>
> [frg. 26][54]

"Die" in this passage may be understood within the context of the nightworld, the dreamworld, for this same passage has also been translated:

> Man in the night kindles a light for himself,
> though his vision is extinguished;
> though alive, he touches the dead, while sleeping;
> though awake, he touches the sleeper.
>
> [Marcovich]

In other words: to "sleep" places us in touch with the "dead," the *eidola,* essences, images; to be "awake" is to be in touch with the sleeper, the ego-conscious personality. In the romantic sense: during sleep we are awake and alive; in life, asleep (cf. frg. 1).

In another fragment (89) Heraclitus says: "The waking share one common world *(cosmos),* whereas the sleeping turn aside each man into a world of his own." In one's individual cosmos, there the dream-work takes place. The dream-work's purpose *individualizes* the soul from the daylight and natural perspective. Because of this individuality of the dream, conceptual generalities about dreams must fail. As Heraclitus (frg. 113, Freeman) said: "The thinking faculty is common to all," but (frg. 115, Freeman), "The soul has its own *logos,* which grows according to its needs." By digesting and transforming the day's remainders, according to the logos (intelligence) of the soul rather than to the laws of common thought, the dream-work makes an individualized soul. This cannot be made only in the dayworld where, as Heraclitus says (frg. 106): "One day is like any other." The deformative, transformative work in dreams constructs the House of Hades, one's individual death. Each dream builds upon that house. Each dream is practice in entering the underworld, a preparation of the psyche for death.[55]

DREAM MATERIAL

One of Freud's fundamental fantasies in regard to the stuff of dreams is expressed by his word *concrete* ("for a dream all operations with words are merely preparatory to regression to concrete ideas" [*TD,* p. 144]). It seems to Freud "as if the dream process were controlled by considerations of *suitability for plastic representation"* (*TD,* p. 143). Bachelard speaks of the dream similarly, as if its shapes rise from the plasticity of the imagination, an imaginary raw material like dough, or clay, or molten metal.[56] *Stuff* is indeed the right word for dreams.

Work on them is hard; we think of them as being difficult, impenetrable, tough to crack. Our ability to understand something from them is inversely proportionate to what Freud called *resistance* (*NIL*, pp. 23–25; *CP* 5:137–38, 152). The dream must be "worked on" and "worked through," and analysts refer to the patient's dreams as "material." Dreams are made by a coagulative process: condensation, intensification (over-determination), reduction (abbreviation), iteration (repetition), concretizing. The synthetic cooking operation of the dream-work—that *bricolage* we spoke of—brings disparate ingredients together and concocts them into new things. These dream things we call *symbols*. They are made, or given, as densities, and the German word *Dicht* ("dense," "thick," "tight") occurs both in *Verdichtung* (Freud's term, which we translate as "condensation") and in *Dichtung* ("poetry"), *Dichter* ("poet").

This dream material is not simple raw material. The stuff is always shaped, imaged, and like alchemy's prime material, always has a specific name. To call this stuff "the chaotic id" or "the collective unconscious" betrays its true face. Chaos, like the id and the unconscious, is an abstraction, a concept about the material, not the material itself, which may appear as an ocean, an abyss, a mudslide, a carnival, a bit of jelly, a madhouse—but always, always as a precise image.

Emotions are crafted into distinct materialized shapes. Their language—shaking like a leaf, boiling with rage, laid flat, sunk—specifies what's the matter in the emotion. The fingers of the complexes may tear one to shreds in the night, for sleepers are workers; but as they tear, they shape each emotion into its form. One woman, betrayed by her lover, may dream her pain as an endless ditch, herself thrown into

weeds, burrs, and empty litter, while another betrayal may
come as a cold room with white walls, the dreamer being
led toward a high marble slab. Your betrayal differs from
mine, because each matters in a different shape, baked in
another mold. The morning brings us each his and her own
dream of cast and hardened images like fresh-crusted bread.

The fantasy of the "raw and the cooked" (Lévi-Strauss)
begins in the psyche's dream, which is not mere nature but
elaborated nature, *natura naturata*. This cooking of psychic
stuff that goes on in the night, because it is a soul-making,
is as fundamental to culture as are the other forms of cooking
and crafting that anthropology upholds.

Even where analysts use all these material terms when
speaking of dreams, they tend to follow uncritically the Cartesian dualism between *res cogitans* and *res extensa*. They tend
to put matter outside into physical earth, so that to gain
matter one is told by the analyst to take a job, train the
physical body, or tend to practical outside matters. Where
airiness and moistness are taken psychologically and metaphorically—a person is full of hot air, up in the clouds, flies
too high, or is sloppy, dewy eyed, and leaks all over the
place—the imagination of earth is conceived literalistically
in projected form upon nature, body, and matter. The material element of psyche is taken as actual earthy material.
But as a person hardly gains psychic air—distance, wit, mind,
perspective—by breathing exercises or sky diving and hardly
gains water by bathing more or drinking Evian or Vichy,
so why should earth be gained by material activities? Even
if the soul be a *krasis* (compound) of elements, can the proper
mixture be achieved by the simple introduction of the opposite
("you are too airy and need earth") or by literalizing this
element into actual earth?

This earth, however, can be gained by working on dream
'material,' for dreams "stimulate work."[57] Through that
work, which is behind all translations and amplifications and

interpretations, we gain internal ground. Our psychic stuff is fashioned more firmly, articulated and differentiated, by our actions with the image. The more we work on our material in an analysis, as well as before and after its hours, the more modeled and even contained the psyche becomes. We are more able to hold things and let them stew, more receptive; we have gained both vessel and ground.

Although a person may be a "natural" and "gifted," we may nonetheless sense his or her soul to be raw, naive, simple, as if there were still a good deal of work to be done, opening its space, solidifying its body, and sophisticating its sensitivity. We want not only "old souls," "good souls," and "great souls," but *worked* souls, in contact with whom we get a sense of what matters.

That is what we are each after—that sense of matter apart from material things and the materialist view of things. We want our lives to matter, our relationships, how we spend our days, and that our death not be immaterial. What we look for is soul-matter. How is this psychic matter made? How do we gain ground and earth, other than by work on our psychic stuff, those "immaterial" dreams that seem so little to matter that they must be sweated over—plowed through, hammered out, wrenched in pieces—in order to gain sense and weight. Whatever we work on begins to matter to us. Work makes matter, and psychic work makes the psyche matter.

We may thus gain earth not only by working the earth of Demeter, the agricultural fantasy of returning to the soil as diggers, being natural. We may become earthy also through Ge, working upon one's fate, the retributive justice connected with ancestral sins, the limitations of nature visited congenitally upon one through the specific geographical and historical locus of one's home, place of attachments, first home ground.

There is a third way of making matter, and this is through *chthōn*, working into cold dead depths of the psyche, the underworld of night and dreams and ghosts, and the incurable changeless essence of character imaged in our chthonic complexes. This is the deep home ground, the House of Hades.

We can move in this direction by means of hermeneutics, following Plato's idea of *hyponoia* (*Republic* 378d), "undersense," "deeper meaning," which is an ancient way of putting Freud's idea of "latent." The search for undersense is what we express in common speech as the desire to understand. We want to get below what is going on and see its basis, its fundamentals, how and where it is grounded. The need to understand more deeply, this search for deeper grounding, is like a call from Hades to move toward his deeper intelligence. All these movements of *hyponoia,* leading toward an understanding that gains ground and makes matter, are work.[58]

As we said above concerning Hercules and as we saw above with Freud (*ID,* p. 148; *EI,* pp. 41, 56; *OTL,* p. 7), work is usually imagined in terms of the ego and his muscles. Because Cartesian earth is still outward in visible reality, personality can only be made by a strong ego coping with tough problems in a real world of hard facts. But the dream-work and the work on dreams returns work to the invisible earth, from literal reality to imaginary reality. Through dream-work we shift perspective from the heroic basis of consciousness to the poetic basis of consciousness, recognizing that *every reality of whatever sort is first of all a fantasy image of the psyche* (*CW* 6:§§ 743, 78; *CW* 11:§§ 769, 889). Dream-work is the focus of this interiorization of earth, effort, and ground; it is the first step in giving density, solidity, weight, gravity, seriousness, sensuousness, permanence, and depth to fantasy. We work on dreams not to strengthen the ego but *to make psychic reality,* to make life matter through death, to make soul by coagulating and intensifying the imagination.

It may be clearer now why I call this work *soul-making* rather than analysis, psychotherapy, or the process of individuation. My emphasis is upon shaping, handling, and doing something with psychic stuff. It is a psychology of craft rather than a psychology of growth. Growth lets the soul do its own thing, like a plant. This organic mystique implies minimal work. Soul-making, too, has a mystique, the mystery of death, which encompasses organic growth and employs its images in the work of soul. *Making* is a term which reflects what the psyche itself does: it makes images. This image making is the first given of all psychic life. *Homo faber,* yes; but what is made are images and what these images seem to be making in us is a psychic reality that requires craft and imagination. The Good Book says the human soul is made in the divine image. Let us understand this also to say: the human being is made *by* the divine images in the soul.

One great value of alchemy as a model for psychological work is precisely that alchemy is an opus, a work upon materials. We believe that the alchemists worked with materials because they projected psyche into matter, or as Bachelard puts it: "the alchemist projects his depth."[59] Psyche is still in matter, although now today in another sense. Matter now is the projected material: our materialisms and materializations, all the concrete fixations of our psychic life in ideas, beliefs, symptoms, feelings, persons. The substantial investment we have in these concretizations is where modern physis is to be found. The primal material today is in everything we take unquestionably, uncritically for "real," everything we do not see through. Here is our opaque matter. These "realities" enter our dreams through day residues, where they are worked on by the imagination. As we work through these bits of physis, primal material is placed into the psychic vessel, both strengthening it and differentiating it, converting *res cogitans* into *res extensa* of inner ground.

In practice, these bits of matter convert to inner ground whenever we take back a "projection," as this work is called in psychotherapy. To find these bits of lost ground, we need only notice where one is concretely literal (heavy, dense, grave, weighty), where one stalwartly claims: "But this is reality." Sometimes it is social and moral conventions, an ethical code; other times diet, health, energy, and habits. This concretism can even appear as a semiphilosophical belief in facts, history, evidence, logic, or personal feelings. Very often it is a personal relation, an idealized figure of truth and trust. Most often it is money, the bottom line. Where a person is concrete, there he has invested body. There is where he says, "This is an unavoidable necessity; it matters above all."

Taking back projections in practice is not as simple as it sounds, since to dissolve a projection is to lose body, to lose that vessel where what matters has been placed. Such projections are like fixed or overvalued ideas. They have a delusional quality, because they cannot be seen through as psychic fixations and psychic values. Here is where we are stuck in physis yet also where dreams can do their work by picking up fragments of these concretisms and imaging them into a fresh sense. In other words, dream material is indeed where we can work on the conversion of matter into inner, psychic depth.

This concern with depth leads us in practice to pay special attention to *whatever is below*. This has been so since the beginning of psychoanalysis, and its notions of suppression, subconscious, and shadow. These are terms for what we see in images: burials, the dead, ancestors; workers in refuse, sewers, plumbers; criminals and outcasts; the lower body, its garments and its functions; lower forms of life that we 'look down upon,' from apes to bugs; the underside of the world, the floor of the sea, the downstairs and cellars, and, in fact anything whatsoever that can be turned over in the sense of *hyponoia* to reveal a deeper significance. The emotions that go with these images of bottoming are reluctance, loathing, sadness, mourning, inhibition, enclosure, lethargy, or that sense of depth that presses on us as depression, oppression, suppression. Our downward imagination has entered the earth. Bottom's dream.

Freud noticed that every dream opens into an unfathomable depth. Even if he usually goes to meticulous pains to interpret every bit of every dream, nonetheless twice he says in the *Traumdeutung* (*ID*, p. 525): ". . . we become aware during the work of interpretation that . . . there is a tangle of dream-thoughts which cannot be unravelled. . . . This is the dream's navel, the spot where it reaches down to the unknown." The core of the dream from which the dream itself sprouts "like a mushroom out of its mycelium," says Freud (in this image of damp fragrant earth), is the unknown. We would say this is the hole into the underworld, the moment of Hades, the opening into what Heraclitus implied is the realm of psyche, pure depth. This then is the *omphalos* (navel) of the psychic world. The *via regia* of dreams leads to this point. Correspondences to the dayworld, clearly, are a wrong-way movement.

All my emphasis upon the underworld and my insistence upon maintaining the dream as an underworld phenomenon is to keep the depth of the dream intact. What we take out of dreams, what we get to use from dreams, what we bring up from dreams, is all to the surface. Depth is in the invisible connection; and it is working with our hands on the invisible connections where we cannot see, deep in the body of the night, penetrating, assembling and differentiating, debriding, stirring, churning, kneading—this constitutes the work on dreams. Always we are doing precision work, but with invisibilities, with ambiguities, and with moving materials. What we know about life is here relatively secondary. Our knowledge is of that field most like the dream, that is, mythical realities, where too everything is sharp but ambiguous, apparent only to the imagination.

Moreover, this formative imaginative work is always at the same time deformative, destructive. Each approach to the underworld is through Styx and must meet the obstacle

of its hateful coldness. This is unavoidable and cannot be
sentimentalized. Every correct move in this nightworld kills
what it touches. We come up against densities, hard resisting
places that are penetrated by insight, an insight that shocks
and brings a sense of death. Something that had been clung
to and lived from has been seen through. Work on dreams
is hard to do by the therapist and hard to take by the patient.
We seem unable to do it alone with ourselves. This may be
because we can never see where we are unconscious; but it
may more likely be because we fundamentally resist the destruction that dream-work involves—the killing of attachments and the revelation of unchanging depths. The Queen
of the Underworld is Persephone. Her name means "bringer
of destruction."

6

PRAXIS

CAVEAT LECTOR

This chapter does not belong in a book about images, for two reasons. First, one cannot speak about images in generalitites—and even specific examples of dreams, when presented as illustrations for practice, become generalities. By definition, an image is a particular and brings with it the criteria and internal relations by which it can be understood. The generalities that follow here can help only in *deepening a perspective* toward certain groups of imageries, but they cannot give an account of any particular image that you may have in a dream. No way. Reader beware, this chapter will not tell you what your dreams mean.

Second, *underworld* refers to the psychic perspective, the attitude of the soul that cannot be said to have a praxis in the dayworld sense. To put the underworld into practice betrays the dream, which is not practical, as we have learned. The previous chapters you have troubled to go through were intended to lower you to soul and soul to underworld. The danger in a chapter called "praxis" is that of seducing the whole book back up and over the bridge into the dayworld, by means of the temptation of "practical hints to help the reader."

Especially, let's watch out for misreading "the death metaphor" (pp. 64 f above). The imageries that follow are not clues to death dreams, as if to dream of a black dog, a sieve or a leaky jar, a mirror, a hole in the ground, were signals of imminent and literal dying. None of the groups of imageries that follow indicate death in a literal sense. Such would be a dayworld and naturalistic approach to the dream: using it for practical life, even if that practical life has turned to mean predicting death. What follows are not even imageries of the underworld, since any dream and any God, including the hero, has a style of leading us there—once we assume the underworld perspective. That is the key. We are not presenting images *of* the underworld (like symbols of the Great Mother, of the Penis, or of the Self), as if the archetype were a general abstraction manifesting itself in definite sets of symbolic images. No, the underworld is a perspective within the image by means of which our consciousness enters or is initiated into the underworld viewpoint. The imageries that follow facilitate this initiation. When they are viewed in this way, they can release radically different insights from what one usually expects.

So here is Chapter 6 despite my hesitancies—and partly for my own sake. The following pages afford a place to communicate a sheaf of insights and reflections in regard to dreams, to counter views I bitterly oppose (because they are so near?), to suggest alternative attitudes toward the darkness in our dreams and in human nature, its shadows, pathologizings, and cold inhuman distance. Second, for your sake, Reader. Traditional books on dreams always tell you something about what dreams mean. To fail to do this would wrong the reader's archetypal expectation from a book with *Dream* in its title. So this chapter tries to sail between not wronging the reader and not wronging the dream. And if you are still so disposed, read it then to feel right, but beware of wronging what you might find in it by putting it in practice.

The word praxis has a bad history. Homer used it for business affairs; Plato made it mean more the technical knowledge of applied sciences. Aristotle then toughened the word further by using it in the context of ethics and politics. It always meant action, and it couldn't be more dayworld, more ego. So here, let's kiss the Greeks goodbye. We may retain the word by shifting its sense to what we do at the piano, in the gym, on the stage: a workout, a trial run for refining skills. We practice in order to notice little things that might otherwise escape. Psychotherapy with dreams is also a praxis. We go through its exercises, not to become practical, but to become practiced.

BLACK

Concerning black in dreams, I would like to bypass both the richness of color symbolism, and the many notions already explored in religious mysticism about darkness and alchemical symbolism about the nigredo, in order to restrict myself to *black persons in dreams.*[1]

It is a Jungian convention to take these blacks as shadows, a convention to which there can be no objection. However, analytical psychology has tended to see these black shadows as earthy in the Ge or Demeter senses and thus as potentials of vitality (sexuality, fertility, aggressivity, strength, emotionality). Moreover, the content of the black shadow has been further determined by sociological overtones. Personal associations to blacks in the culture affect the interpretation of the image. The black shadow today supposedly brings spontaneity, revolution, warmth, or music—or frightening criminality. In other eras, black figures in whites' dreams might have been loyalty, or apelikeness, or lethargy, servility, and stupidity, or been translated into superb force and wholeness, the Anthropos or "original man." Blacks have had to carry every sort of sociological shadow, from true religion and faithfulness, to cowardice and evil. The sociological vogues all have forgotten that The Black Man is also Thanatos.[2]

As we saw above, the inhabitants of the netherworld in Egypt were black, and in Rome they were called *inferi* and *umbrae.* Cumont says this "term implies, besides the idea of a subtle essence, the notion that the inhabitants of the dusky spaces underground were black, and this is in fact the colour often given to them. It is also the colour of the victims offered them and of the mourning garments worn in their honour."[3]

I think it would be archetypally more correct, and so more psychological, to consider black persons in dreams in terms of their resemblance with this underworld context. Their concealed and raping attributes belong to the "violating" phenomenology of Hades, of which we have already spoken, just as their pursuit resembles the hounding by the death demons. They are returning ghosts from the repressed netherworld—not merely from the repressed ghetto. Their message is psychic before it is vital. They bring one down and steal one's "goods" and menace the ego behind its locked doors.

In other words, their terrifying aspect might be where their true dynamic lies, although our sociological prejudice will not allow this possibility. Coming from death's kingdom as creepers in the night, of course they frighten. But anxiety, as we have known ever since Freud, signals the return of the repressed, and the repressed nowadays, goodness knows, is certainly not sexuality, not criminality, not brutality—all those things we say that black figures "represent." They present death; the repressed is death. And death dignifies them.

Following this through then, black persons in dreams would no longer have to carry the sociological shadow of primitivity (for the developmental fantasy of the ego), vitality (for the ego's heroic strength), or inferiority (for the ego's moral or political fantasy). In other words, we would move away from a pseudo negro-psychology to a genuine shadow-psychology, an attempt to restore to the black figures "the idea of a subtle essence."

SICKNESS

Concerning sickness in dreams, whatever appears wounded, sick, or dying may be understood as that content leading the dreamer into the House of Hades. (Sick animals and children in folklore are occasioned by a death demon.) These are contents with the most psychological importance, having been singled out by the dream-work as its material for its *opus contra naturam.* These are the images that are bringing about a change in us (rather than our trying to change them), and so they are doing the work of the *psychopompos.* The contents in a dream that have the most potential for soul-making are those that are pathologized (this idea has been treated more fully in another work).[4]

An archetypal perspective from the underworld puts us in a position to correct the analytical interpretation, for example, of the "sick anima." We need not take it so personalistically or naturalistically. As Herzog says, "there are a large number of accounts in which it is said of Huldren, Frau Holle and Frau Werlte that their backs are hollow or rotten, or full of worms and snakes and putrefaction."[5] The usual move when encountering such figures, also in the interpretation of fairy tales, is to declare a "sick anima," that the image is showing how rotten the anima (feeling, femininity, eros, or what you will) is in the individual who had the dream or in the culture that "had" the fairy tale.

Instead of regarding this image as a neglected soul needing saving, medical attention, or development, an appeal through guilt to the ego to do something, we may see this as a soul going through the *putrefactio,* a movement like Persephone's fall into the chasm. The hollow, the snake, and the worm of the underworld are already entering her, unseen, behind the back.

ANIMALS

In considering animals, let us remember that the animal kingdom is bigger than ours. We are members of it and subject to it, so that we may pass only a few cautiously respectful remarks about their images, as one of their fellow citizens with whom we human animals have fallen on rather bad terms.

Generally, animal images are interpreted in depth psychology as representatives of the animal, that is, instinctual, bestial, sexual, part of human nature. Evolutionary theory and Christian prejudice are assumed by this interpretation. I prefer to consider animals in dreams as Gods, as divine, intelligent, autochthonous powers demanding respect. The undeviating patterns that are followed by animals in nature are like the laws of *dike* and *themis,* which keep the Gods within bounds. Ecology is like polytheism: both show interpenetrating and interlimiting patterns of autochthonous powers, each power a qualitative splendor, a presence that is both a unique example and a universal genus at once. Like the Gods, the animals require each other, and everyone follows a divine justice within the limits of its kind.

The above paragraph is not farfetched, for the history of art and religion (fields that are historically hard to separate) show that Gods come in animal forms, that animals are what

Gods want most in sacrifice, and that the relation with animals requires a sensitivity and ritual similar to the relation with Gods.

Since I prefer not to consider animal images as instincts inside us, I do not use the hermeneutics of vitality for responding to their appearance in dreams. Here, I am trying to move away from the view that animals bring us life or show our power, ambition, sexual energy, endurance, or any of the other *rajas,* the hungry demands and compulsive sins and vices that have been put off upon animals in our culture and continue to be projected there in our dream interpretations. To look at them from an underworld perspective means to regard them as carriers of soul, perhaps totem carriers of our own free-soul or death-soul, there to help us see in the dark. To find out who they are and what they are doing there in the dream, we must first of all watch the image and pay less attention to our own reactions to it. As from a duck blind or when downwind stalking a deer, our focus is on the image, acute to its appearance, ourselves abashed, eclipsed in that intensity in order to follow the precise movements of its spontaneity. Then we might be able to understand what it means with us in the dream. But no animal ever means one thing only, and no animal simply means death.

In our tradition of underworld myth and folklore, only a few kinds of animal crop up regularly: The *dog* of Hekate, Cerebros of Hades, and the blue-black dog-jackal, Anubis; the *horse* of Hades' chariot, the horsemen of death, and the nightmare images in horse form; little *birds* are souls and large ones are winged death demons; the serpent as chthonic side of the God, the part that slips away into invisibility through holes in the ground and embodies the soul of the dead person. Then we also find special animals sacred to Gods and Goddesses who have strong underworld affiliations: pregnant cows to Tellus; pigs to Demeter; dogs to Hekate. In some fairy tales, death comes as a fish, as a wolf, as a fox. An unspecific, black, horned animal is frequently an animal image of death. Sometimes this figure is imagined as a black goat. Goats, says Farnell, were never loved by heroes.[6] Especially in the classical world, black animals were sacrificed to the chthonic powers.

The dream spider deserves singling out, because it is usually not associated with underworld symbolism. Spider images have generally been woven into a great mother web of spinning illusions *(Maya)*, paranoid plots, poisonous gossip and entrapping, clinging relations, as well as anal power fantasies. Jungians sometimes see a dream spider in terms of the negative Self (black, eight-legged creature making mandala forms). They would say the spider comes as long as one dreads the unconscious force of integration.

Although most natural spiders live in the earth, dream spiders usually appear in the air, a nightworld air like the chthonic, pneumatic underworld. There is an underworld intellect, a chthonic mind of nature that must spin out its patterns, constructing networks that can catch and hold any winged fantasy flying by. Remember the Platonic idea of Hades whose mind is so marvelous that souls never want to leave his domain? Abandon all hope ye who enter here. No way out of the spider's web, and the fly-weight *puer* spirit is most afraid of the chthonic mind. So, when the spider comes to your dream, do not diagnose it. Turn to the other half of the tandem, yourself, the dream ego. Are you Miss Muffet content on your tuffet, or a little buzz of thoughts afraid of the synthetic imagining power of the deep mind weaving your fate into the organizing intelligence below nature?

The main point here is that there are many animal ways into the underworld. We may be led or chased down by dogs and meet the dog of fear, who bars the way to going deeper. We may be driven down by the energetic rapture of hard-riding horsepower; go down through the air like a bird in its many modes—twittering, sailing, diving—a sudden seizure of the spirit, the impulse suicide of a quick mental move. We may descend by means of our own piggishness, which has a hidden holiness, too, in its depths. Again, the descent and death that the animal constellates is not necessarily of our physical being because an animal is a physical being. This would be to take the animal image literally. Rather, the animal presents a *familiaris,* a dumb soul-brother at our side, or a soul doctor, who understands psychic laws other than those of the dayworld ego and which are a death for that world.

The wide belief that animals embody the souls of the human dead should give us a special respect for the animals that come to us in the night. From a nightworld perspective, they are presentations of specific soul qualities and behaviors, essentials that cannot better present themselves than in this animal shape.

The appearance of an animal restores us to Adam. We recover the first man in the cave, tracing out the animal soul on the underground walls of the imagination. Of course, the different animals present styles and shapes of vitality, so one tends to say, "Animals in dreams represent instincts. They stand for our bestiality and primitivity." No, they do not; first, because they are not ours or us; second, because they are not images *of* animals, but images *as* animals. These dream animals show us that the underworld has jaws and paws, opening our awareness to the fact that images are demonic forces. The least we can do for them is to pay them that primordial respect of the cave man drawing in the dark, face to the wall, that respect of Adam, so closely considering them that he could find for each one its name. We need large caves and loving attention. Then they may come and tell us about themselves.

A preparation for the underworld may be initiated by an animal sacrifice in a dream. It would not be right to take this only from the dayworld view of giving up a piece of one's vital desire. For example, a woman began an analysis with a dream of "having to put her dog away." It was her old family German shepherd, now owned by her daughter. In the dream, she takes it to the animal doctor who "puts it to sleep." This dream combined the Demeter-Persephone motif, the family spirit of protectiveness and guardian watchfulness that kept her sheepish and in the flock, and the dog as guiding spirit into the realm of the dead. The dog went to Sleep and Death, and she was led there too by feelings of loss, lethargy, and aloneness. The animal doctor is also a doctor-animal or one who has animal wisdom, able to perform the death rites of therapy in regard to the animal. After this dream, there followed encounters with many family ghosts, dead relatives, perverse desires, ancient sins. She was no longer protected by the dog from the dog. The dog was now ruling her land of sleep, her sleeping earth, digging up all sorts of bones and dirt. A *nekyia* had begun.

BODIES OF WATER

Concerning *bodies of water* in dreams (oceans, rivers, lakes, pools, baths), let us bypass the symbolisms of lustration and baptism, of doctrinal wisdom and uterine mother, and also the too general meanings of life energy, Mercurius, and the unconscious. Instead, let us take a lead from Heraclitus (frg. 36): "To souls, it is death to become water . . . , " and (frg. 77, Freeman): "It is delight, or rather death, to souls to become wet. . . . " Jung has expanded upon the death of the soul through water in his classical work on the *Rosarium philosophorum* (*CW* 16) where he offers a host of remarkable psychological insights on the many implications of water. There, too, he refers to Heraclitus.

If we connect Heraclitus' statements about water and death

with the familiar alchemical motto—"perform no operation until all has become water"—then the opus begins in dying. When a dream image is moistened, it is entering the *dissolutio* and is becoming, in Bachelard's sense, more psychisized, made into soul, for water is the special element of reverie, the element of reflective images and their ceaseless, ungraspable flow. Moistening in dreams refers to the soul's delight in its death, its delight in sinking away from fixations in literalized concerns.

Entering the waters relaxes one's hold on things and lets go of where one has been stuck. The "waters" that one goes into may be like a new environment or a new body of doctrine that wraps one round and which may both hold one up or suck one into its deeps. It may be like a new sexual relationship, in which the naked body is immersed, a river that carries one rushing along (Poseidon was a river and a horse), or on which one floats feeling a deep and moving support. The waters may be cold or warm or hot, turgid, shallow, clear—as Bachelard says, the language of water is rich for metaphorical reverie. The underworld differentiates at least five rivers: the frigid Styx; the burning Pyriphlegethon; the mournful, wailing Cocytus; the depressive, black Acheron; and Lethe (q.v. Remembering and Forgetting). Again, we must pay attention to the *kind* of water in a dream—nor may we merely assume that rivers always mean the flow of life.

Because initiation into the water usually brings a refreshing new liquidity, dream interpreters have identified water with emotion (affects, feelings), but the movement has an impersonal elemental quality, as water itself does. If one looks carefully at the dream, the emotion is usually located in the dry ego-soul as it dissolves, not in the waters, which often are simply *there*, cool, dispassionate, receiving.

So the image-soul's delight is the ego-soul's dread. In dreams, it fears drowning in torrents, whirlpools, tidal waves, which again interpreters (have they such dry souls?) often translate to mean the dreamer is in danger of being over-whelmed by the unconscious in an emotional psychosis, flooded with fantasies—no ground, no standpoint. Heraclitus, however, like alchemical psychology, sees death in water as the way of dissolving one kind of earth while another kind comes into being. Fragment 36 (Freeman) continues:

> To souls, it is death to become water;
> to water, it is death to become earth.
> From earth comes water, and from water, soul.

Literal fixations in earthbound problems do stop the soul's movement, and so "it is death to become earth." The soul does want to flow on and move through. Now, since death also means the perspective of soul, these very same fixations put soul into earth and earth into soul, giving to matters a new psychic sense. A psychic matter forms, i.e., "from earth comes water." We begin to see and feel psychologically what matters in the soul's fixations. This regenerates water, as well as soul.

Literalizations that kill the flow and bury the soul always need dissolving; at the same time what is dissolved always finds new earthworks to stop flow. This is an ever recurring process, as in alchemy, describing a cycle of soul-making, for which dissolution in water is necessary. To fear the dream's waters is to fear being surrounded and sunk into the body of this cycle in which the soul delights.

REMEMBERING AND FORGETTING

The entire question of remembering and forgetting may also be reexamined, this time from the perspective of Lethe, who, you remember, forms part of the Orphic group: dreams, sleep, death, and forgetfulness. Of course Lethe played a po-etic part in romanticism, but she also has had a significant role in the development of depth psychology, which began with Freud's investigation of the forgotten (in hysteria) and of the slips and holes, the tiny forgetfulnesses of consciousness *(Fehlleistungen) (OPA,* p. 261). Jung went in the same direction, following the forgotten in the lapses of attention of the word association experiments and in his cultural research into the collectively forgotten areas of psychology (Gnosticism, alchemy, mythology). By following Lethe they were led into the underworld.

Unfortunately psychology emphasizes attention and recall; the dayworld wishes to have, must absolutely have, a "good memory"; a bad memory is more devastating to success than is a bad conscience. Forgetting therefore becomes a pathological sign. But *depth* psychology based on an archetypal perspective might understand forgetting as serving a deeper purpose, seeing in these holes and slips in the dayworld the means by which events are transformed out of personal life, voiding it, emptying it. Somehow we must come to better terms with Lethe, since she rules many years, especially the last years, and we would be foolish to dismiss her work only as pathological. The romantics took Lethe most seriously.

Kerényi[7] conjectures, in an article devoted to Lethe and Mnemosyne, that they had a meaning in antiquity converse to our current dayworld view. Forgetting then must have meant the vain running on of life, like a river, like the water of the Danaides, whose vessel was a leaky sieve—another underworld mythologem reminding of unmade, unfinished souls.[8] This running on of life leads to an unquenchable thirst for more life and to the drinking of the waters of forgetfulness that only increase the compulsion to seek new inflows and outflows. What is forgotten is not this fact or that face but archetypal remembrance itself, Mnemosyne, the mother of the musing mind, which alone would satisfy the thirst. This understanding of Lethe lends support to our idea that what is being forgotten out of the dayworld of our lives may be making possible the inflow of another sort of remembrance—once we turn our attention from chasing the lost bit of data to the empty, sinking feeling that forgetting leaves behind and which is also the mother of musing.

In dreams, evidences of forgetting (lapses of attention, misspoken words, mistaken identities, dozing, drunkenness, including forgetting the dream itself) would belong not only to complex indicators (which after all are readings from the dayworld's value upon attention) and to a severe censor at a firm threshold, but are means of delivering events to another archetypal realm.[9] The forgotten dream is the dream resisting to be remembered, perhaps because memory has been put into the yoke of the dayworld and the forgotten dream refuses this service. It will not deliver its contents to the ego's strengthening. The more we are moistened by the underworld, as in an analysis, the less Lethe resists. Dreams come more easily, for we are now in a better relation with the entire family to which Lethe belongs. That forgetting and dreaming have so close a relationship implies that dreaming itself, as we said earlier, is a process of forgetting, of removing elements out of life so that they no longer hold such interest, of letting slip, washed downstream, a movement out of ego into psyche.

RETARDATION

If, as Freud said, the underworld knows no time, then punctuality and retardation do not belong there. Yet, these are common experiences in dreams. We are too late for the plane, rush for an appointment only to get more entangled and delayed, misread the clock and are an hour off for the examination (performance, conference) and so cannot make the beginning. Worst of all, we try desperately to catch up, only to find our legs don't move in their molasseslike, paralyzed slowdown.

These emotions of hurried anxiousness need to be read from the image. Then we learn that the dream-ego is terrified of slowness, especially the slowness in its own lower body. We learn that images of punctuality are ideal adjustments to the time of others, fixations on the clock that keep the dream-ego ticking. Dream-punctuality shows a dream-ego in accord with daylight consciousness, and retardation shows a dream-ego drifting into the disorientation of underworld timelessness, despite panicked efforts. Underworld has begun to affect upperworld which now is throwing off its commitment to time and slowing its compulsion to be in accord with clockwork order.

So, when in dreams we find sentences like these: "There wasn't any time left," "I'd be late and had to hurry," "My watch must have been wrong," "I now would miss the start," we may read them as statements that time is coming to a stop. One's "watch" is off guard or its mechanism has stopped. The experience is that of having lost time and being lost without time in a psychic place where forward movement cannot go on. There is no longer a start nor a new beginning. One's lower limbs are in secret league with what is pursuing, for the legs have stopped their running on. Now there is stasis. Progression and regression become invalid constructs. They have nothing to do with the underworld.

This movement in time from the upperworld to underworld by means of being late and running out of time can be compared with the movement from story to image by the means of taking the words of time out of a story. Stories unfurl in time. First this happens, then this and this, and then that. Each *then* is related to a subsequent one. "Then" has a wholly temporal implication; it always refers to something later following upon and often the result of something earlier.

The image approach to "then" is quite different. This approach always puts "then" into relation with "when," rather than into a series of other "thens." The events that occur in a dream are imagined to be taking place without concern for time, as if all at the same time, where their temporal succession doesn't matter, rather than in the straight linear connection of story.

For instance, when in a dream you (the dream-ego) rush to the doctor's, then you are late; and when you are late, then you rush to the doctor's. Rushing and being late inseparably require each other. They develop out of and intensify each other. They occur together in an image with "the doctor's," but neither comes first with then the other following from it.

Another dream instance: when the conference is called for 3 P.M., then your elevator gets stuck and can't rise to it; when your elevator gets stuck and you can't move up, then you feel the call of the three o'clock conference. Being stuck and being called (to "3") appear together in the dream, but neither comes first, causing the other.

From the imagistic perspective that reads the dream as a statement of essence, neither chicken nor egg comes first. For we are not in a story-time but in an image-space, where chicken and egg mutually require each other and are simultaneous correlatives. Notions of origin and of causality are also invalid constructs in an underworld perspective, for which time does not enter and the image presents an eternal (always going on, repetitious) state of soul.

This move into image-time frees temporal events in dreams from dayworld attitudes, that is, a naturalistic fallacy that refers to "real" time and "real" clocks. Instead, the phenomena of retardation are kept within the image of the elevator or of the doctor's, for that is where being stuck and being late takes place. Time problems are placed somewhere. We ask: in connection with whom and what specifically is punctuality demanded and hurry constellated? What exactly does not respond to the dream-ego's intentions: the ability to read directions, the automatic lift (elevator), the car starter, the watch(ing) mechanism, feet and legs? We search for the place of failure, for this is the place of pathologizing, where the dream-work has begun its breakdown of daylight time.

If the dream does not unfurl in time because the underworld is timeless, then there is nowhere to go with it, in the sense of goal. We have to abandon our hopes for the future when working on it. The dream stops time, and we have to stop too, else it slips into a story and carries us into the stream of time. We can stop time by not reading the dream as a story. Then the dream has no end. This means both that it is not going anywhere else and that it is always going on. A dream is stuck within itself, its actual imagery, and has to be read in terms of what is going on in it. It is stuck within the limits of its framework, like a painting in which nothing comes first and nothing comes later and which is read by articulating and deepening the internal relations of its image.

If the dream isn't going anywhere, then neither is the dream-ego, who too is fastened within the limits of the dream, trapped in the image that halts the upperworld time-story of the clock and its regular procession through the numbered hours. The dream-ego tries to escape the image with a temporal panic. It rushes to catch "up" for fear of slowing "down."

By concentrating upon the image in which time is embedded, part of which imagery is *number* symbolics, we are stressing the quality of time, as did Artemidorus and other ancient dream interpreters who always asked about the hour when the dream took place. Was it soon after falling asleep, deep in the night and far removed from daylight, or toward morning? Although it seems as though they were fixing the dream at a certain level of sleep in accord with their theories, they were also asking the dreamer to notice the time quality of the dream images. These time qualities refer to distinct psychic moments: at breakfast, when school is out, after the late show. They present moments of feeling consciousness, matutinal, post-meridional, toward evening and the close of day. A 2 P.M. examination both examines one in terms of the duplicities and tensions of twoness and takes place after the zenith, the day already moving imperceptibly toward its fall, though unnoticeable in the accumulated brightness and warmth still blazing from a noon now past.

I am trying here to regain a feeling for the differences among the hours.[10] They too are mythical persons (Horae), with distinct personalities. Times in dreams refer to regions of the night, places with qualities, like the twelve subterranean domains traversed by the Egyptian sun God in his ship of the night.[11]

ROUNDNESS

Jung's research into the symbolism of the self has established an interpretative convention: roundness = self. The basis of this hypothesis is to be found in Jung's discussions of the mandala (Sanscrit for "circle"). Since Jung's time, roundness is applied categorically to all sorts of manifestations from traffic circles and doughnuts to pearls and UFOs. Any mandala form appearing in a dream tends to be interpreted with a categorical literalness in accordance with Jung's statement that such circular figures are an "attempt at self-healing." A part of Jung's premise here is the close linguistic association of heal, hale, heil (German for save), and whole.

The mandala belongs to the psychic geography of Tibet, to its underworld mystery religion and a culture based on that religion. The self depicted in a mandala is therefore a differentiated pattern of polytheistic persons and places (and not a simple monotheistic circle, ring, or sphere corresponding with Western desires for a unitarian monism). Since the image derives from an underworld culture, it can only rightly be read from an underworld perspective. The appearance in a dream of a mandala-shaped object or pattern may indicate an integration, as Jung said, but the integration is into the Bardo world of death. This is a loss of reality in our usual daylight sense of reality. So, if the spontaneous manifestation of the circle is an attempt at self-healing, that healing means dying in the way we have been elaborating it in this book.

When we make the move, following Jung, from mandala as circle to mandala as integration, the move from an image of roundness to the idea of wholeness, we shall have to bear in mind the shadow of death that is implicated in the mandala. Wholeness taken only from the natural perspective as growth—the all-round person, where roundness means filling out rather than emptying out—becomes a defensive integration, a strengthening by packing with fillers the holes in our natures, which are ways we keep in touch with the underworld. Jung himself points out the defensive use of the mandala and also warns against "artificial repetition or deliberate imitation of such images" (*CW* 9,i:§ 718). Defensiveness is in the very nature of the circle itself. It easily becomes a paranoid closure of meaning, which by including everything in its wholeness, keeps at bay the very underworld that it presents. As the Tibetan mandala is a meditative mode that protects the soul from capture by demons, so the Self as an all-embracing wholeness keeps the demonic nature of psychic events from getting through to the soul. Roundness, whether in mandala or Self, is protective, a *temenos* that always offers most protection to our paranoid tendencies. A circle is centered, complete, in need of nothing beyond itself. It is the perfect system. So, it is not only our dayworld misuse of the mandala that is "wrong"; this wrong possibility is given with the circle itself.

In archaic Western symbolism, the circle is a place of death. We find it in the sepulchral ring or burial barrow later recapitulated in Christian circular churchyards.[12] Both the wheel and the ring (especially as wreath) may be read as underworld expressions. To be put on the wheel in punishment (as Ixion) is to be put into an archetypal place, tied to the turns of fortune, the turns of the moon and fate, and the endless repetitions of coming eternally back to the same experiences without release. Everything moving and nothing changing; all life as *déjà vu*. The underworld implication of the circle is especially pronounced among the Celts, says Margarete Riemschneider.[13] In Celtic myth, the wheel or that which rolls has uncanny, sinister intention. Rings are closed circles and the circle closes on us whether in the marriage band, the crowning laurel, or the wreath on the grave. No way out, which is also how necessity has been defined. The collar ring yoking the neck of a captive slave or prisoner is the oldest meaning of the word *necessity (ananke)*. A wheel puts the closed circle into motion, and now we are in a cyclical, compulsive rolling, no end to it. Caught in a mechanism, whether the predictions of doom that accompany technical advancement (which begins with the collared slave even before the wheel) or the sense of tragedy that accompanies the laurels of victory.

The wheel is a worldwide mode of taking the measure of time, representing it as a cycle in which the days and nights turn. We turn with time and, as Bachelard said, space is our friend, but time has death in it. So, the analytical hour, that peculiar ritual of time basic to psychotherapy since Freud, has death in it, like the sand in the hourglass. The dentist, internist, and surgeon do not allot time in the same way. There, it is a matter of time needed for the job; the medical man does not break off the work according to the clock. But psychotherapy comes in hours. It accords with the great wheel. Each of its hours, by evoking death, evokes soul. The "hour" remains even when therapists try to free themselves from it (the 45-minute hour, the unscheduled appointment), as if the clock circle and hourglass that analysis implies is essential to its healing-dying process.

Sometimes, spontaneous images of roundness bring a healing beyond paranoid defensiveness, beyond safety within one's private scheme of personal integration. These images must therefore afford another, an impersonal kind of integration. The individual free soul moves into a perspective of cosmic necessity. We become part of the circle we move in, whatever that circle might be—neurotic, social, intellectual. We have become necessary to it and taken into it.

The circular states of repetitiveness, turning and turning in the gyres of our own conditions, force us to recognize that these conditions are our very essence and that the soul's circular motion (which is its native motion, according to Plotinus) cannot be distinguished from blind fate. It is as if the soul frees itself not from blindness but by its continuing turning in it. Ultimately, if the spontaneous mandala heals, it does so because it compels a recognition of the limitation of consciousness, that my mind and heart and will turn only in a circle, and yet that same circle is my portion of an eternal necessity.

PSYCHOPATHY

A static essence of personality may appear in dream figures, which the waking-ego judges to be psychopathic because they are not affected by the moral values of the dayworld and because they do not change. Such figures are fulltime inmates of the underworld. In dreams, we meet them as killers, nazis, and as crooks with beguiling charm.

I should interject here that I am using the concept of psychopathy interchangeably with that of sociopathy, preferring the former because it keeps the description to the psyche rather than relating it primarily with the field in which this "pathic" behavior shows itself, society. The nature of the psychopathic personality is one of the most riddling questions in psychiatry. Yet, acute schizophrenic episodes and antidepressive pharmaceutica, and even minor circumscribed syndromes, receive far more space in the literature. Psychiatry's brightest minds from Jung to Laing have always given far less attention to this incorrigible, destructive component that cannot learn and does not change.

Psychopathy is traditionally characterized by two main traits. First, it is supposedly congenital and static in that it shows no learning from experience, no process either of improvement or worsening. Second, it is a condition of "moral insanity," as it was first called by Prichard in 1835, showing an amorality that can go to extremes of egotism and cruelty without remorse or expiation. This combination of timeless repetition, amoral self-centeredness, and inherent destructiveness indicates that the psychopathic is fittingly perceived from an underworld perspective and, as well, that the underworld is not only a realm of soul but also one of psychopathy. Freud recognized this psychopathic underworld within the id that contains "immoral, incestuous and perverse impulses . . . murderous and sadistic lusts" (*CP* 5:155). He speaks of the "evil in the id" and holds the dreamer morally responsible for the content of his dreams (*ibid.*, 156–57).[14]

If other imagery in dreams may not be translated upward into the natural language of the waking-ego, then why should the "evil in the id" be taken literalistically? Is it not too an analogic language? Dream incest, as Jung pointed out, means the union of likes and kinship libido. Similarly, perverse impulses in dreams may refer to unnatural connections that are needed to twist nature into psyche. Murderous, sadistic lusts may also be understood analogically, as part of the desire to de-structure that is necessary to the alchemical *mortificatio* and *putrefactio* processes, where parts turn against each other in order to achieve radical separations. Disguise, deception, cold, cruel surprise—we are now in a place beyond human warmth and decency, yet where psychic operations still take place, even though we cannot tell the difference between the kid's switchblade and the ritual knife.

In order to come to terms with the base of the psyche, we must not turn a moral eye upon its baseness. Rather, it will be necessary to look at the underworld as did Polygnotus in his famous painting at Delphi, which shows no trace of moralism,[15] just as the "judging of the dead is foreign to Homeric poetry;"[16] just as the cult of Hekate is amoral; just as Hermes takes and Hades receives, regardless of moral character, each of us as we are. Freud too affirmed that the depths of the psyche are without good or bad, without moral codes or even negation. There even the same word can be ultimately deceptive, meaning opposite things at the same time, and Jung often enough said that dreams lead us astray as much as they exhort (*CW* 10:§ 835). As a piece of objective nature, they have no moral ax to grind.[17] Therefore, to take a moral point of view toward the dream does not correspond to the dream or speak to it in a language of resemblances. Let us keep Hermes in mind; paradox, black and white at once.

To call a dream "good" or "bad," to draw from a dream a conclusion for choice, to find in the dream a rectification of attitude is all moralizing; it interjects into the underworld an alien point of view. We then are demanding from the dream that it assume a moral responsibility and be our spiritual director. Conscience and superego are indeed psychic factors, and these concepts do find their foundations in dream figures of law, governing order, and superior moral authority, but we cannot magically free ourselves from the burden and dignity of moral questions by shifting their onus onto dreams. We wish them to steer us onto the paths of righteousness and to warn when we are wrong. "I had a warning dream," we say. Just here is "psychopathy" of an insidious kind: instead of making up our mind, we pretend the dream is doing it for us. (My dreams say we should separate, have an affair, move out, and the like.) Instead of living the risks of social interest, we fall back on the assumedly superior—and objective—inner voice of the private dream. Here is social amorality, that is, irresponsibility, given pious and incontrovertible psychological sanctions. Images, like the Gods, do make claims on us, just as the dream asks to be worked; but dreams do not tell us what to do.

Let us keep in mind the primary perspective exposed in this book and said by Freud long ago when he was considering the morality of dream-wishes: *"Psychical* reality is a particular form of existence not to be confused with *material* reality" (*ID*, p. 620). Freud's and Jung's affirmations of the amorality of the underworld say that moral positions and psychological understanding are incommensurables. Therefore, reactions to images in terms of morality are inappropriate reactions. This necessitates a preparatory task before working with any dream: we must de-moralize the soul from entrenched upperworld standards owing to its two-thousand-year solitary confinement in the cells of theological Christianity, where all its introverted imagination was morally appraised. But Freud's "immoral, incestuous and perverse impulses" in the deeps of the soul's dreamings are psychic images, not moral actions.

The de-moralized dream becomes a psychopathic danger only in the hands of the translator who turns images into messages for social actions. Psychopathic behavior in the world results less from the image than from its translation into material realities. Again, actual psychopathy has more to do with the heroic ego, whom we admire for his positive actions, than with the underworld figures, whom we fear for their negative fantasies. The dream killer translates into life as a psychopathic tendency, but the killer in the underworld of "psychical reality" is one of the mythical guises of death, the grim reaper being only a more clichéd way of saying it.[18] The murderer in the dream is not merely the hostile, evil, or "amoral shadow" of the dreamer that needs recognition and integration. There is a divine death figure in the killer, either Hades, or Thanatos, or Kronos-Saturn, or Dis Pater, or Hermes, a death demon who would *separate consciousness from its life attachments.*

Similarly, the figures who return ever and again without change: the boys and girls from adolescence who did not age as we have, the hard father or cold mother still demanding our blood. These figures, like Ajax still nursing his grievance, Dido turning her back, Tantalus endlessly reaching for what can never be attained, are the unchanging psychopathic aspect of the complex. Work at changing the unchangeable is wholly misplaced, an ontological confusion that can lead psychotherapy into the myth of Sisyphus. The death instinct seeks, in Freud's (*CP* 2:260) and Fechner's notions, *stability;* in Plato's language, the souls in Hades are incurable (*Gorgias* 525e). They do not change. We have come to call this essential aspect of the complex that is beyond morality and change "psychopathy," yet here is psyche at its purest and most stable permanence, what philosophy would call the realm of essence. To insist that the psychopathic essence recognize the moral values of the upperworld or move from its stabile fixities is to act like Hercules or Christ in the underworld, attempting to rescue the dead rather than to learn from them. Plato (*Cratylus* 403–04; cf. *Phaedo* 80d) saw this fixity not only in the saddening sense because souls are unable to leave Hades, but also because Hades is of such intelligence and such a wise benefactor that the soul desires to remain there forever.[19] It is in the unchanging fastness of the psychopathic that we have most to learn about the nature of the soul.

To learn from the underworld means to learn from the psychopathic. This is a tall order. In dreams, I may fall into paroxysmal stabbing, see an unknown man my age pursue a child with sexual intent or my son falsify a signature and smilingly deny it—these and worse crimes occur and repeat.

Just here I may draw recurrent insights and profound realizations about personality and behavior and go deeper into the shadow and the essential limits it sets me. That these dreams repeat shows the stability of my psychopathy, that it is now settled down to essences of character. If character is our guardian daimon and our fate, as some have translated Heraclitus (frg. 119), then these repetitive patterns are actually tutelary spirits having more to do with how my fate works out than will my upperworld connections and projects.

The dayworld ego digs in its heels, however. It says: although these moral horrors appear, something must be done about them. The moral shock forces an attempt to change an incurable image. Again we see how the moral reaction is inappropriate, even used as a defense against the image, for now enters the real menace: the social-worker complex constellated by the moral horror. As soon as we are shocked, we step away into a social perspective and distance ourselves by means of causes, cures, and literal action. This, however, is precisely the same perspective as psychopathy! Both social worker and sociopath say: it's all out there, and it's all wrong. Both are always "doing something." Owing to this literalism of action, the sociopath cannot learn and the social worker cannot dent the psyche of the problem. The dayworld ego's attempts to deal with the amoral shadow become as fruitless as the repetitions of the underworld. In fact, the underworld myths harden into recividism, the eternal return of the psychopath to his amorality and the eternal attempts at correction by the moralisms of society.

The urge to cure the incurable keeps us from recognizing the essence of our limitations, and the limits that come with the psychopathic essence of personality. Even worse: this urge conceals an imposter who, like a quick-change artist, transforms itself into social worker. The repetitious sense of despair and the repetitious desperation to cure have the same source: the nonprocess, amoral nature of the underworld.

These few paragraphs on a thoroughly perplexing subject at least may suggest why psychopathy has remained such an enigma for psychology: it is because psychology has projected the underworld wholly outside into the sociological underworld, seeking to fathom psychopathy there. However, if psychopathy belongs to the psychological underworld, then investigations of it begin where Freud left off: the death drive—not morality.

ICE

When images of ice appear in dreams, one is likely to imagine that they refer to regions of the spirit: high mountains, remote polar purity, and the thin splendor of the clean. There is another realm of ice—deep, deep down. Below the water (q.v.), the hell fires, and the mud (q.v.), there is the ninth circle of the Inferno that is all ice. According to Dante, this is the place of Cain, Judas, and Lucifer. Gnostic writings also describe a snow-and-ice region of the underworld.[20] This frozen *topos* is another way of imaging psychopathy (q.v.). But there is more to it.

The descent to the underworld can be distinguished from the night sea-journey of the hero in many ways. We have already noticed the main distinction: the hero returns from the night sea-journey in better shape for the tasks of life, whereas the *nekyia* takes the soul into a depth for its own sake so that there is no "return." The night sea-journey is further marked by building interior heat *(tapas)*, whereas the *nekyia* goes below that pressured containment, that tempering in the fires of passion, to a zone of utter coldness.

Therapeutic analysis remains incomplete if it is satisfied with bringing balm to burning problems. It has still to venture into the frozen depths that have so fascinated poets and explorers and that in depth psychology are the areas of our

archetypal crystallizations, the immovable depressions and
the mutisms of catatonia.

Here we are numb, chilled. All our reactions are in cold
storage. This is a psychic place of dread and of a terror so
deep that it comes in uncanny experiences, such as voodoo
death and the *totstell* reflex. A killer lives in the ice. Or,
this ice may be experienced as a paranoiac distance, such
as Nietzsche describes in Zarathustra's Night Song: "Light
am I . . . this is my loneliness to be begirt with light. . . .
Alas, there is ice around me, my hand burneth touching
iciness."[22]

We may recall here that the Styx is a river of icy hatred
that protects the underworld and is holy and eternal as are
the God's oaths that they swear by that frigid river. If the
ice serves a function in the underworld, then the icy area
of our nature serves a function in the soul. Glacial cold—
psychopathic, paranoiac, catatonic—is not absent feeling or
bad feeling, but a kind of feeling of its own. Cain, Judas,
and Lucifer are beyond human warmth and psychology's
techniques of sharing the heart, as if humanism would recon-
struct the globe so that all humanity lived in the tepid balance
of the temperate zones. Cain, Judas, and Lucifer are not
tepid, not temperate; they have another kind of heart. The
icy chasm of Christianism's shadow is a realm of radical
importance that cannot be reached with Christianism's bleed-
ing heart. An archetypal approach to this zone follows the
homeopathic maxim: like cures like. The *nekyia* into Hell's
ice requires coldness. If any connection is to be made, we
must be able to work with the cruel extremities of ice itself.
We can meet Cain, Judas, and Lucifer by being aware of
our own desires to be false and to betray, to kill our brother
and to kill ourselves, that our kiss has death in it and that
there is a piece of the soul that would live forever cast out
from both human and heavenly company. These desires that
seek no redemption and have abandoned all hope also move

in the therapist's heart—not only his charity and faith. These desires of the Ninth Circle give that cold psychological eye that sees all things from below, as images caught in their circles, an eye that glitters with the inhuman insight of Lucifer, light bearer.

The heart has a coldness, a place of reserve like the refrigerator that preserves, holds, protects, isolates, suspends animation and circulation, an alchemical congelation of substance. The cruelty and mean despising are the surroundings of a private sense of ultimate deepening. Maybe in my ice is my fairytale princess, whom ego psychology wants to kiss into life; but maybe she is otherwise engaged in her frigid stillness, deepening toward the Ninth Circle, below everything moving; a detachment and stability reminding of the cold body of death. Here is a soul figure who is neither flighty, nor sensuously rippling, nor brooding moods and emotions. Instead the glitter of ice reflects perfection; nothing but crystallized insights and sharp-edged truths are good enough. Desire for absolutism, absolution in perfection. The ice-maiden is a terrible taskmaster, frigid and unresponsive; but since her region is on the map of psychic geography, polar coldness is also a place one can be. Therefore the urge to warm the cold and melt the ice (oppositionalism again) reflects a therapeutic effort that has not been able to meet the ice at its own level. The curative urge conceals the fear of the Ninth Circle, of going all the way down to those depths that are so quickly and surely called psychotic.

Pagan and early Christian tomb inscriptions speak of the dead soul as refrigerated: *in refrigeratio anima tua; deus te refrigeret; in refrigerio et in pace.* The literary tradition also used *refrigerium* and *refrigerare* for the condition of the released soul after death. The source of this convention is supposedly the translation into Latin of Greek words akin to psyche that mean "cool." (*Psykter* = wine-cooler; *psychos* = wintertime, cold weather; *psychros* = cold, unreal, cold hearted, frigid.) The basic form, *psychō,* means something like "blowing cold" or "cooling breath." Indeed there is an ancient connection between the dimension of coldness and the soul *(anima, psyche).*

Psyche not only was in a cold place or was a place of coldness in various senses of the word. It was also given a cooling drink of sweet psychic refreshment, for instance, by Osiris. These cold drinks return in our dreams. Are we supposed to understand Cokes, ice cream, Kool-aid against this antique background? The problem here is the literalization of sweetness into sugar (or its synthetics), i.e., the problem of the naive, naturalistic attitude of the child, to whom, if something is sweet, it must taste sweet, and if it is cold, it must be sensed concretely as cold. When the place of ice is also the place of sugar, there is a confusion between the psychic needs of the underworld and the emotional needs of the child. The dream image shows them concocted together. (The problem will be given a clue by the color and name of the drink, as well as by the location of the image.) The dream-ego, sipping its chocolate ice-cream soda, is one that has to take its dark ice with a creamy sweetener, but at least the dream-ego is imbibing the cold drink of death.

CEREMONIAL EATING

The analytical hermeneutic in regard to ceremonial eating (banqueting, revelry) also needs an archetypal correction. As long as Dionysos and Hades are the same, rituals that seem to celebrate the joy and force of life have also an underworld shadow. This shadow is implicated in eating with dead persons and in preparing and partaking of foods that were especially associated with underworld mythologems: honey, seeds, pomegranates, corn, small cakes, also apples. Mushrooms, by the way, for forest peoples (e.g., the Dayak), are the souls of the dead springing up into the land of the living. These damp, fragrant, spontaneous puffballs, these "midnight mushrooms" (*Tempest,* act 5, sc. 1) of airy earth or earthy air, were called "sons of the Gods" by the Neoplatonist Porphyry; and in Italian folklore the spot in the earth where a mushroom appears indicates a specific metallic body below, i.e., the planetary figures or archetypal bodies of the underworld.[23] Freud, as we saw above, reverted to the mushroom as an image for the mystery of the origin of dreams.

Other foods that we can find mentioned in Greek chthonic cults and "banquets for the dead" are cooked vegetables, eggs, cocks, occasionally fish.[24] Drinks include a mixture of honey-water, milk, and wine. Black sheep were slain and burnt completely in sacrifice.[25] As we see, the menu can be long and varied. It receives different emphasis depending on place, cult, and historical period. An amplification of any of these items, such as honey or milk, would require a good twenty pages.

We should not get too kosher about which foods belong only to the underworld and which not; the point is sensing the *sacrificial atmosphere* that transforms eating into a ritual for the psyche. Such foods and such meals may then be understood as referring to Hades, "the hospitable," the hidden host at life's banquet. Then these ritual communions may open the way into an easier fellowship with one's "dead persons." These are usually experienced as family influences from the past, as the unlived life, the unfulfilled expectations of the ancestors that one carries unwittingly. By sitting at table with them, we are now feeding them and beginning to be fed by them.

The psyche needs to be fed. This idea appears not only in the widespread practice of leaving food and utensils for preparing it in the graves of the dead. It appears as well, for instance, in the annual ceremony *(Anthesteria)* in Greece of feeding the souls *(keres)* that returned from the underworld to their former abodes—a ritual that still occurs on All Souls' Night, or Halloween, when we placate masked persons with token edibles. The alchemists had an operation called *cibation* ("feeding") and one called *imbibition* ("soaking" or "steeping"), in which the psychic stuff that one was working on required the right food and drink at a certain moment during the opus of soul-making.

In Eden, eating was the first sin and our human life begins with the first bite, by which I certainly do not mean in the developmental sense of orality and nipples. Eating dreams need to be expanded beyond such simple notions as the oral phase and the gratification of demands. Food is so fundamental, more so than sexuality, aggression, or learning, that it is astounding to realize the neglect of food and eating in depth psychology. Therefore, we need to look very closely at such dreams, realizing how little we can be helped by our psychological tradition.

So, we will want to notice precisely what the persons in a dream are eating, and where, when, and with whom, for this tells us how the feeding process is going on. We may learn what the dream-ego feeds on, from, and with. Does it feed from a waitress who takes his order (or won't take his order); does he go "out" to eat; does he eat "at home" and can he "cook himself"; does he grab sweets in the street; go into his *refrigerium* in dead of night to find what he desperately hungers for?

Foodstuffs evoke concrete, naturalistic associations: "I hate liver: it's too rich and has a sweet taste," "I never take tea for breakfast, so why did I dream it?" "Orange juice is healthy, even if I am gulping it in the dream." It is hard to see through to the dream-liver that is (among other things) the great bloody organ of living passion (whether one hates dayworld liver or not); it is hard to recognize that tea in the morning is a new ritual for breaking into the day and that gulping orange juice is just what it says—a manic compulsion for bright sunlit "juice," like the souls in Hades thirsty for life. Penetrating into a specific food image is unusually difficult, because it is concrete; yet what we eat in dreams is not food but images.

The Egyptian underworld shows the corpse being given food and drink by the Ba (*Ba,* p. 146). Again, we can see how the Egyptian underworld turns the dayworld upside down. The idea depicted is not one of the soul living from the body's matter, an epiphenomenon of diet—you are what you eat. Rather, we are shown that the body draws upon the soul for its nourishment. The life of the body needs the soul stuff of images.

Earlier we quoted a romantic notion that images are the soul's best food. May this mean as well that foods are the soul's best images? With this I am suggesting that eating in dreams nourishes the mouths of our ghosts, giving back to the other souls and our own dream-soul some part of what grows in our psyche. It is a sacrificial, ceremonial act. Whoever eats in a dream, wherever and whenever it takes place, psychic persons are being nourished by the dream's images. Eating in dreams would therefore have little to do with a hunger instinct and much to do with a psychic need for nourishing images. Food, whatever its kind, is precisely the image of nourishment. The possible origin of the dream-food is Pluto's cornucopia.

The Gods too want their proper food—remember the revenge they took on Prometheus when he tried to pass off something second rate? Nor was Cain's cooking favored. Although the fruits, the slaughter, and the burning be natural, what nourishes them is not literal, but sacrificial, metaphorical. The ceremony is of concrete images, food as ritual token; so in our dreams, eating is a moment of transubstantiation, where what is only natural becomes also metaphorical. It is a primordial ritual for keeping the Gods alive, keeping in communion with presences beyond our selves, and treating them as part of the family in need of regular meals.

REVELRY

Now we come to several kinds of revelry (music, carnival, circus, clown). We should bear in mind throughout that the theme as a whole is characterized by the word *revelry* itself: riotous rebellion (revel/rebel), discord, upset, the revolt of mirth and breakdown of laughter.

To begin with music. It cannot archetypally be reduced to only Orpheus or Apollo. There are kinds of music: meditative, martial, love, funeral, dithyrambic, simple ditties and chanteys. The many Muses say there are many ways of musing, but a particular sort can be more closely connected with the underworld. Pounding drums, ringing bells and chimes, and high-pitched fifes have been used both to ban the demons of the dead, as well as waken them. This kind of discordant, uncanny music sometimes comes in dreams together with peculiar processions (like a Mediaeval scene of pilgrims and cripples in a Bergman film)—a grotesque parody, a Bedlam, which word too has come to mean a craziness of sound. I take these weird scenes of music as a rite in process, a movement gathering together the deformed and outcast elements of psyche and assembling them into the process of soul-making. The alchemical *massa confusa* is now en route, moving.

But even a simple song in a dream comes under suspicion as having a deeper sense, an under-meaning *(hyponoia)*. The Toda in India believe that only the dead sing in dreams.[26] We may therefore listen to dream music of any sort with an ear cocked toward death, an ear for psychic tones. This means that we do not need literal sound in a dream in order to tune into the dream's music (its phrasing, rhythm, discords, dominant and recurring themes, its hidden harmony). We need only the musical ear that makes what happens into music.[27] When music does sound in a dream, first of all the dream is stating it can be heard. Let us say, it wants to be listened to.

Carnivals, masked balls, traveling fairs and shows—the underworld as a mad, upside-down liveliness of autonomous figures, disguised, spontaneous, fascinating and frightening, drifting through the night or set up during the night right in the middle of town. The freaks and cheats have come, and the animals (q.v.) and the mechanical circular (q.v.) rides.

In the dream of a woman attached to her immediate family, its comfortable bourgeois standards and the values that go with such standards, the ego is chased through the streets of a shady district by obscene and menacing carnival figures. The dream-ego takes refuge from pursuit by slipping into a chair and with pretended nonchalance takes up witty conversation with the intelligentsia at the table (a European's dream, of course).

The menacing raucous humor and the body bawdiness of the shady district are reflected in the dream-ego as aboveboard, witty talk. It too is in disguise (pretending nonchalance). Her defense works, for it stays in the style of the menace: in the street, using wit, and with consciousness of pretense.

Another young woman, who had come to analysis to "control loose habits" (drinking, overeating, pills, sleeping around), hears the frightening tinny music of a riotous Mardi Gras band, coming closer. The dream-ego wakens her in panic, and she believes for an instant that she is in the analytical room. The riotous process from which the dream-ego flees into analysis is still getting closer despite analysis. Looseness is not coming under control as she had planned. In fact, the analytical room and the band that riots are part of the same image. The image required her to give an analytical ear to what the loose music, this band of her soul, was playing in her and with her. The Lenten ashes of Ash Wednesday and the carnival music of Fat Tuesday belong in the same image and construct each other.

A third young woman, whose ideal was communal relationships based on sincerity and open truth, dreamt of being at a costume party in which all the figures are masked. People dance individually, alone in corners like madmen. The dream-ego is whirled around in a dance with a partner whom she does not recognize or cannot see and awakens in terror because no one is real.

Death, as the masked dancer, the invisible, the separator, forces each of us into a dance without partners in the individual shape of our mask. This dance is not "real" in the sense of the dayworld, to which reality the ego flees by waking. Carnival emphasizes both a communal event—many figures, crowds, balls, and yet an event that is unrelated and impersonal, no couples and pairings or even intimate groups. The personal level is broken up for another kind of experience.

When Dionysos entered Thebes, there was also this kind of terror and excitement. Identities became uncertain. Young women left their family attachments and personal relationships to take to the streets and the hills. Dionysos and Hades are the same, so these dreams remove the dream-ego from daily life to a seeing through of its standards in rebellion, or revelry.

When the carnival pursues and the masked dancer invites, the dream-ego is in the role of Persephone being chased by the invisible spirit's demands. Were the spirit unmasked, it could be taken at its face value, literally. We would know what it seeks by the face it presents. It is masked in order to stimulate inquiry, the search to discover. This is the adequate spiritual response to the masked or invisible spirit; one learns how to dance with its demands, which is not the same as worship or slavery. This is terrifying to the ego, however, and it calls the masked stranger, Death, or the Negative Animus, or a Vampire. Dionysos in Thebes was called the Stranger.

The word *carnival* derives from *carnem levare*, "to put away the flesh, or meat." It refers to a moment of psychisation that removes the naturalistic attitude. Thus it feels like a death. The carnival figures that force this "putting away" are resisted by the body emotions of the dream-ego. They are in panic for their 'life,' defending themselves against this strangeness by taking "carnival" to mean only an exuberance of flesh.

The upside-down experience described in the Egyptian underworld is nowhere better displayed than in the circus.[28] There everything seems concentrated toward one aim: turning the natural way of things topsy-turvy, an *opus contra naturam* that overcomes gravity and establishes a thoroughly pneumatic world. The elephant rises on two hind legs or stands on a ball filled with air. One man holds up eleven others above his head. Another piles more and more household trivia vertically upward, all on the point of one chair leg. The human fly walks upside down and nothing falls from the juggler's hands. The human cannonball shoots through the air and human birds perch on the highwire or swing through space from the trapeze. Beasts leap through fire. The horse is white and goes round in a ring.

Meanwhile, the clowns with white faces of death, mute like souls in the underworld, making strange music, falling down and coming apart, always too slow and forgetting, repeating the same mistakes, on the edge of diarrhea (q.v.), hold the reflective mirror up to life by mimes of our upperworld behavior.

Where else but the circus will we ever see the underworld in daylight: the tent of enclosed space (q.v.), the rings, everyone as close to death as his or her art will allow, the freaks of nature that are beyond nature, and above all, the precise performance of repetitive nonsense, as if Ixion, Tantalus, and Sisyphus had once worked for Ringling Brothers.

In the dreams and imaginations of therapy the upside-down motif occurs more frequently than one might expect. We need only to look for it. A man is turned upside down in an elevator. His feet are now higher than his head. His head now takes a lower place and yet becomes the base for his feet. What now goes on in his mind is his new standpoint, and it is the standpoint of below. This happens in an elevator, confirming Heraclitus, who said that the way up and the way down are the same. Another man dreams of standing on his head after three precise sommersaults. Later, he tells me that he then tried it and experienced blood rushing into his ears. He had never imagined his head with blood in it before; now it became a blood-filled organ, rich, red, round. He began to think of thought in a new way and started to have what he called bloody red thoughts, that were both rebellious and also like obscene pranks. The passionate intellect was coming to him through the clown.

A woman, doing an initial active imagination, meets a monkey hanging by its tail. It explains to her that it is right side up in its world and that she has to learn to move this way too if she wants to be with the monkey. She feels frightened and unbalanced. This seems the way to craziness—but it is such a joke. Another woman dreams of a circus clown descending from the high wire. He descends upside down, supported by a guide line at his Achilles heel. The way of descent is the way of human frailty. What is weakness to the hero is the support system to the clown: the most tender spot is guide when one is upside down.

As I write this, there is a movement afoot shown by images from my practice, to say nothing of those by Fellini and the arts, towards clowns, mimes, and circus. Like small boys we want to run away and join the circus, but identification with the clown is miming the mime. Heraclitus (frg. 130, Freeman) warned about this, supposedly saying, "It is not proper to be so comic that you yourself appear comic." To enact the clown literalizes the guide to the underworld. The comic spirit can take us there, but we are not the guide—not Harlequin, Trickster, or Hermes Psychopompos, not even a Clown. The comic spirit masquerades in all things we do and say; we are each a joke and do not need to put on a white face.

The matter is not one of becoming a clown but of learning what he teaches: making an art of our senseless repetitions, our collapsing and our pathologizings, putting on the face of death that allows the dream world in and watching it turn ordinary objects into amazing images, our public persons into butts of laughter.

We follow the clown into the circus by entering a perspective of rebellion against the dayworld order; rebel without cause or violence. Turning topsy-turvy, we deliteralize every physical law and social convention in the smallest things that we take for granted. Through him we enter the perspective of the fantastic soul, clown as depth psychologist. Imagine, Freud and Jung, two old clowns.

DOORS AND GATES

A word about doors and gates. One epithet of Hades was "he who closes the door."[29] It was at the gates to the underworld that Hercules wrestles with Hades. In order for Hercules to be taken (if he was) into the Eleusinian mysteries, he had first to be adopted by a God-father, Pylios,[30] a doorman, so that Hercules would be able to pass through the gates of Hades.

The problem of the underworld for the Herculean ego is at the threshold, at the borderline, which for him separates two kinds of consciousness. For Hermetic consciousness, there is no upperworld versus underworld problem. Hermes inhabits the borderlines;[31] his herms are erected there, and he makes possible an easy commerce between the familiar and the alien. Unlike Hercules, who wards off evil and saves us from sickness, Hermetic consciousness finds no threshold,

no gates on the other side of which are conditions called
"sick" (q.v.) and chronic (or retarded q.v.), for here the experience of life and death are inseparable. Pathologizing keeps
them together. Borderlines are a place of open intercourse
also for the Trickster, the Dancer, and the Harlequin. For
Hercules, however, it is a wrestle and a sweat to move in
and out, to entertain differing alternatives, languages, cus-
toms—psychic realities and physical realities—at the same
time. His world is oppositional. He does not know how to
pass through the gates without an *enantiodromia* ("opposite
flight") into madness, into mystery, into the female sex.

Doors and gates are the places of "going through," of "passing over" as one called it in Victorian times. They are the
structures that make possible a rite of passage. The underworld perspective begins at the gates of entry, where entry
signifies initiation. At the beginning, one must move into
the Janus-faced double nature of the gate, so that everything
within is able to be understood in a double sense, hermetically,
metaphorically.[32] The gates make possible the underworld
perspective.

We meet the gates less in dreams than at the moment of
awakening from them. Then we experience the wrestling at
the threshold. Awareness struggles between nightworld images and dayworld plans. We have most trouble recollecting
dreams when we are in our Herculean stance, actively getting
up and going. Hence, periods when we can't recall our dreams
may point to the presence of Hercules, rather than to Hades
shutting us out. Hades would shut the door—not so much,
I believe, to keep the dream from escaping as from escaping
via Hercules and into his ego that interprets the dream into
actions for solving its problems. This robs Hades and cheats
death of the dream's work in soul-making. By capturing Cerebros, the guardian of the gate, Hercules reveals his most
fundamental threat to Hades: the destruction of the threshold,
opening the underworld forever to incursions from above,

the realm of soul always available to practical life. Christ's mission that eradicated Hell was indeed foreshadowed by Hercules'. This is not just myth, back then. As Sallust said: myth never happened but always is. The destruction of the gates and of the underworld and soul occurs any morning. We capture the dog of night terror and turn straight into the day, muscles flexed, rising up from the bed, our projections reinforced by the dream.

Again, compare Hermes, for whom there is no two-world problem, two attitudes and a fight between them. There is but an hermetic mode that sees all worlds through hermeneutic eyes.

It may seem that the threshold struggle is one between inner and outer attitudes, but the Herculean perspective is not simply extraversion. It is the literal way of regarding images, such as we saw above in his behavior in the underworld. Therefore, the same heroic ego appears in introverted literalism, as when taking dreams at their word, to be spiritual messages, synchronistic foretellings, oracles of individuation, Self-instructions, memories of the past, statements of our feelings, and the like. Yes, dreams are wonderful, and they make us wonder, but they are not wonders, or miracles, or revelations, or truth. They belong to soul and its images, not to spirit; the spiritual phenomena that may appear in dreams are also deliteralized by the images in which the spirit appears. Introverted literalism loses the image in the message.

Introverted literalism (for want of a better phrase) occurs at another place in the Hercules stories. Later antiquity converted Hercules from "an arcane strong man to a symbol of mystic salvation."[33] Conversion, however, is only *enantiodromia*. The style of consciousness is untouched. Its realm of action has changed, but the attitude in the new realm is the same. So Hercules still catches us when we see the dream, no longer as message for the muscles in life, but now as "symbols of mystic salvation."

For Hercules, the key to the door is in Persephone's hand. There was much question in antiquity whether Hercules had ever seen Kore-Persephone;[34] for had he, then he would have been an initiate. This implies for us that the battle at the gates—that oppositionalism between two worlds—can only be left behind when there is a shift in the anima from Hebe to Persephone, when fantasy itself begins to yearn neither for outward success nor inward salvation but for depth.

MUD AND DIARRHEA

We referred in the section on Dream Material (Chapter 5) to Bachelard's idea of the plasticity of psychic substance, that it is like paste, clay, dough, molten metal. This bears upon descriptions of the underworld as a realm of mushy or fecal matter. Plato (*Rep.* 363c–d) describes it as mud. Aristophanes' *Frogs* depicts a swamp of everflowing excrements. Kerényi describes Hercules crossing the marshy waters of Acheron and compares them wth the swamp of Stymphalos,[35] and I would add the shit-filled stables of Augeias. The *nekyia* text which Dieterich translated provokes him to the observation that the early Christian-Orphic fascination with purgation and with the underworld as a filthy hellhole of blood, dirt, and shit, reflects the double implication of diarrhea both as an objective image of loathsome warning and a subjective symptom of fright in face of that image.[36] We may also recollect that, to the Egyptian underworld imagination, the dead walked upside down so that the stuff of their bowels came out through their mouths.

The labyrinthine tract of the bowels has already been considered an interiorized underworld, with their heat, deep location, and sulphuric stench.[37] There is a long association in our tradition between the bowels and insanity,[38] even ideas of the bowels as the seat of the soul.[39] The word that medicine still uses for rumblings in the intestines (borborygmus) is the word Plato (*Phaedo* 69c) and Aristophanes used for filthy mire in the underworld. A late Orphic hymn calls the Goddess of the realm of death *borborophoba,* which we can render in the double sense of shit-fearing: she who keeps it at bay, and she who makes it flow in panic.[40]

In view of this background, let us see through dreams of diarrhea as radical compelling movements into the underworld or as an underworld that has come to sudden and irrepressible life within us, independent of who and where we are. Like death, diarrhea strikes when it will and all alike. Shit is the great leveler.

We are crossing a border. Diarrhea signals the daylight order at its "end." The old king falls apart and shits like a baby—decomposition and creation at once: incontinence, humiliation, ridicule, from Saturn, lord of privies and underwear, to Saturnalia. It feels like mere anarchy is loosed upon the world, and the wish is for nothing more than an enclosed and private space to take down one's pants. Like the northerner gone south, the long-dreamt, long-wished vacation is fulfilled in a toilet. The toilet as death of the wish, as death wish,[41] as joke, place of the clown.

What I am trying to suggest here in the dirty joke mode of toilet humor, is an extension both of our Freudian notions, which couple bowels with anality, and Jungian notions, which relate them and their products with creative expressions, *prima materia,* and alchemical gold. "Toilet dreams"—those in which there is an immediate need to defecate, or a backed-up sewer and fecal flood, or an embarrassing, frustrating search midst others for "a place to go," or the discovery that one has soiled oneself, and the like—can be read as underworld initiations. These are indeed death experiences for the dayworld ego, whose cleanliness is next to its Godlikeness. In the language of Egyptian imagery, the anal has now reversed into the oral, what was held back is spewed forth, and we are released into the repressed. Do you remember Freud's panic that Jung's ideas might cause his psychoanalytic science to lose its hold over the deep psyche, letting loose the "black tide of mud of occultism"?

The great pile of interpretative ideas about feces, what shit is supposed to "mean" (the crap about shit): the gift of love to the parent; creative expression beginning with smearing and coloring; the control of wealth and the origins of conscience; the death within; the birth of the non-I, making possible separation and objectivity; the negative Self of values hidden in the most vile and rejected; the shadow that follows after one, at one's behind; as well as the scatological rites of all nations, and the inexhaustiblity of outhouse humor— all this is an embarassment of riches. Just this suggests an archetypal background in the richness of Hades, in Pluto's wealth. Of course, the underworld is also made of excrements, for they are a richness for continual fantasy images. From this viewpoint, feces is not translatable into another term. As residue of residues, feces suggests an essence permanently present and continually forming anew. Its appearance in dreams reflects an underworld to which we daily bend in homage, never to be rid of.

SMELL AND SMOKE

This leads us to smell and to smoke. Statistical studies show that by far most dreams are "seen," or at least use the language of visual perception. Only occasionally do we hear, touch or taste in dreams, and, rarest of all, do we use the sense of smell. Yet, Heraclitus says (frg. 98, Wheelwright); "In Hades souls perceive by smelling," and further (frg. 7); "If all things became smoke, the nostrils would distinguish them."

Antiquity, as we saw above, generally regarded the dead

shades as pneumatic beings. Cumont writes: "They are compared to the wind, for the wind is the air in motion, to a vapour, to a smoke which escapes as soon as restraint is attempted."[42] Plato (*Crat.* 404d) suggests that the etymological meaning of Persephone is "seizing that which is in motion."

But how do we grasp the soul's motions; how perceive air? The early Greek idea of "I perceive" (the expression for which is retained in our words *ether* and *esthetics*) signified more generally "taking in" or "I breathe in" (*OET*, pp. 74–75). Perhaps the issue raised by Heraclitus is not what kind of sensation does the soul have at its disposal in the afterlife (Kirk's rather concrete, naive, and Christianized reading),[43] but rather what is the best analogy for psychological perception. Perhaps, psychic depths that are not revealed to the more visible, tangible senses, require a perceptual mode, such as that of smell, that discriminates amidst what is hidden, a perception of intangibles by intangible means. Psychological work would call for a keen nostril, an ability to perceive subtle bodies, or the body subtly, tracking down what is essential. That word *essence* is used both for an elemental substance at the core and for fragrance. Perhaps too, this metaphorical valuation of smell accounts for the curious belief among psychiatrists that olfactory hallucinations in schizophrenics may be actual perceptions made more acute by autistic withdrawal from other senses, as if through a retreat by the patient to the pneumatic underworld where souls perceive by smelling.

Perception of this subtle sort can be attributed to the invisible Gods, who recognize through the power of scent what was given them in burnt offerings and incense: "God takes various shapes just as fire does, which, when it is mingled with spices, is named according to the scent of each of them" (frg. 67). Again: it is the nostrils which discern the spirits.[44]

Thus when Heraclitus says (frg. 96): "Corpses are more fit to be cast out than dung," we cannot be satisfied with a usual sort of interpretation, i.e., that Heraclitus implied something we already know: the dead body is less useful than dung. Rather, in his usual paradoxical style, he might well be saying that dung, e.g., the smell of rot, is worth more than the material that gives rise to it, or, not the simple, physical body has value but the soul that is released through *putrefactio*. The *fumus* ("smoke") or subtle vapor is etymologically intercognate with the *fimus* ("dung"), the dying matter from which it rises (*OET*, pp. 510–11). A psychic process takes place in shit (as we saw above) that is recognized only by a psychic mode of perception which, following Heraclitus, we are calling "smell."

The rare dreams in which we smell something ought to be inspected from this vantage point. If only the nose knows, then besides imagining what is happening in the dream only as a base event of the animal or anal, or an old event of memory, or as the arrival on the scene of the intuitive function, I would consider the dream event as something essential, pneumatic, esthetic, even ethereal. When we smell something, we are taking in its spirit, so it is just as well to know what we are smelling. Ethereal may also mean otherworldly and uncanny in the diabolic sense; the devil too is recognized by his smell. So the phenomenon that comes with a smell comes from the underworld, calling for an intense psychic acuity to discern its nature.

Smell is the undersense, the *hyponoia* (p. 137 above) that perceives psychic realities when "all things become smoke" (frg. 7). Smoke refers, on the one hand, to conditions that are obscured and confused to the daylight eye of physical perception and, on the other hand, to vaporized or psychized conditions, where the dead soul or image soul leaves the body's matter. (There may be more in it than "meets the eye" when clinicians claim they can diagnostically smell a psychosis.)

Smoke is the first visible result of fire on matter. It is both thin matter and thick air, an intermediate substance between spirit and body. So it is quite a good likeness to the soul itself, an observation that did not escape alchemy.[45] Wheelwright says: ". . . smoke, cloud, and vapor are but different forms of the state of being of things intermediate between fire and water, and soul belongs ontologically in this area. Being vaporous a soul is also smoky. . . ."[46]

In dreams where there is smoke, there is not only a hidden fire (concealed passion, as they say). Smoke is important in itself independent of the fire it is supposed to signify. Soul-making is going on, an irreversible change in natures, and a rising that is at the same time a blinding and suffocation if one gets too close by identifying oneself with the elemental change. (I am not touching here upon the pleasures, rituals, and addictions of smoking tobacco.)

SPACE

An idea that Freud absorbed from Fechner—that the dream takes place in its own *topos*—makes us consider space as a basic dimension in all dreams. Almost every dream has its psychical locality, where its images come into being (see p. 15 f). Images are somewhere, and they have their own characteristic spatial quality. The underworld itself is a topography: the House of Hades, the Halls of Valhalla, the rivers, islands, ever descending levels. The fundamental language of depth is neither feelings, nor persons, nor time and numbers. It is space. Depth presents itself foremost as psychic structures in spatial metaphors. This is so basic and evident that we tend to miss it, passing right by the depth that is at hand in the specific space of each image.

We may lose this spatial dimension, the "whereness" of the dream, when we amplify it with symbolism. An apple, a fish, or a crazy-faced lady, if archetypes, are everywhere—

and nowhere. But this apple, this fish, and this crazy-faced lady take up a specific place within a specific dream, and the depth of these images emerges only within that space, as does an apple in a painting by Cézanne, a fish in a painting by Braque, and the crazy-faced lady in one of Picasso's portraits.

The fundamental image of all underworld is that of *contained space* (even if the limits are shrouded and undefined). Continuing with our principle of resemblance, every response to the underworld should resonate from a similar contained space, whether this be the consulting room itself, the close therapeutic relationship, the hermetic vessel in which the work is done, the dream-journal, or the going inward in imagination. All these derive from the deep and closeted underworld. We may experience the dream *topos* as being "cabin'd, cribb'd, confin'd" (*Macbeth*, act 3, sc. 4), as an incubation, a labyrinth, pregnancy, or claustrophobic catacomb for exploring ancestral skeletons. So we talk of "going in" to analysis or of finding no way "out" of analysis, for the depths of psychotherapy have become one of the "places" today of experiencing psychic space.

These experiences of limited space are essential to dreamwork. Here I am not referring to ideas of emotional containment or of a religious *temenos*. Rather, something more ordinary; I have come to believe the psyche must be crowded, pushed to the wall, from outside by others, shoved and jostled in the vale of the world; from inside by its multitudinal trinkets, its collections of imageries and cross-current trips. Chaff, lots of chaff; day-residues, *i.e.*, junk and garbage make our dreams. The spirit would free us from this oppression. It wants more air, more space. "I can't breathe in my marriage," says the wife; "If I don't leave this house, I'll suffocate," says the daughter; and then each moves into a little room of her own with a window giving onto a wall.

We keep our dream-journals in tight little script, observe

tiny machinations of our symptoms, treasure a single insight, such as a grain of sand on which a whole world turns. Vast cosmic perspectives are of course necessary, too; we must fill the lungs. Still, dream-work is an art of the small, and sometimes we become small and precise only under pressure. Perhaps, the tightness is a preparation for death so that we become small enough in soul to fit in the shrunken body that goes in the box, small enough to slip through the little window cut for souls to exit from the death room. Perhaps the sense of limited containment belongs to the experience of the psychic body, that awareness of a concealed interiority laying low within every word and gesture.

Bachelard, in his *Poetics of Space,* has elaborated some images of interior space (joyful ones only). His work helps move psychology into new metaphors for its work, permitting yet another archetypal correction of analytical psychology. We have too long borrowed terms for analyzing dreams, abstractions such as "opposites," "compensations," "elements," "poles," "energies," and the like.

If the dream-place is basically an enclosed scene, as Ludwig Binswanger pointed out,[47] then we need to speak of our dreams less in terms of psychodramatics so as to experience their scenic setting. Look at the dream as if it were a theater program. Setting: My Mother's House; My Lover's Hatchback Car; On a Green Field—these scenes already define the psychic position of all the events in the dream. Everything that happens, happens *there.*

The movement from drama to scene is like the movement from story to image and from heroic agonist to shadows. (We have already noted that "scene" and *skia,* "shade," are cognates.) This movement frees us from the dramatic view of the dream even while it retains the deeper notion of theater. The dramatic view keeps the dream moving in time through four phases toward a *lysis* or resolution. This view takes the space or setting of the dream only as a preliminary to its plot. For the underworld view, however, what matters is not how the story comes out, but where it is taking place, what region of the soul is now on stage, so that I may know "where I am at" in regard to my dream-soul. A feel for scenes, even an hysterical feeling that creates stagy and melodramatic scenes, attempts to revert the dream-work to Dionysos and Hades, to the sense of life as an enactment of masks, and dreams as these masks. Theater creates that dissociative illusion of being in and out at the same moment, both souls there at once. We are both wholly in the dream and yet aware that it is, we are, only an act.

ATTITUDE TOWARD DREAMS

Finally, concerning the attitude toward any dream whatever, let us meet it on its side of the bridge in its own country. If we follow it into the nightworld, our consciousness will be vesperal, a consciousness going into night, its terror and its balm, or a consciousness of Persephone, the excitement of pursuing images into their depths and mating there with the intelligence of Hades. This dark attitude pervades, even if the dream's images are shot through with sunlight. Dreams are children of Night, and we have to look at their brightest dayworld image also through our selfsame smoky glasses. So we work into the dream without forethoughts of *Aurora consurgens,* for Eos (Dawn) prefers heroes and takes them up. Instead: the resurrection of Death. Instead of turning to the dream for a new start and for foresight to warn of pitfalls and regressions, there will always be a going downward, first with feelings of hopelessness, then, as the mind's eye dilates in the dark, with increasing surprise and joy. The helpless feeling that indicates the underworld is already present begins right in the moment of looking at a dream. There is a darkening of consciousness that makes the dream seem so utterly foreign and incomprehensible. Prometheus and Pandora, helper and hoper, left behind on the other bank. Consciousness will be less visual; the sacrificial connection with "the deities of the dead was made with averted face; no looking, only the voice. . . ."[48] The underworld whispers; there is no emotional *thymos* there, a world far indeed from such raucous notions of therapy as the primal scream, which has as archetype coming into day and the birth of the child. This therapy, like all counseling and training of perceptual awareness, prepares the ego for life, but dream-work goes differently as we have seen.

The place of one's sensitivity may move from eye to ear and then through the senses of touch, taste, and scent, so that we begin to perceive more and more in particulars, less and less in overviews. We become more and more aware of an animal discrimination going on below our reflections and guiding them.

This retraining of the senses, learning to tune in and get in touch, to sniff out and long savor, to accord with the hidden and invisible sense in an image that makes it really matter, may relieve our sensational materialism at its very source.

Sensual imagination restores to the image its primacy as *psychic basis of sensation*. To take our senses only on the level of natural sensations is a naturalistic fallacy. It's like believing that we have to see an image to imagine or hear music to listen musically. The image makes possible the sensing of it.

This turns upside down what psychology has been teaching ever since Aristotle: images result from sensations and soul is built of the bricks of sense experience (dayworld residues). Once we deliteralize sensation and take our senses too as metaphorical modes of perceiving, we are finally across the bridge and can look back on the all-too-solid brick structure where we live our lives as manmade defenses against the soul, as an "anthropomorphism called reality."[49]

Not easy this—and so esoteric, occult. But dream theories, if they reflect dreams at all, must seem strange to dayworld consciousness. Freud's theory was shockingly unpopular. Sex was too much for his peers and his generation. The first edition of his great book was not read. Jung's theory was too difficult because of its intellectual demands. One had to learn not only his new terms but also be comfortable in the history of universal culture, so as to recognize symbols and archetypes. His main great works are still barely read. At their inception, Freud's theory was perverse and Jung's complex; now both are taken for granted.

Because the perspective in my essay derives in part from both Freud and Jung, it carries over their inheritance. It is both shocking and difficult, but now for the reason of death. Besides the inheritance, this book adds its own reason for rejection. What I have been proposing is farfetched, impractical, and visionary. The approach bespeaks the territory of its origin, chthon, the faraway pneumatic world that is a dimension not available in itself and so cannot be rightly presented; it can only be a shadowed perspective emptying out other positions. It is a killer.

Both Freud and Jung attempted with their works to give us a positive knowledge of the psyche. In their own and different ways, they contributed to science, to *knowing* something about dreams: their nature, structure, dynamics, symbols, language, intentions, internal mechanisms, meanings. In contrast this book attempts to elaborate an *attitude* toward dreams in which any positive knowledge would be a daylight move, wronging the dream and wronging the soul. When we believe we know the invisible, we begin on a ruinous course. We are now reaping the ignorant delusions of the last century's positive knowledge of nature, which loves to hide. We thought we knew invisibles like the atom, the cell, and the gene, and off we went riding the horse of hubris, and now there may be no road back. If we believe in a positive knowledge of the dream or of the psyche, are we not riding that same horse on that same ruinous course—and a century late, anachronistically approaching the psyche with attitudes that have already been invalidated in regard to nature. Essential for working with what is unknown is an attitude of unknowing. This leaves room for the phenomenon itself to speak. It alone may keep us from delusions. Hence my stress upon two things: the dark eye that makes our brightness unsure; and careful precision in regard to what is actually there, a method that Lopez-Pedraza felicitously calls "sticking to the image."

The absence of positive knowledge in this book, its blatant neglect of fact, of statistical prediction, of propositional falsifiability and historical authority, even of evidence and example, may further contrast what has been going on here with what Freud and Jung were doing, although neither did they rely on these methods for their psychologies of the dream. Nevertheless, they each had a coherent metapsychology on which their methods of dream analysis depended. Where they built a coherent system, we are suggesting instead a consistent perspective in keeping with a specific mythic domain, the underworld. Rather than a coherent psychological theory, our aim is a consistent psychological attitude.

The difference between a coherent theory and a consistent attitude is that the latter is both more modest in its ambition and more daring in its practice. Our perspective can allow dreams to belong to whatever theory one likes (Freud's, Jung's, or another's), because the metapsychological stories that explain dreams—their nature, function, dynamics, symbolisms—are irrelevant to the dream and its images. Any theory will do so long as it does not disturb the consistent underworld perspective of the dream as image. We stick with tactics, the imaginative, soul-making work with the dream. Never mind the strategy. The underworld is not a theory, nor even a story. It is rather a mythic place, where only psyche matters and nothing else. A consistent perspective will be consistent with this image-sense of psychic reality, regardless of the more elaborate theory one constructs about psychic reality (Freudian, Jungian, and others).

Our metapsychology is wholly mythic and imaginative. It insists on such unsystematic unknowables as depth, soul, and death. The perspective conforming with this background is shackled in its ambition. What kind of theory could we construct, when we can't describe, let alone define, the basic terms in our vocabulary? We have to enter the battle without directions from headquarters, as if there were no headquarters and no battle plan. Ever on watch for the undersense, we must grapple with each dream bare-handed, daring our way through from image to image solely by means of our imaginative craft and consistent viewpoint, without theoretical goals saying how it should all come out and when the engagement is over. Having no theory, we can only stick to the dream.

Here a difference with Freudian and Jungian praxes becomes most obvious. I mean the relation between the dream and a person's remembrances, or anamnesis, is different in our way of working. Although Freudians have always paid especial attention to dreams, and Jungians have categories called "initial dreams" and "big dreams" that they use as decisive, predictive images,[50] neither take the radical bridge-burning step that our attitude forces on us. While they put the dream in the patient and his life context, we place the patient and his life in the dream. Our first psychotherapeutic move is to imagine him in a dream. His dayworld stories are regarded as further places where his dream is dreamt, his problems further analogies of his images. These images are his psychic context and his psychic reality, which we, as therapists of psyche, consider to be our first and last concern. Our image theory means that we have nowhere to place the patient except in his images, in the midst of his 'material', and both of us must stay in the underworld, foregoing whatever metapsychological aims the dream might be serving: ego development, integration, social interest, individuation.

This means forsaking anamnesis in the sense of case history, the usual gathering of a context of social realities and personal experiences in which to put the dreams. To our perspective, none of this is more important than the dream or even helps to understand it. The phenomenon to be saved is the dream, saved from its dayworld links, which distort the images in personal recollections. Our anamnesis is the dream itself, and we get to know the patient through his dreams, from below, turning to his psyche before his dayworld life. This move constellates the underworld from the beginning and initiates the whole analytical procedure as a descent into unknown space.

In the darkness of this initiation, the two people instinctively move nearer to each other. A bond forms, as if an eros between the dying, something that is other than the transference of past emotions, other than love between pupil and guide, between patient and doctor, a quite rare and inexplicable feeling brought by the mystery of the image.

I do not know what this kind of loving is, but it is not reducible to other more familiar forms. Perhaps it is an experience of the eros in thanatos. Perhaps it is an experience of telestic eros, of which Plato speaks in the *Phaedrus*, the eros of the mysteries and initiations of the soul; or, it may have something to do with the creative eros that always occurs when one is close to soul, the myth of Amor and Psyche moving through our emotions (*MA*, pp. 49–111). Whatever the nature, there is a loving in dream-work. We sense that dreams mean well for us, back us up and urge us on, understand us more deeply than we understand ourselves, expand our sensuousness and spirit, continually make up new things to give us—and this feeling of being loved by the images permeates the analytical relationship. Let us call it *imaginal love*, a love based wholly on relationship with images and through images, a love showing in the imaginative response of the partners to the imagination in the dreams. Is this Platonic love? It is like the love of an old man, the usual personal content of love voided by coming death, yet still intense, playful, and tenderly, carefully close.

"Old men ought to be explorers," said T. S. Eliot. Let us imagine them as explorers of the image, lovers of the dream. Prospero, rather than Ferdinand in Miranda's arms; or sailing to Byzantium. This love does not reach only toward unifying, as we have all been so tediously taught. When we love, we want to explore, to discriminate more and more widely, to extend the intricacy that intensifies intimacy.

But imagine! Therapy sessions that let be mother and childhood and sexual guilts, that come late to the personal battles now being fought at home, and the depressions and headaches that the patient wants to cure—therapy that seems just to dwell in dreamland. And imagine only gradually and deviously getting into the patient's remembered history and the crises of his personal development. Our way of anamnesis is indirect, following the wandering course of the dreams, giving them their own legs. Whatever of the anamnesis the soul needs for its movement appears in its own time. All the bits of case history[51]—mother and father, past loves and present complaints—find their way into therapy via the dream, becoming thereby images. What we ask for in the first meeting is the dream, and what we start first with in meetings thereafter is the dream. This moves the entire therapeutic encounter onto the psychic ground of the underworld. Into that context goes the past history and the present day.

Often the images forget what the dreamer believes are his traumas, as if the dreams don't care at all about the failures that have brought him into therapy. The dreams are already working at forgetting the patient's remembered life. For therapy to return directly to these deeds and sufferings only reconstitutes the heroic ego. Forgetting is the underworld procedure, which means we do not want to keep the patient in his memories, but want to dissolve the memories in his dreams.

To start with the dream may not be as radical as it sounds. We may only be conforming with a Platonic fact of nature. To Plato and to some modern behavioral research, the dream comes anyway before conscious life. From the kicking, twitching, and electrical brain patterns of animals during their sleep, it has been concluded that they are dreaming. Because similar behavioral signs are present in infants and in the human fetus, the hypothesis has been drawn that they too are going through a process analogous, if not identical, with adult dreaming. Before the dayworld begins even factually and developmentally, the dream is at its work.[52] Psyche precedes its manifestations in the life of external and social experience. The soul is imagining before the contexts we try to put it in.

Despite these differences between the practising of classical psychotherapy (Freudian and Jungian) and what we are here sketching, we and they alike rely on the method of reversion, turning the dream back to myths beyond the dream. All of us offer visions that restore dreams to a most universal and profound metapsychology of myth, and so all three are essays in epistrophe, such as we discussed at the opening of this book.

The myth to which we all revert dreams is the same one, the underworld. This is the base and common ground of depth psychology, in which the dream has always played the most important part. Freud and Jung, however, tended to translate the mythic into the conceptual, the underworld into the unconscious. This first dayworld move led to further conceptualizations: repression, opposition, ego, libido, and led further away from both dream and myth. So, in came more myths, Oedipus, eros and thanatos, the primal horde, the hero, the *anima/animus* pair, the *unus mundus* and the four-fold root. Each built cosmologies and metapsychologies of mythic principles.

Freud and Jung usually recognized they were doing this, but they couldn't leave myths as myths, although Jung especially tried to develop an overt mythical mode by means of his personified archetypes. They could not free themselves from psychological conceptualizing, and so they tended to conceive myths metapsychologically (whereas we are trying to imagine our metapsychology mythically). They translated myths into superordinate principles, and dreams became illustrations of these principles. They employed dreams as positive evidence. For them the dream could contribute to a science of psychology, helping its advancing knowledge of psychological laws. This attitude to the dream as "empirical material" may never have been uppermost in their therapy; it nonetheless was an attitude we find throughout their writings on dreams. Even when dreams were connected with myths, it was to demonstrate this relationship, showing that myths work in the psyche. The dream was always witness to their metapsychology.

Just here a little crack begins to widen in our common ground. As it divides their way from ours, it may open to a chasm, because it also divides two eras of consciousness. Theirs is of far greater magnitude, *kein Vergleich;* but their huge genius is also restricted by the positivistic attitudes of medical empiricism. Even these giants could not tear loose from their historical period. So their epistrophe reverts to myths positively imagined: systematic, objectively established, and literally believed as true. The Oedipus situation is declared to be worldwide fact, the archetypes to be instinctual universals. The libido is *not* theoria, it *is;* the self is *not* belief, it *is.* So the base to their dream theories must be called by its right name: metaphysical mythology, which loses the "meta" to the substantiations of "physis" and loses "myth" to the literalisms of their "ologies."

Now the myth to which we revert the dream is no more substantial than the dream itself. Neither dream nor its background in the underworld can be brought in as evidence in support of each other. All that we have claimed for the dream cannot be established by experience or be grounded in myth. Myth doesn't ground, it opens. We remain in the perspective of depth, with nothing more reliable under our feet than this depth itself. We take depth psychology literally at its word, because depth is a metaphor that has no base.

That last sentence reflects the gap between the founders of depth psychology and us, who follow in this nonliteral, hermeneutic era. They had to have bedrock, although they knew and sometimes said that these bedrocks were images, no more substantial than fantasy. Therefore our way of working with dreams can only make baseless claims and, like each dream each night, asks you to accept "the baseless fabric of this vision." Image is psyche and cannot revert except to its own imagining.

This last chapter on praxis has been an exercise in imagining, not interpreting; and this last section of the last chapter is an attempt to recapitulate the entire book's intention: to present an attitude that keeps the dream working in the soul. At times I have fallen into old modes of talking about dreams, explaining what a dream might "mean" and treating its images as symbols. As I warned the reader, this mode is forced upon one by the genre of the dream book. Besides, there is a desire in each of us to know something for sure, positively.

Yet if we think back on any dream that has been important to us, as time passes and the more we reflect on it, the more we discover in it, and the more varied the directions that lead out of it. Whatever certainty it once might have given, shifts into complexities beyond clear formulations each time the dream is studied anew. The depth of even the simplest image is truly fathomless. This unending, embracing depth is one way that dreams show their love.

Because we cannot know dreams in the positive way that we wish, we form an attitude to them in response to our frustration. Instead of knowing more about dreams, we want to get deeper into dreams by working out ever more penetrating and subtle forms of inquiry. Our attitude leads to a hermetic method. So, our insistence on the dream as dark is not an obscurantism, nor is it a cynical despair that gives up because it cannot know and a romantic *laisser aller* that only wants to wonder at dreams and be loved by them. No, the darkness of the dream encourages more inquiry and hard work. Go at it, face on, without malice aforethought, without the positions that we have learned from inadequate theories and dayworld textbooks, which always fit dreams into psychological systems of knowledge.

I do not consider dreaming as a piece of the psyche like a textbook chapter listed along with memory, perception, emotion, and the like. Dreaming is the psyche itself doing its soul-work. We do not understand enough of this soul-work because we are not altogether in its place; we are not "dead," not all psyche, once we have left the underworld and returned to our various other soul parts as listed in the textbook.

Therefore our task is less to integrate dreams and dreaming into a psychological system that could give us a positive feeling of knowing about them, than it is to see those systems as "dreams." My argument here sounds like theory too—of several souls in different regions, of wholes and parts—but it is meant as an heuristic device to encourage an attitude that can live with the defeat of our desire to know. Then we can dissociate the dream from our dayworld attempts to grasp it, letting our desire die away into its images, which seem to be the only positions a dream ever takes.

Despite Freud's and Jung's lifelong concern with human darkness and with the psyche as a field of depth, psychotherapy—including Freudian and Jungian—has become more and more life involved, keeping psyche attached to life, and so, reading dreams in service of life. In its intemperate optimism, psychotherapy more and more forsakes the depths of its founders. If, as Jung said, modern man is in search of a lost soul, this soul is lost partly in life; the attempts of modern psychotherapy to connect dreams to life only strengthen ego at the cost of soul, following *thymos* and not *psyche*. The underworld aspect of each complex, where it touches death, is also where psyche is in its unchanging essence and where soul can be refound. The underworld and its imagery holds the deepest riddles and eventually becomes the prime concern of anyone engaged in soul-making.

As the dream is guardian of sleep, so our dream-work, yours and mine, is protective of those depths from which dreams rise, the ancestral, the mythical, the imaginal, and all the hiding invisibilities that govern our lives. Dreams are sleep's watchful brother, of death's fraternity, heralds, watchmen of that coming night, and our attitude toward them may be modeled upon Hades, receiving, hospitable, yet relentlessly deepening, attuned to the nocturne, dusky, and with a fearful cold intelligence that gives permanent shelter in his house to the incurable conditions of human being.

January 1972—December 1977

NOTES

1. BRIDGE

1. H. Corbin, *En Islam iranien* (Paris: Gallimard, 1972), 3:215. "In *ta'wil* one must carry sensible forms back to imaginative forms and then rise to still higher meanings; to proceed in the opposite direction (to carry imaginative forms to the sensible forms in which they originate) is to destroy the virtualities of the imagination." H. Corbin, *Creative Imagination in the Sufism of Ibn'Arabî*, trans. R. Manheim (London: Routledge and Kegan Paul, 1970) p. 240.

2. FREUD

1. Aristotle, *De div. per somnum* 2, *Parva Naturalia* 464b.

2. These three positions regarding the dream are presented by Freud briefly (*OD*, 2–3). Cf. my "Methodological Problems in Dream Research," *Loose Ends*, (Zürich: Spring Publications, 1975).

3. E. S. Casey, "Freud's Theory of Reality: A Critical Account," *Rev. Metaphysics* 25, no. 4 (1972):659–90.

4. Cf. "Preconscious Stimulation in Dreams, Associations and Images," by O. Pötzl, R. Allers, and J. Teler, intro. Charles Fisher, monograph, *Psychological Issues* 2, no. 3 (New York: International Universities Press, 1960).

5. *BPP,* p. 40, Freud makes "an exception to the proposition that dreams are fulfilments of wishes" in his discussion of traumatic neuroses.

6. H. Steffens, *Caricaturen des Heiligsten* (Leipzig, 1821), 2:696 (quoted from Béguin, *Traumwelt,* trans. mine). Steffens was a Norwegian who made his academic career in Halle, Breslau, and Berlin, having studied in Freiburg and Jena. His typically romantic traits are his following Schelling, wandering from place to place, conversion to and from Catholicism, writing fairytales and autobiography, and his many-sided interests that ranged from natural science to theology.

7. Gustav Theodor Fechner (1801–1887), German physicist, philosopher, and experimental psychologist. "Man lives on earth not once but thrice. His first stage of life is a fast sleep, the second an alternation between sleep and waking, the third an eternal waking . . . The transition from the first to the second stage of life is called birth; the transition from the second to the third is called death." (Q.E.D.: the transitional phase characterized as an alternation between waking and sleeping is called life.) G. T. Fechner, *Das Büchlein vom Leben nach dem Tode,* 3d. ed. (Hamburg and Leipzig: Voss, 1887), pp. 1–2 (trans. mine). Largely because of this book, W. Wili (*EJ* 13[1945]:50) counts Fechner with the Neoplatonists, H. Corbin (*EJ* 22[1953]:97f.) quotes from another of Fechner's later works, *Über die Seelenfrage, ein Gang durch die sichtbare Welt, um die unsichtbare zu finden* (Leipzig, 1861), as a Western link with Iranian revelation. Curiously, the references in Jung at Eranos (*EJ* 14[1946]:394) to Fechner take him from his other, scientific side *(Elemente der Psychophysik).* Even Freud (*BPP,* p. 3) referred to Fechner's more romantic writing, *Einige Ideen zur Schöpfungs- und Entwicklungsgeschichte der Organismen* (1873), which presents Fechner's position in regard to Darwinism.

8. A. Béguin, *L'Âme romantique et le rêve,* 2d ed. (Paris: Corti, 1939). I have used the German translation by J. P. Walser, *Traumwelt und Romantik* (Bern and Munich: Francke, 1972), in which the bibliography has been reworked and the German quotations are in modern spelling. Béguin, a Swiss, himself committed suicide.

9. G. Durand, *Les Structures anthropologiques de l'imaginaire* (Paris: Presses Université de France, 1963).

10. Mainly collected in *Kleine Schriften* von Dr. Mises (Leipzig: Breitkopf und Härtel, 1875).

11. These details are taken from Fechner's own "Krankheitsgeschichte" ("case history"), written by him in 1845 (two years after his recovery), and printed in his nephew's biography of him (J. C. Kuntze, *Gustav Theodor Fechner* [Dr. Mises] [Leipzig: Breitkopf und Härtel, 1892], pp. 105–35.)

The illness is reported upon by Ellenberger, *The Discovery of the Unconscious* (London: Allen Lane, 1970), and recounted without additional biographical information by K. Lasswitz, *Gustav Theodor Fechner* (Stuttgart: Frommann, 1896), pp. 41–48, and M. Wentscher, *Fechner und Lotze* (Munich: Reinhardt, 1925), pp. 31–37.

Concerning the ham: Fechner ate it every day for quite a while, the good woman bringing it to him regularly. "Gradually I learned to digest other stimulating and spicy meat dishes and sour (acid) drinks, not merely bland and mild foods. For a long time, plain water, bread and floury dishes could not be tolerated, whereas meat of all kinds, especially strongly peppered, I digested well" (Kuntze, *op. cit.*, pp. 111–12). The sudden turn for the better after a dream of meat and then eating meat (against a resistance) after a long bland diet parallels precisely what happened to Gopi Krishna upon whose crisis—and this meat detail—I have commented elsewhere. There are other striking parallels; both undergo torture, and are unable to read, both are preoccupied with what takes place in their heads, both are nursed by their wives, both come out with new relationship to light. (Cf. my "Commentary" to Gopi Krishna's *Kundalini* [London and Berkeley: Watkins and Shambala, 1970], pp. 204 f. on the meat, and n. 42 below.)

12. G. T. Fechner, *Die Tagesansicht gegenüber der Nachtansicht* (Leipzig: Breitkopf und Härtel, 1897), p. 22. The typical romantic contrast of the day- and nightworlds, the contrast to which Fechner's is the reverse, is put at full length by G. H. von Schubert (see Béguin, *Traumwelt*) and by F. Splittgerber, *Schlaf und Tod oder die Nachtseite des Seelenlebens*, 2d. ed. (Halle: Julius Fricke, 1881). This work is not mentioned by Béguin.

13. Psychological, visionary, or imaginal geography has been described most fully by H. Corbin. An introduction in English to his ideas on the subject with further references can be found in "*Mundus Imaginalis:* or the Imaginary and the Imaginal," *Spring 1972* (New York and Zürich: Spring Publications, 1972), pp. 1–19. See also "Visionary Geography," in his *Spiritual Body and Celestial Earth*, trans. N. Pearson (Princeton, N.J.: Princeton University Press, 1977), pp. 24–36.

14. For two other ways of understanding Freud's reference to the underworld at the beginning of his *Traumdeutung*, see Carl E. Schorske, "Politique et parricide dans 'L'Interpretation des reves' de Freud," *Annales* 28, no. 2 (1973): 309–28, and K. A. Grigg, " 'All Roads lead to Rome': The Role of the Nursemaid in Freud's Dreams," *J. Amer. Psychoanalyt. Assoc.* 21 (1973):108–26. Schorske's well-argued point is that the underworld which Freud overcame by means of his self-analysis and dream book was the father and the political world, enabling Freud finally to become profes-

sor within the state university and finally go to Rome, the symbolic center of political history. By situating the *Traumdeutung* within the *zeitgeist* of the end of the century and Freud's own occasional political imagery, Schorske enriches our understanding. Nonetheless the difficulty remains: the book on dreams and its author's own dreams are accounted for in terms of dayworld constructs, contents, and concerns. For Schorske, the political level in Freud's work determines its mythical milieu and psychological result. For us the reverse is more likely the case, since the deliberate *topos* of Freud's work is not the father, professional world, politics, and Rome—but dreams. After his *nekyia*, Freud, like Aeneas (who carried his father on his back), could finally enter "Rome." Grigg's paper reduces Rome, politics, and underworld all to Freud's early incestuous wishes for his Roman Catholic nursemaid.

15. *Lex*, s.v. "Unterwelt," pp. 81–2. The speech of the dead is a whisper, and Roman poets (Ovid, *Meta.* 5. 356; Virgil, *Aen.* 6. 264, 432) refer to the dead as the mute. T. S. Eliot picks this up again in his *The Hollow Men*, IV (1925), where the dead figures "grope together/And avoid speech."

16. K. Kerényi, *The Heroes of the Greeks* (New York: Grove Press, Evergreen ed., 1962), p. 283; *Cults*, 3:287: ". . . and Hades is distinguished by no attribute at all, but merely by the gesture of the averted head. . . ." An Egyptian text (*ERE*, pp. viii, 22a) says that death "turns not his face towards them, he comes not to him who implores him, he hearkens not when he is worshipped; he shows himself not, even though any manner of bribe be given to him." Here is another, an underworld, background for the dispassionate scientific objectivity of psychoanalytic treatment method.

17. *Lex*., s.v. "Unterwelt" pp. 67, 79.

18. This passage by Freud reads: "This theory occupies a peculiar position in the history of psycho-analysis; it marks a turning-point. With the theory of dreams, analysis passed from being a psycho-therapeutic method to being a psychology of the depths of human nature. Ever since then the theory of dreams has remained the most characteristic and the most peculiar feature of the young science, something which has no parallels in the rest of scientific knowledge, a new found land, which has been reclaimed from the regions of Folklore and Mysticism. The strangeness of the ideas which are necessarily involved in it has made it into a shibboleth, the use of which distinguishes those who might become believers in psychoanalysis from those who are incapable of comprehending it. Speaking for myself, I always found it a thing I could hold on to during difficult times when unsolved problems of the neuroses used to confuse my inexperienced judgment. Whenever I began to have doubts about the correctness of my

tentative conclusions, the moment I managed to translate a senseless and complicated dream into a clear and intelligible mental process in the dreamer, I felt, with renewed confidence, that I was on the right track." (*NIL*, pp. 15–16). The passage may be read as a confession of Freud's faith and the mode of practising this faith. If one substitues the words "religion" and "religious" where Freud has "science" and "scientific" and replaces "vision of the underworld" for his "theory of dreams," the credo nature of the passage and its tone becomes even more evident.

19. Ernest Jones, *Sigmund Freud: Life and Work* (London: Hogarth Press, 1953), 1:351.

20. Preface to the third English edition of *ID*.

21. Preface to the second edition of *ID*.

22. According to H. F. Ellenberger, *The Unconscious*, p. 218: "Freud took from Fechner the concept of mental energy, the topographical concept of mind, the principle of pleasure-unpleasure, the principle of constancy, and the principle of repetition. A large part of the theoretical framework of psychoanalysis would hardly have come into being without the speculations of the man whom Freud called the great Fechner."

There is a good deal in Fechner relevant as well to Jung's thought, besides that to which Jung refers. Fechner examined the laws of causality and wrote a humorous little paper on the fourth dimension and one on the proposition that the shadow is alive; another paper is called *extrema sese tangunt* (Jung ever and again says "les extrèmes se touchent"); Fechner satirically suggests in another paper that the world might have been created through the destructive principle; he uses the crystal as an example of the soul's peculiar powers ("Zur Seelenfrage," in *Die Tagesansicht, op. cit.* n. 12). Fechner was, by the way, the son and grandson of a country parson. Fechner's father, however, was a parson of the Enlightenment, appearing in the pulpit without a wig, having his children inoculated against cholera, and installing a lightning rod on the church tower. Fechner, like Jung, did not study theology but medicine.

Further on Fechner (including translations of excerpts into English), see Walter Lowrie, *Religion of a Scientist: Selections from Gustav Th. Fechner* (New York: Pantheon Books, 1946). Articles on Fechner have recently appeared in the *J. Hist. Behav. Sci.* 10 (1974).

3. PSYCHE

1. *CW* 7²: § 410; H. F. Ellenberger, *The Unconscious*, p. 562 n. The Oxford English Dictionary, Supplement A–G, fixes the first use of "depth psychology" (*Tiefenpsychologie*) in Freud to 1923 (*The Ego and the Id*),

English version, but it appears already in "Repression" (1915, *CP* 4:106).

2. B. Snell, *The Discovery of Mind* (New York: Harper & Row Torchbook, 1960), p. 17.

3. I am indebted to Paul Kugler for insights into the possibilities of archetypal phonetics; cf. his "Image and Sound," *Spring 1978* (Dallas: Spring Publications, 1978), pp. 136–51.

4. Aristotle, *De anima,* a2, 405a25.

5. *RP,* Ch. 3.

5a. Jung, *CW* 7: §303, implies Hades when connecting the "invisible" soul, "having no ties with our mortal substance," with "a world of invisible things."

6. Cf. M. P. Nilsson, *Geschichte der griechischen Religion,* 2d ed. (Munich, 1955), 1:452.

6a. Cf. "The Misfortunes of Mint," Ch. 4 of Marcel Detienne, *The Gardens of Adonis* (London: Harvester Press, 1977).

7. *Lex.,* s.v. "Hades."

8. *Cults* 3:286.

9. *Cults* 3:283.

10. Cf. *PW,* s.v. "Thanatos".

11. *Cults* 3:287.

12. E. Herzog, *Psyche and Death,* trans. D. Cox and E. Rolfe (London: Hodder & Stoughton, 1966), p. 39 f. on etymology of various death demons. For full discussion of the etymology of Hades, see Hjalmar Frisk, *Griechisches Etymologisches Wörterbuch* (Heidelberg: Carl Winter, 1973), 1:33–34. Plato is important authority for the etymological identification of Hades with the "unseen" or "invisible" (*Gorgias* 439b, *Phaedo* 80d, 81c). L. Wächter, "Zur Ableitung von 'Hades' und 'Persephone'," *Zeitschrift f. Relig.- u. Geistesgeschichte* (1964):193–97, derives *Hades* not from "invisible," but via Semitic roots from the underworld "waters" that rise from the deep. This derivation does not alter the equation: underworld = unconscious or id; for Freud often spoke of the id as a "reservoir," just as Jungians speak of the unconscious as a "source" and as "coming up."

13. H. Lloyd-Jones, "A Problem in the Tebtunis *Inachus*-Fragment," *Class. Rev.,* n.s., vol. 15, no. 3 (1965):241–43.

14. B. C. Dietrich, *Death, Fate and the Gods* (London: Athlone, 1967), p. 360.

15. For a full discussion of the brood of Night, see *Lex.* s.v. "Nyx," and E. T. Reimbold, *Die Nacht im Mythos, Kultus and Volksglauben* (Cologne: Wison, 1970). For an iconography of sleep and death with their mother Night, see H. von Einem, "Asmus Jacob Carstens, Die Nacht mit ihren Kindern," *Arbeitsgemeinschaft f. Forschung des Landes Nord-*

rhein-Westfalen 78, 24 plates (Cologne: Westdeutscher Verlag, 1958). The tradition in statuary goes back to Sparta where sleep was paired with death, as sleep was paired with dreams in Sikyon (Pausanias 3. 18, 1; 2. 10, 2). Kirk, *Pre-Socratic Philosophers, op. cit.* "Abbreviations," pp. 19–24, gives a short, valuable treatment of Night and its cosmogonical meanings, based on a collection of passages from ancient writers. According to Reimbold (p. 25), the powers born of Earth and Sea in general are aggressive, vitally dynamic forces and disruptive to the world order; the powers born of Night, her brood in general, are apathetic, heavy, sleepy, lethal, lethargic. Cf. C. Ramnoux, "Histoire antique de la 'Nuit,' " *Cahiers Internat. de Symbolisme* 13 (1967):57–68.

16. *The Mystical Hymns of Orpheus,* trans. T. Taylor, (London: Dobell, 1896), pp. 159–63—Hymns 85, "To Sleep;" 86, "To the Divinity of Dreams;" 87, "To Death."

17. Cicero, *On the Nature of the Gods* 3. 17.

18. L. Preller, *Griechische Mythologie* 1 (Berlin: Weidmann, 1860); 621 ff.; *Demeter und Persephone* (Hamburg, 1837), pp. 189 ff. U. v. Wilamowitz-Moellendorf, *Der Glaube der Hellenen* 1 (Berlin: Weidmann, 1931): 202–11.

19. Wilamowitz-Moellendorf, *Der Glaube,* p. 210, cited by W. K. C. Guthrie, *The Greeks and Their Gods* (London: Methuen, University pb., 1968), p. 218. Guthrie reports on Wilamowitz' view but sides against him and with Rohde. The disagreement among classicists is repeated in the disagreement between Freud and Jung, who overtly broke over the 'nature' of sexuality. Did it belong to Ge, as fertility, literal, physical, and earthy or did it belong to chthon, expressing a spirit deeper than its bodily manifestation? Jung, with A. Jaffé [*Memories, Dreams, Reflections,* transl. R. & C. Winston (New York: Pantheon Books, 1961), p. 168] writes: "But my main concern has been to investigate, over and above its personal significance and biological function [Demeter and Ge], its spiritual aspect and numinous meaning, and thus to explain what Freud was so fascinated by but was unable to grasp. . . . Sexuality is of the greatest importance as the expression of the *chthonic* spirit. That spirit is 'the other face of God,' the dark side of the God-Image [Hades]. The question of the chthonic spirit has occupied me ever since I began to delve into the world of alchemy." My italics and insertions in square brackets show a way of reading the Freud-Jung difference. Freud later recovered chthon and Hades in his death drive. This was inevitable, because he had taken sexuality only on the Ge level. Jung did not have to make this move, for he had started below Ge with chthon from the beginning.

20. Euripides, *Hekuba* 70.

21. Cf. Dietrich, *Death*, pp. 232–39.

22. Wilamowitz-Moellendorf, *Der Glaube*, p. 211, cited by Guthrie, *The Greeks*, p. 218.

23. For studies of the Demeter-Ge-Chthon complex, see especially *Lex.*, s.v. "Gaia"; Dietrich, *Death; Cults* 3, J. E. Harrison, *Themis*, Ch. 11 (Cambridge: At the University Press, 1927).

24. P. Berry, "What's the Matter With Mother," Lecture No. 190 (London: Guild of Pastoral Psychology, 1978).

25. Cf. Kirk, *Pre-Socratic Philosophers, op. cit.* "Abbreviations," p. 50, where he tries to sort out the relations between Ge-Chthonie-Demeter-Hera.

26. R. T. Rundle Clark, *Myth and Symbol in Ancient Egypt* (London: Thames & Hudson, 1959), p. 257.

27. E. Rohde, *Psyche*, trans. W. B. Hillis, 8th ed. (London: Kegan Paul, 1925), p. 158.

28. *Ibid.* Rohde, however, soon enough returns to the dominant fantasy of his period—fertility. Cult of souls is reabsorbed by "underground spirits" (p. 183). Thereby, Rohde loses the distinction between natural life and psychic life, a distinction he had already implied himself in what he wrote about Ge. He maintains the archetypal perspective of the Magna Mater, for whom death and even soul are part of the fertility round and for whom naturalistic literalism is the appropriate mode of thought.

29. *Lex.*, s.v. "Tartaros," p. 2444.

30. B. Gladigow, "Pneumatik und Kosmologie," *Philologus* 111 (Wiesbaden, 1967): 1–20, gives a thorough examination of the phenomenology of air in the fantasy of the underworld from Hesiod on, even to Dante. (Greek epitaphs often refer to Hades' *wings;* cf. Richmond Lattimore, *Themes in Greek and Latin Epitaphs* [Urbana, Ill., University of Illinois Press, 1962], p. 147.)

31. For an interesting derivation of the Christian hell fire from Stoic theories of passion (as a feverish sickness of soul), *see* H.-J. Horn, "Die 'Hölle' als Krankheit der Seele in einer Deutung des Origenes," *Jahrb. Antike u. Christendom* (1968/69), pp. 55–64.

32. *Lex.*, s.v. "Tartaros," p. 2445.

33. Gilgamesh Epic, Tablet 7, col. 4, 31–41.

34. F. Cumont, *After Life in Roman Paganism* (New York: Dover Press, 1959), p. 79.

35. *Ibid.*, p. 80.

36. J. Zandee, *Death as an Enemy according to Ancient Egyptian Conceptions* (Leiden: Brill, 1960), p. 73. Cf. B. George, *Zu den Altägyptischen*

Vorstellungen vom Schatten als Seele (Bonn: Habelt, 1970).

37. Walter F. Otto, *Die Manen* (Darmstadt: H. Gentner, 1958), pp. 70–73.

38. *Cults* 2:519.

39. The thymus gland in the throat of humans is vital only in childhood, disappearing with maturity. The thymus gland that we eat as sweetbreads is the growth gland of the calf. Growing youth, its calf love and calf eyes, favors the wetness which Heraclitus says is so costly to psyche. For him, "The dry soul is wisest and best" (frg. 118), perhaps because it is near to the fire. For further passages emphasizing thymos as moisture, see OET, pp. 46–48.

40. The translation here of frg. 15 combines Freeman's first half of the passage with Marcovich's second half. Albert Cook, "Heraclitus and the Conditions of Utterance," *Arion*, vol. 2, pt. 4 (Boston: Boston University Press): 472, translates even more affirmatively the unity of Hades and Dionysos: ". . . sang a hymn to the pudenda, most shameful things would have been done. Hades and Dionysos are the same, to whichever *(hoteo)* they rave . . ." Further, A. Lesky, "Dionysos und Hades," in his *Gesammelte Schriften* (Bern and Munich: Francke, 1966), pp. 461–67, for a discussion of the problem. It is of course discussed also in the literature on Heraclitus mentioned below (see Abbreviations) and, particularly relevantly for depth psychology, by W. F. Otto, *Dionysus,* transl. R. Palmer (Bloomington, Ind.: Indiana University Press, 1965). On Dionysos as Lord of Souls and the dead, see Rohde, *Psyche,* p. 168.

41. It is curious to find, even in the later Rome of the Empire and despite the influence of *terra mater* (Tellus), that Dionysos remained a Lord of the Underworld, as witnessed by sarcophagi: ". . . of all mythological subjects in ordinary domestic decoration the ones most used were scenes from his [Dionysos'] cycle of myths" A. D. Nock, "Cremation and Burial in the Roman Empire," *Essays on Religion and the Ancient World* (Oxford: Clarendon Press, 1972), 1:290. Other common mythologems depicted on Roman sarcophagi (and therefore of relevance particularly for underworld psychology) were (p. 291) ". . . episodes from the Trojan cycle, the story of Hippolytus, the rape of the Leucippids, the visit of the Moon to Endymion, Eros and Psyche, the rape of Proserpine." Also Heracles, Attis, Adonis, and occasional Egyptian motives. (Interestingly, The Great Mother does *not* seem to figure so largely as modern psychology has led us to expect.) Jewish sarcophagi during this period also show Dionysian scenes, E. R. Goodenough, *Jewish Symbols in the Greco-Roman Period* (New York: Pantheon Books, 1965), 12:30–37.

42. *Cults* 3:288. See also D. L. Miller's profound insights in his "Hades and Dionysos: The Poetry of Soul," *J. American Academy of Religion* 47(1978).

43. The ham (from an animal sacrificed to the chthonic deities), cooked in the juice of lemon (an apotropaic fruit against death) and wine (the life-force of Dionysus), and strongly spiced (souls in Hades perceive by smelling, according to Heraclitus, frg. 98), all add up to the "right food" for restoring Fechner's disturbed body (alimentary system). His disturbance of spirit remained and took another year-and-a-half and another channel for its remedy.

44. *Metamorphoses* 4:5, 443: "errant exsangues sine corpore et ossibus umbrae/." Nilsson, 4.5, 443 *Geschichte*, finds this description follows the traditonal Greek model.

45. Dieterich, *Nekyia* (Leipzig: Teubner, 1893).

46. For any hero who wants to take this trip, an initial itinerary is provided by S. G. F. Brandon, *The Judgment of the Dead* (London: Weidenfeld & Nicolson, 1967).

47. Cf. Detlef-I. Lauf, *Geheimlehren Tibetischer Totenbücher: Jenseitswelten und Wandlung nach dem Tode. Ein west-östlicher Vergleich mit psychologischem Kommentar* (Freiburg in Breisgau: Aurum, 1975).

48. We must be aware here that *psyche* had no more a clear single meaning, even in the Homeric epic, than does psyche or soul today: ". . . as the semantic base of *psyché* shifts within the Homeric poems, it is dangerous and misleading to take it as a constant in an attempt to interpret 'Homeric' psychology. . . ."—J. Warden, *"Psyché* in Homeric Death-Descriptions," *Phoenix* 25, no. 2. (Toronto, 1971): 100. Not only Homer, but later Athens too: "I think we must admit that the psychological vocabulary of the ordinary man was in the fifth century in a state of great confusion, as indeed it usually is."—E. R. Dodds, *The Greeks and the Irrational* (Boston: Beacon Press, 1957), p. 138. Eric Havelock (*Preface to Plato,* Ch. 11 [Oxford: B. H. Blackwell, 1963]) considers Socrates' idea of soul—as a self-conscious, thinking subjectivity akin to our modern notion—to have been the culmination of a long development away from the Homeric *psyche.* W. F. Otto's *(Die Manen)* distinction of two Homeric usages of *psyche,* one in the context of life and one in the exclusive context of death and the underworld, supports the two-soul theory. His view shows interpretative disagreements with Onians *(OET),* whom I generally follow. David Claus's study on the entire question in Greek antiquity, to be published by Yale University Press, was not available to me at the time of this writing.

Otto's two senses of the word *psyche* does find a parallel in the feeling of the contemporary usage of the terms "psyche" and "soul." Psyche has come more and more to be used in an Aristotelian sense, as a set of objective functions bound to the biological life of the body. It can be described rationally and presented in textbooks of psychology. Soul, however, evokes a sense of privacy and inwardness. It reminds of religion, love, and death—though at the same time it is immediately given in the animated, personified relation with the world. I generally use psyche and soul interchangeably, trying to restore to psyche (and psychology) its ancient sense akin to soul and *anima*, see my *Suicide and the Soul*, 2d ed. (Zürich: Spring Publications 1976), pp. 43–47; also my two essays on "Anima" in *Spring 1973* and *Spring 1974* (New York and Zürich: Spring Publications, 1973, 1974); and *RP*, pp. x–xi *passim*. Despite this attention to the roots of the word *psyche* and its vicissitudes in signification, we cannot get to "what *soul* really means" by any means whatsoever—semantic, theological, etymological, anthropological. The word was and is symbolic, an image that cannot be grasped in its depth, as Heraclitus said. Psyche (or soul) is the subject of our experience, that which experiences, as Jung said, and is not an object of experience able to be defined. This "unknowable" sense evokes that other prime unknowable, death.

49. According to Žabkar *(Ba, pp. 111–13)*, Ba does not mean the "soul" of our Christian and Western usage—a departed ethereal spirit. Ba does not mean a spiritual component in a person opposed to a material one. There is "no internal dualism in man" for the Egyptian. Rather, the Ba is the personification of a deceased person's vital forces that is usually confined to the underworld; Ba is a "mortuary concept" (p. 120) and it comes into existence at death (pp. 119–22). The Ba, so to speak, is one's death personality. It is a personified entity, a quality of a person, and a mode of existence (pp. 1, 8). Here it compares with the Homeric underworld *psyche* and with primitive ideas of a soul that exists in death as the whole person and not as an element or component part of a person (cf. Otto, *Die Manen,* p. 87). This emphasis upon the soul as the whole person indicates that the perspective of the underworld is a complete mode, reflecting the entire human being, presenting full personal reality *as a psyche*— as a being that experiences psychologically. The underworld viewpoint is thus not a partial one opposed to a natural one, a social, physical, and dayworld one, as if there are different and partial points of view coming from different parts of personality. The psychological one is that quality of the whole person present in the midst of all viewpoints, reflecting them in its underworld mirror, enabling a consciousness that sees through. That Ba and Psyche are also personifications suggests that the personified mode of communicating with oneself and with other souls belongs to this mode of consciousness. The realm of the dead is full of persons; paradoxically,

everything in the dead's world is animated. There are no dead objects, and there is no objective death in the sense of corpses as things without souls.

50. Cf. R. H. Lowie, *Primitive Religion*, 2d ed. (1948), in response to Ernst Arbman, "Untersuchungen zur primitiven Seelenvorstellung," *Le Monde oriental* 20 (1926):85–226; 21 (1927):1–185, as discussed by Ivar Paulson, "Untersuchungen über die primitiven Seelenvorstellungen mit besonderer Rücksicht auf Nordeurasien," *Ethnos* vol. 1, no. 2 (1956):147–57.

51. Cf. H. H. Walser, "An Early Psychoanalytic Tragedy—J. J. Honegger and the Beginnings of Training Analysis," *Spring 1974* (New York and Zürich: Spring Publications, 1974), pp. 243–55.

52. W. Freeman, "Psychiatrists Who Kill Themselves" (Paper delivered at the Symposium on Suicide, San Francisco State University, October 1967).

53. Cf. P. Berry, "The Rape of Demeter/Persephone and Neurosis," *Spring 1976* (New York and Zürich: Spring Publications, 1976), pp. 186–98; also *RP*, pp. 205–10. As Berry points out, it is only after the Hades rape, and because of it, that one is able to experience one's natural, habitual modes of consciousness as defenses against initiations into a less literal and more psychic sense of reality. This new sense is at one and the same time an emptying loss (Hades) and an enrichening (Pluto). These psychological approaches to the Greek mysteries may be our best way of understanding them. After all, they were first of all events of the soul. Although sacred, they could not have been so esoteric as to be removed from popular comprehension. They were a mass event, and therefore must correspond with a common possibility in each of us still. Instead, scholarship has literalized "The Mysteries" by mystifying them into mysteriosophy, a sacred preserve of scholarship; or it has taken them as a mystery-story, requiring archeological and textual detective work.

54. R. Lattimore, *Themes*, pp. 147, 161–64.

55. For a study in comparison between contemporary personal experience and the Persephone-Hades mytheme, see R. U. Hyde, "Hades and the Soul" (M.A. thesis, Sonoma State College, Calif., 1977).

56. The material on Hekate to which I refer can be found in English in *Cults* 2:501 ff. Berry, *op. cit. sup.* gives additional references and insights in her notes.

57. Homeric Hymn to Hermes 14; Apol. Rhod. 4. 1732. See further, B. Büchsenschutz, *Traum und Traumdeutung im Alterthume* (Berlin: Calvary, 1868), p. 6, for a series of passages from classical texts on Hermes

as Bringer of Dreams. One also could invoke Hypnos to bring dreams, cf. *PW*, s.v. "Hypnos," p. 325.

58. Büchsenschutz, *Traum:* "in keinem Falle hat der Volksglaube die Träume zu selbsständig handelnden Gottheiten gemacht, denn auch bei den Dichtern erscheinen sie nur im Dienste anderer Götter. . . ."

59. Martin P. Nilsson, "The Immortality of the Soul in Greek Religion," *Opuscula Selecta* (Lund: Gleerup, 1960), 3:41; cf. K. Kerényi, "Eidolon, Eikon, Agalma," in *Griechische Grundbegriffe* (Zürich: Rhein Verlag, 1964), p. 37.

60. As soul is made from depressive and negative experiences, so depth psychology has required "negative" kinds of conceptualizations. Cf. P. Berry, "What's the Matter with Mother"; also my "Psychotherapy's Inferiority Complex," *Eranos Jahrbuch 46*, 1977 (Leiden: E. J. Brill, in press); "Three Ways of Failure and Analysis," in my *Loose Ends* (New York and Zürich: Spring Publications, 1975), pp. 98–104.

61. F. M. Cornford trans., from his *Plato's Theory of Knowledge* (London: Kegan Paul, 1935), p. 327.

62. G. Bachelard, *On Poetic Imagination and Reverie*, trans. by C. Gaudin (Indianapolis, Ind.: Bobbs-Merrill, 1971), p. 21.

63. ". . . the very word *oneiros* in Homer nearly always means dream-figure, not dream-experience. This dream-figure can be a god, or a ghost, or a preexisting dream-messenger, or an 'image' *(eidolon)* created specially for the occasion. . . ." ". . . it exists . . . independent of the dreamer." Dodds, *The Greeks*, p. 104. Important here is the idea, corrective to ours, that the dream is not part of "me."

64. J. M. C. Toynbee, *Death and Burial in the Roman World* (London: Thames & Hudson, 1971), p. 46.

65. Lucian, "Menippus, or The Descent into Hades," trans. A. M. Harmon (London/Cambridge: Loeb Classical Library) 4:93.

66. *Ibid.*

67. Menippus goes down dressed as Hercules in a lion skin, like Dionysos, who too wears the Herculean disguise in *Frogs*. (Menippus also wears the hat of Ulysses and carries Orpheus' lyre.)

68. Hesiod, *Theogony* 383 ff. Cf. *Lex.*, s.v. "Styx," for further references to this tradition and on Styx in full amplification.

69. Pausanias 8, 18 describes the source of Styx in a *lofty cliff* to which Frazer adds: "enormous beetling crags of grey rock . . . I have seen nothing to equal it anywhere." This image 'locates' hatred in our lofty cliffs, our stone-wall verticality (*Verstiegenheit*).

70. Dodds, *The Greeks*, p. 109.

71. For complete lists of such epithets in Greek and Latin, see *Lex.* 7:s.v. "Epitheta Deorum."

72. D. P. Walker, *The Decline of Hell* (Chicago: University of Chicago Press, 1964).

73. Cf. R. J. Sardello, "Death and the Imagination," *J. Inst. Man* 10, no. 1 (1974): 61–73, for an excellent presentation of the death metaphor. Sardello points out the dangers to the soul when the death metaphor has been voided of images and treated only abstractly. He shows the importance of having an imagination of death in order to sense one's human vulnerability and to play and fantasize, suggesting that without an imagination of death, there is a death of imagination.

4. BARRIERS

1. *Lex.*, s.v. "Tellus"; cf. W. W. Fowler, *The Religious Experience of the Roman People* (London: MacMillan, 1933), pp. 120–22. G. Dumézil, *La Religion romaine archaique* (Paris: Payot, 1966), p. 363, gives a good bibliography on Tellus.

2. Dumézil, *La Religion*, p. 113.

3. On the psychology of the matter-mother relation, see Berry, "Mother," *op. cit.*

4. Cf. E. Neumann, *The Great Mother* (New York: Pantheon, 1955), where every sort of female figure and image become 'symbols' of the "Great Mother." If one's research shows results of this kind, i.e., where all data indicate one dominant hypothesis, then it is time to ask a psychological question about the hypothesis. Of course one finds the "Great Mother" everywhere if the "Great Mother" is the archetype dominating the searcher's vision. Because psychology is a hermeneutical discipline having to do with interpretative meanings, with significances, there are no objective data independent of the subjective vision of the gatherer. A psychologist will be bound to see his own myth in his material.

5. Eva Neumann, *The Masked Dancer* (Philadelphia: St. Joseph's College Press, 1965), p. 7.

6. Cf. R. Lenoble, *Esquisse d'une histoire de l'idée de Nature* (Paris: A. Michel, 1969).

7. D. Konstan, *Some Aspects of Epicurean Psychology* (Leiden: Brill, 1973), pp. 22–27, *passim.*

8. The question of oppositions as a whole has been treated by C. K. Ogden in a useful small book, *Opposition* (Bloomington, Ind.: Indiana University Press, 1967). Logic texts cover only the formal aspects.

9. Quoted from *ibid.*, p. 64.

10. The only attempt that I have found to engage Jung with his background in the psychology of Heraclitus is that by Garfield Tourney, "Empedocles and Freud, Heraclitus and Jung," *Bull. Hist. Med.* 30 (1956):109–23.

11. The more detailed logic of this systematic vision can be found in Gabriel Tarde, *L'Opposition universelle,* the basic idea of which Ogden epitomizes as follows (p. 41): "Opposition is not to be defined as the maximum degree of difference, but as a very special kind of repetition, namely of two *similar* things that are mutually destructive in virtue of their very similarity. . . . . There can be no essential, innate, absolute, or natural opposition between nations, races or forms of governments; for every real opposition implies a *relation*. . . ." (Italics mine; they stress the conjunction or identity of opposites.)

12. Cf. David L. Hart's careful analysis of compensation in Jung (and Adler, Freud, Rank, Maeder, and others), *Der tiefenpsychologische Begriff der Kompensation* (dissertation, Universität Zürich, 1956).

13. Cf. P. Berry, "On Reduction," *Spring 1973* (New York and Zürich: Spring Publications, 1973), pp. 67–84, for a critique of the balance fantasy in Jungian therapy.

14. Cf. Selma Hyman, "Death-in-Life—Life-in-Death, Spontaneous Process in a Cancer Patient," *Spring 1977* (New York and Zürich: Spring Publications, 1977), pp. 27–45, for a brief exemplary account of a case.

15. A. Adler, *The Neurotic Constitution,* trans. B. Glueck and J. E. Lind (New York: Moffat, Yard, 1917), pp. 24–26, 334–60.

16. Tertullian, *De anima* 55, Ante-Nicene Christian Library, ed. A. Roberts and J. Donaldson (Edinburgh: Clark, 1870). Tertullian himself was one of the few fathers *not* holding to this position, but in his usual brilliant way sums up, by the sentence quoted, his opponents' majority view. Tertullian *(ibid.)* held that "to no one is heaven opened" and that the "sole key to unlock Paradise is your own life's blood." In other words, for Tertullian, Christ had not made safe, sure passage by his journey to the underworld. Tertullian's remarks on the Hades of Homer are in these Chapters 54–56. The matter is treated succinctly in F. Huidekoper, *The Belief of the First Three Centuries concerning Christ's Mission to the Underworld* (New York: James Miller, 1876), pp. 112–28, an essential study documenting Christianism's position.

17. *Luther's Works,* "Commentaries on I Corinthians 15" (St. Louis: Concordia, 1973), 28:202.

18. *Idem,* pp. 206–07.

19. The Septuagint translation of Hosea 13:14 reads *"hadē"* for the Hebrew *"sheol,"* not all versions do.

20. *The Interpreter's Bible, Corinthians; Galatians; Ephesians* (Nashville, Tenn.: Abingdon Press, 1953), 10:253.

21. *International Critical Commentary, First Corinthians,* 2d ed. (Edinburgh: T. & T. Clark, 1929), p. 378.

22. *Ibid.,* p. 375.

23. *Interpreter's Bible, loc. cit.*

24. For some consequences of the spirit/soul conflict, see my "Peaks and Vales: The Soul/Spirit Distinction as Basis for Differences between Psychotherapy and Spiritual Discipline," in J. Needleman, ed., *On the Way to Self Knowledge* (New York: Alfred A. Knopf, 1976), pp. 114–41, which includes a discussion of the conquest of sleep (for the sake of the spirit) by the Desert Saints. See also Origen's comments on I Peter 1:18–19 and the ransoming of the spirit at the price of soul, Huidekoper, *Christ's Mission,* pp. 87–88, 152.

25. Barnabas 5:6; Justin, *Apol.* 1, 64.

26. Cf. S. G. F. Brandon, "The Personification of Death in Some Ancient Religions," *Bull. John Rylands Lib.* 43, no. 2 (Manchester, 1961): 332–33. Thomas Carlyle's *On Heroes and Hero Worship* makes the Hercules background to Christ paramount in his notion of Jesus as "the greatest of Heroes," but Adonis, Eros, Dionysos, Orpheus, Apollo, Asclepius had also been imagined as backgrounds of Christ.

27. H. Schär, "Bemerkungen zu Träumen der Bibel," in *Traum und Symbol* (Zürich: Rascher, 1963), pp. 173–79.

28. There are only four uses of *psyche* in the Pauline Epistles. In the entire New Testament, *pneuma* appears almost five times more often than *psyche.* "So much is this the pattern that Paul comes to call *psychikoi* bad and *pneumatikoi* good (I Cor. 2:13–15; cf. I Cor. 15:44–46)." David L. Miller, "Achelous and the Butterfly," *Spring 1973* (New York and Zürich: Spring Publications, 1973), p. 14.

29. *The Homeric Hymns,* trans. Charles Boer, Dallas: Spring Publ., 1979.

30. A. Jaffé, "Bilder und Symbole aus E. T. A. Hoffmann's Märchen 'Der Goldene Topf'," in *Gestaltungen des Unbewussten,* ed. C. G. Jung (Zürich: Rascher, 1950).

5. DREAM

1. A. J. Ziegler, "Rousseauian Optimism, Natural Distress, and Dream Research," *Spring 1976* (New York and Zürich: Spring Publications, 1976), pp. 54–65.

2. The approach described in this paragraph has been presented and

carefully criticized by Mary Watkins, *Waking Dreams* (New York: Harper & Row, Colophon Books, 1977), which is the only thorough and fair examination of the field. Another intelligent work, showing the practice of therapeutic imagining that is more subtle than ego-psychology, is that of Bianca Garufi, "Reflections on the 'rêve éveillé dirigé' Method," *J. Analyt. Psychol.* 22 (1977):207–29.

3. G. Róheim, *The Gates of the Dream* (New York: International Universities Press, pb., 1973), ch. 1.

4. In place of all these operations, Patricia Berry has elaborated imaginal operations that take the dream as an image rather than as a compensation. See her "An Approach to the Dream," *Spring 1974* (New York and Zürich: Spring Publications, 1974), pp. 58–79.

5. My critique of humanistic psychology can be found in *RP*, so I spare the reader here.

6. Eva Neumann, *The Masked Dancer.*

7. The Ba performs "physical actions, particularly those of a sexual nature," and the Coffin Texts state that "he copulates with himself," and "takes sexual pleasure" (*Ba*, p. 103). Sexual activity in sleep can be considered in the domain of the Ba, where "he copulates with himself" refers to sexual relations among images, in imagination.

8. "A general characteristic of the Christian (as well as Islamic and Buddhist) mission in northern Eurasia is the indicative fact that most north Eurasian peoples have held on to their old primitive ideas of soul parallel with their monistic concept. They know to keep the two modes distinct when one inquires. Kept especially vivid are the ancient primordial traits of the free-soul, even if only as death-souls, the death-ghost beyond the grave." I. Paulson, "Untersuchungen . . . Nordeurasien," my trans., p. 155. Jung (*CW* 7:§ 302–03) revives the free-soul notion, conceiving the anima as an "autonomous entity" in relation with the realm of invisibles "beyond the grave," i.e., "beyond [dayworld] consciousness."

9. Ernst Arbman, "Untersuchungen zur primitiven Seelenvorstellungen mit bes. Rücksicht auf Indien," 2 vols., *Le Monde oriental* 20–21 (Uppsala, 1926–27): 85–226; 1–185; I. Paulson, "Untersuchungen . . . Nordeurasien," pp. 147–57. Åke Hultkrantz, *Conceptions of the Soul Among North American Indians,* monograph (Stockholm: Ethnolog. Museét, 1953). (Cf. I. Paulson, "Swedish Contributions to the Study of Primitive Soul-Conceptions," *Ethnos* 19 (1954):157–67; Otto, *Die Manen,* pp. 37–83, supports the two-soul concept.

10. Bernhard Ankermann, "Totenkult und Seelenglaube bei afrikanischen Völkern," *Z. Ethnolog.* 50 (1918):89–153.

11. Paulson, "Untersuchungen . . . Nordeurasien," p. 148.

12. Arbman, "Untersuchungen . . . Indien," (1926), 1:183.

13. Paulson, "Untersuchungen . . . Nordeurasien," p. 148. Paulson finds that north Eurasians attribute the same kinds of souls to animals. To be expected, for "primitives" generally do not make such a cleft between human and animal as do our "advanced" civilizations. Cf. I. Paulson, "Die Vorstellungen von den Seelen der Tiere bei den nordeurasischen Völkern," *Ethnos*, vol. 2, no. 4 (1958):127-57.

14. Charon the Ferryman, of course, shuttles back and forth, so one might be tempted to imagine the interpreter's role as a translation between two banks of the river. Charon, however, never leaves the underworld, and his traffic goes one way only—deeper still, to the farther shore. Charon's manner of transporting the ego-shade into an underworld attitude is by fouling, rusting, dirtying, frightening—for such is his description in Vergil's *Aeneid*, bk.6, ll. 298–303. The besmirching attacks we make on ourselves are attempts to lower ourselves to an underworld.

15. K. Kerényi, *The Heroes of the Greeks* (London: Thames & Hudson, 1959), p. 177. The Introduction to this book should not be missed!

16. L. R. Farnell, *Greek Hero Cults and Ideas of Immortality* (Oxford: Clarendon Press, 1921), pp. 15–16; cf. Rohde, *Psyche*, pp. 116, 121–22; also Kerenyi, *Heroes* (London), p. 14.

17. Kerényi, *Heroes* (London), pp. 4–5.

18. *Ibid.* p. 3.

19. Farnell, *Greek Hero Cults*, p. 104. Hercules was also called *Champion* and *Bright-eyed;* these epithets as well as a three-column list of his actions can be found in *Pausanias's Description of Greece*, translation and commentary by J. G. Frazer (New York: Biblo and Tannen, 1965), 6:74–75. Of all his murders, rapes, conquests, slaughters, and the like, one epithet is most curious: *Nosedocker*. He cuts off noses. He deprives one of the underworld mode of perception of essentials; see pp. 185 f on Smell and Smoke.

20. See ch. 6, n. 28.

21. Marcovich groups and translates this fragment altogether differently. See his frg. 1. Wheelwright (14) has: "One should not act or speak as if he were asleep."

22. Steffens, *Caricaturen*, p. 698, quoted from Béguin, *Traumwelt*, p. 108.

23. Nilsson, *Geschichte*, p. 455: ". . . der König der Unterwelt greift aber nie handelnd ein. . . ." Nilsson stresses the passivity of Hades, which gives an important psychological hint about the Hercules-Hades opposition.

24. Cf. the "mildness joined with melancholy" (Farnell) cited above in the section on Hades. Anubis was also gentle, "a benevolent deity who

cared for the dead," and was depicted "with his arm around the shoulder of the dead man." Brandon, "Personification of Death," pp. 334–35.

25. Rohde, *Psyche*, p. 169.

26. Kerényi, *Heroes* (London), p. 178.

27. Farnell, *Greek Hero Cults*, p. 155.

28. Lucian, *Erotes* 4. Cf. Birgitta Bergquist, *Herakles on Thasos*, Boreas 5 (Uppsala: Acta Univ. Studies, 1973), p. 66; the *lex sacra* at Thasos stated that neither goats nor pigs were allowed to be sacrificed, nor could women partake in the cult.

29. Cf. L. D. Hankoff, "The Hero as Madman," *J. Hist. Behav. Sci.* 11 (1975):315–33. Hankoff examines the madness of Odysseus, David, Solon, Kai-Khosrau, and Brutus. He considers the madness of the hero to be feigned; a ruse the hero uses in order to shift consciousness "from physical power to mental agility." He also considers the "descent into the chaos of feigned mental disorder" to be an initiatory ritual after which the hero comes to full blossoming. Whether or not we read heroic madness as Hankoff does, we can at least see that madness is built into the heroic story. A strong ego seems only able to get out of itself by means of its own oppositionalism, i.e., conversion into ego-disintegration or madness. This generalization needs further precision by observing in detail the extremely differing styles of madness in, say, Hercules and Ulysses. When we look at insanity from the heroic perspective, madness seems more a function of the strong ego than the so-called weak ego that psychotherapy is often so busy trying to bolster.

30. On the *shtula/suksma* distinction, see C. G. Jung's psychological discussion in his "Commentary on Kundalini Yoga," *Spring 1975* (New York and Zürich: Spring Publ. 1975), pp. 5–7.

31. On the *molk/malakut* distinction, see H. Corbin, *Spiritual Body and Celestial Earth*, trans. N. Pearson (Princeton: Princeton University Press, 1977), pp. 211, 244; also his *"Mundus Imaginalis,"* Spring 1972 (New York and Zürich: Spring Publ., 1972), pp. 6–10.

32. Marcovich contests this reading, believing Hypnos a corruption. He reports however, that Snell translates it by *Traum*, Zeller by *Traumbild*, Reinhardt by *Trugbild*, and Kranz as *Dämmerung*. Burnet translates: ". . . all we see in slumber is sleep."

33. K. Bradway & J. Wheelwright, "The Psychological Type of the Analyst and Its Relation to Analytical Practice," *J. Analyt. Psychol.*, 23/3, 1978, p. 218.

34. Narcissism does not account for Narcissus and even falsifies the story. Narcissus does not know that it is his own body he sees in the pool. He believes that he is looking at the beautiful form of *another* being.

So it is not self-love of his 'own' image (narcissism), but the love for a vision that is at once body, image, and reflection. See further, Louise Vinge, *The Narcissus Theme in Western Literature* (Lund, 1967). Since Vinge, two important papers on the theme deepen our understanding even further: M. Stein, "Narcissus," *Spring 1976* (New York and Zürich: Spring Publ., 1976), pp. 32–53; P. Hadot, "Le Mythe de Narcisse et son interprétation par Plotin," *Nouvelle rev. psychanalyse* 13 (1976):82–108. Hadot (p. 90) connects Narcissus with Dionysos and Persephone because of the "chthonic" elements (moisture, narcotic drowsiness, death) in his character. I would add, the chthonic essence of "narcissism" is further revealed in the signal importance given to the *image*, which takes one into the depths.

35. Franz von Baaders, *Tagebücher aus den Jahren 1786–1793* (Leipzig, 1850), quoted from Béguin, *Traumwelt*, p. 109.

36. G. H. von Schubert, *Die Symbolik des Traumes* (Bamberg, 1814). Cf. Béguin, *Traumwelt*, pp. 137 ff., especially p. 142.

37. I am suggesting a scrutiny of dreams that combines psychiatric syndromes with poetic genres; cf. Annabel Patterson, *Hermogenes and the Renaissance—Seven Ideas of Style*, Princeton: Princeton Univ. Press, 1970, pp. 44–68.

38. "He who listens to the stream cannot be expected to understand the one who hears the singing of the flame: they do not speak the same language"—Bachelard, *On Poetic Imagination*, p. xxiii (from *La Psychanalyse du feu*, p. 178).

39. Cf. Bachelard, *L'Air et les songes* (Paris: Corti, 1943): Ch. 1; "Imagination et mobilité."

40. Bachelard, *On Poetic Imagination*, p. 83. (from *L'Eau et les rêves*, p. 17). Cf. his *La Poetique de l'espace* (Paris: P.U.F., 1967), p. 3: "The poetic image is in its essence *variational.* It is not, like a concept, *constitutive*" (my trans.).

41. Bachelard, *On Poetic Imagination*, p. 83 (from *La Terre et les reveries du repos*, p. 83).

42. Philostratus, *Imagines* 1. 27, Loeb Library (London: Heineman).

43. Cf. C. Levi-Strauss, *The Savage Mind* (London: Weidenfeld, 1966), pp. 16–36; also *RP*, p. 164 and n.

44. Bachelard, *On Poetic Imagination*, p. 19: "Imagination is always considered to be the faculty of *forming* images. But it is rather the faculty of deforming the images offered by perception, of freeing ourselves from the immediate images: it is especially the faculty of changing images."

45. "Torment," "torture," "torsion," and "tort" (wrong, injury) are all etymological cognates of "tortuous" and "tortoise" (the twisted and slow movement of the soul). Similar cognates are: writhe, wrest, twist, wreathe, wrinkle, wring.

46. Farnell, *Cults* 2:556.

47. Bachelard, *On Poetic Imagination*, p. 21.

48. Cf. my "Essay on Pan," with W. H. Roscher, *"Ephialtes,"* Pan and the Nightmare, Two Essays, (New York and Zürich: Spring Publ., 1972).

49. M. Marcovich, *Heraclitus, op. cit.* "Abbreviations", p. 51.

50. Cf. H. Corbin, *Avicenna and the Visionary Recital* (New York: Pantheon Books, 1960), pp. 28–35.

51. See n. 1 ch. 1 above.

52. Bachelard, *On Poetic Imagination*, p. 97 (*La Poétique de la rêverie*, pp. 106–07).

53. Heraclitus' style itself is psychological and often was ridiculed by more straight-thinking philosophers. He was called the Riddler and the Dark by the apologetical Bishop of Rome, Hippolytus. He puns; although his meanings are ever and again ambiguous, his imagery is nevertheless sharp. He uses metaphors and similes. His way of talking brings together the black and white, or what Freud called the contradictory meaning of root ideas. Heraclitus is a Dionysian thinker, as he has been called by F. M. Cornford (*From Religion to Philosophy*, [New York: Harper & Row, Torchbook, 1957], p. 183). Or as B. Snell puts it: "So ist Heraklits Vorliebe für Wortspiele nie ein geistreicher Scherz, sondern ein ständiges Hinweisen auf dieses merkwürdige Doppelwesen des Logos, der eindeutig ist und doch doppeldeutig" ("Die Sprache Heraklits," *Hermes* 61, [Berlin, 1926]:373). W. K. C. Guthrie also discusses Heraclitus' style in terms of paradox, symbol and brilliant obscurity: *A History of Greek Philosophy* (Cambridge: Univ. Press, 1962) 1:410–13.

54. Cornford's paraphrasing in his *Greek Religious Thought* (London 1923), p. 81.

55. The idea that dreams are a preparation for death appears both among the romantics and the Greeks. Cf. C. A. Meier's remarks on Mnesimachos and on J. E. Purkinje (with references) in *Die Bedeutung des Traumes* (Olten: Walter, 1972), pp. 32, 118. We may understand this now less literally and more as the removal of elements *(Tagesreste)* out of life and giving them soul values.

56. G. Bachelard, *La Terre et les rêveries de la volonté* (Paris: Corti, 1948), pp. 74–104; cf. *On Poetic Imagination*, p. 80 f. and *ibid.*, p. 80 (Gaudin's footnote), and Bachelard, "L'espace onirique," in his *Le Droit de rêver* (Paris: P.U.F., 1970), pp. 195–200; Bachelard, *La Poétique de la rêverie* (Paris: P.U.F., 1968), p. 144; *The Poetics of Reverie*, trans. D. Russell, (Boston: Beacon Press, 1971), p. 167.

57. C. Gaudin, "Introduction" to Bachelard, *On Poetic Imagination*, p. xxiv.

58. One approach to *hyponoia* or "undersense" is by deforming usual sense. We work at a decomposition of the usual way we compose our sentences, their punctuation, spelling, and parts of speech. Then the latent sense of an image may emerge from the wrapping shrouds of our sentence constructions to stand forth as a resurrected epiphany. We suddenly hear a new sense in usual words. They become images again. T. E. Hulme urged this on poets, and James Joyce performed it. Important and ground-breaking for this deliberate *hyponoia* of language is Jed Rasula's "Spicer's *Orpheus* and the Emancipation of Pronouns," *Boundary 2*, 6,1 (Binghamton: SUNY, 1977), especially section 4; cf. also my two articles on the verbal work with images in *Spring 1977* and *Spring 1978* (Zürich and Dallas, Tex.: Spring Publications, 1977 and 1978).

59. *Ibid.*, p. 53 (from *La Terre et les rêveries du repos*, p. 51).

6. PRAXIS

1. Cf. *Realms of Color, EJ 41* (1972).

2. Cf. Herzog, *Psyche and Death*, p. 196, for a dream in which the pursuing black man is death, The Black Man.

3. Cumont, *After Life*, p. 166.

4. *RP*, Part 2, "Pathologizing."

5. Herzog, *Psyche and Death*, pp. 199–200.

6. Farnell, *Greek Hero Cults*, p. 155. (The goat "belonged" to Pan and to Dionysos.)

7. K. Kerényi, "Mnemosyne—Lesmosyne: On the Springs of Memory and Forgetting," *Spring, 1977* (New York and Zürich: Spring Publications, 1977), pp. 120–30.

8. Eva Keuls, *The Water Carriers in Hades: A Study of Catharsis Through Toil in Classical Antiquity* (Amsterdam: Hakkert, 1974); an excellent book. Also I. M. Linforth, "Soul and Sieve in Plato's Gorgias," *U. Calif. Publ. Classical Philol.* 12 (1944).

9. R. Graves, *Greek Myths*, §14.b.4: Plutarch calls Dionysos "a son of Lethe" (which Graves takes in terms of wine). Although the meanings of Lethe here are surely more complex than drunkenness, the remark does again link Dionysos with Hades and the underworld.

10. Cf. Silvio A. Bedini, *The Scent of Time, Trans. Amer. Philosophical Soc.* 53, no. 5 (1963). Unlike our Western tradition of sundials that rely upon bright daylight, Chinese, Korean, and Japanese cultures measured time by water and fire, both of which work as well at night. By means of the incense, timekeepers intricately adjusted for the seasons of the year (varying lengths of the night); one could know the hour of the night by

its scent. (See pp. 185 f on the underworld and smell.) The hours of the night were as differentiated as those of the day: for instance, the Japanese time system *Rokuji* (six times) names six different periods, four of which are nightworld times: evening, early night, midnight, after night. Early Chinese night watches divided the night into five equal watches: sunset, dusk, after dusk, waiting for dawn, dawn.

11. B. George, "Die Bahn der Sonne am Tage und in der Nacht," *Studia Aegyptica* (Budapest, 1974), 1:104–16; *Ba*, p. 74.

12. A. H. Allcroft, *The Circle and the Cross,* Vol. 1 (London: Macmillan, 1927).

13. M. Riemschneider, "Rad und Ring als Symbol der Unterwelt," *Symbolon* (Basel and Stuttgart: Schwabe, 1962), 3:46–63. On Italic vases, wheels were often depicted on the ceiling of the House of Hades or over the heads of Hades and Persephone, cf. Keuls, *Water Carriers,* pp. 78, 88, 92. Her interpretation of the wheel follows the perspective of Ge (Jane Harrison and the fertility cult cycle). A collection and analysis of these depictions can be found in Konrad Schauenburg, "Die Totengötter in der unteritalischen Vasenmalerei," *Jahrb. des Deutschen Archäolog. Inst.* 73 (1958), pp. 48–78. See further Goodenough, *Jewish Symbols,* vol. 13 (Index), s.v. "Round objects," for multitudinal references to their symbolic association with death and burial.

14. Cf. *ID,* pp. 620–21, where Freud, earlier, does not hold the dreamer responsible for his dreams, because the ethical question is wrongly posed in regard to them. It should be posed in regard to actions. These thoughts are on the very last pages of his *Traumdeutung,* as if to say the book closes on that note, but leaves—as last pages do—a question open. He covers previous literature on the moral issue and dreams *ID,* 60–72.

15. Rohde, *Psyche,* pp. 241–42, based on Pausanias 10. 28–31. The classical treatment of the subject is Carl Robert, *Die Nekyia des Polygnot,* 16. Hallisches Winckelmanns progr. (Halle, 1892).

16. Cumont, *After Life,* p. 76; cf. Brandon, *Judgement,* p. 194.

17. "One can sometimes dream that he does something that shows his worst aspects. But the dream . . . has no ethical intentions. . . . Dreams are like plants, products of nature. One can make out of it an ethical, a philosophical or some other problem, but it isn't inherent in the dream." From the "Notes" by H. H. Baumann, translated into English by H. Henley, of a *Seminar on Children's Dreams,* held by C. G. Jung (Eid. Tech. Hoch, Winter, 1936–37).

18. Herzog, *Psyche and Death,* pp. 28–37, 149–59, 202.

19. On the wisdom of Hades, see Edgar Wind, *Pagan Mysteries in the Renaissance* (Harmondsworth: Penguin, 1967), pp. 280–81: ". . . the god

Consus, a special deity for dispensing good counsels, was worshipped by the Romans underground."

20. Dieterich, *Nekyia*, p. 202.

21. Friedrich Nietzsche, *Thus Spake Zarathustra*, sec. 31.

22. Dieterich, *Nekyia*, p. 96; cf. Farnell, *Greek Hero Cults*, p. 376. For a full study see André Parrot, *Le "Refrigerium" dans l'au-delà* (Paris, 1937).

23. Cf. Robert Hertz, *Death and the Right Hand* (London: Cohen & West, 1960); Angelo de Gubernatis, *La Mythologie des plantes* (Paris: Reinwald, 1882), 2:58.

24. For a full chapter on these "banquets," see W. H. D. Rouse, *Greek Votive Offerings* (Cambridge: At the University Press, 1902), pp. 3–36; also Goodenough, *Jewish Symbols* 6:166–172.

25. Rohde, *Psyche*, pp. 168–69.

26. A. Waymen, "Significance of Dreams in India and Tibet," *Hist. Rel.* 7, no.1 (1967): 6; cf., W. B. Emeneau, "Toda Dream Songs," *J. Amer. Oriental Soc.* 85, no. 1 (1965): 39–44.

27. Cf. Tom Moore, "Musical Therapy," *Spring 1978* (Dallas, Tex.: Spring Publications, 1978), pp. 128–35.

28. Literature on the theme of circus and clown that has helped me is William Willeford, *The Fool and his Scepter* (Evanston, Ill.: Northwestern University Press, 1969); D. C. McClelland, "The Harlequin Complex," in *The Study of Lives: Essays in Honor of H. A. Murray*, ed. R. W. White (New York: Prentice Hall, 1963), pp. 94–119; Marie-Cecile Guhl, report on a lecture by Jean Starobinski, "La fonction mythique du clown," in *Circé I, Cahiers du Centre de Recherche sur l'Imaginaire* (Chambéry, 1969), pp. 285–89. Late to hand but especially noteworthy is David L. Miller's "Clowns and Christs: Wit and Humor in the Religious Imagination," 1978 Panarion Conference tape, Los Angeles.

29. M. P. Nilsson, *Geschichte*, 1:454.

30. Kerényi, *Heroes*, p. 178.

31. The borderline consciousness of Hermes is best shown by R. Lopez-Pedraza in his *Hermes and His Children* (Zürich: Spring Publications, 1977); N. O. Brown, *Hermes the Thief* (New York: Random House, Vintage Books, 1969).

32. The double, Janus nature of the gate was also expressed as a door, neither open nor closed, ajar, waiting, always an open possibility; cf. B. Haarløv, *The Half-open Door. A common symbolic motiv within Roman sepulchral sculpture* (Odense, Denmark: Odense University Classical Studies 10, 1977).

33. Keuls, *Water Carriers*, p. 161.

34. Cf. discussion with references, Keuls, *Water Carriers,* p. 162–63; K. Kerényi, *Eleusis,* trans. R. Manheim (New York: Pantheon Books, Bollingen Series, 1967), pp. 53, 83–84; H. Lloyd-Jones, "Heracles at Eleusis," *Maia* 19 (1967): 206–29.

35. Kerényi, *Heroes,* p. 179.

36. Dieterich, *Nekyia,* p. 83 n.

37. Gilbert Durand, *Les Structures anthropologiques de l'imaginaire* (Paris: Presses Université de France, 1964), pp. 273–86.

38. E. Fischer-Homberger, "Zur Geschichte des Zusammenhangs zwischen Seele und Verdauung," *Schweiz. med. Wschr.* 103 (1973):1433–41. She discusses the theories of "copro-psychiatry," i.e., autointoxication caused by fecal matter in the bowels and leading to psychopathological conditions. Treatment was Herculean: enemas that washed out the filth.

39. Ernst Bargheer, *Eingeweide. Lebens—und Seelenkräfte des Leibesinneren* (Berlin and Leipzig: de Gruyter, 1931), pp. 101–113.

40. Cited by Dieterich, *Nekyia,* p. 81.

41. Cf. N. O. Brown, *Life Against Death* (Middletown, Ct.: Wesleyan University Press, 1959), "Excrement," e.g., "In the last analysis, the peculiar human fascination with excrement is the peculiar human fascination with death."

42. Cumont, *After Life,* p. 166.

43. Kirk, *Pre-Socratics,* p. 211 (*op. cit.* "Abbreviations"). Cf. also p. 207 for his translation of the (forged?) frg. from Sextus *Adv. math.* 7. 129: "For in sleep, when the channels of perception are shut, our mind is sundered from its kinship with the surrounding, and breathing is the only point of attachment to be preserved, like a kind of root. . . ." Cf. Burnet, p. 152 (op. cit. "Abbreviations").

44. See Philo's treatise *On Dreams* (London: Heinemann, Loeb Classical Library, Vol. V) pt. 1, pp. 47–60 on the metaphor of smell. Philo interprets Haran (Genesis 11–12) as the realm of ordinary sense perception. Abraham's departure from this "land" (stance, position, perspective) is by means of seeing through, or better "smelling through" the literalism of usual sense perception. His way out had already been foreshadowed by his father, Terah, whose name means "scent-exploring." Philo equates Terah, this father of the first father, with Socrates and self-knowledge. The journey into awareness is fathered by the exploration of scent that sniffs at invisibles hidden in sense perception itself. Cf. further my *Emotion* (Evanston, Ill.: Northwestern University Press, 1961), p. 235n. on smelling and psychic perception, and David L. Miller's extraordinary excursus on the sense of the nose in his "Clowns and Christs," *op. cit.*

45. On the soul (anima) as smoke in alchemy, see *CW 12:* 278 n.

46. P. Wheelwright, *Heraclitus*, p. 66.

47. L. Binswanger, *Wandlungen in der Auffassung und Deutung des Traumes* (Berlin: J. Springer, 1927), p. 62. Cf. E. S. Casey, "The Image/ Sign Relation in Husserl and Freud," *Rev. Metaphysics* 30, no. 2 (1976): 218, who draws attention to the importance of the "scene" for an image to be wish fulfilling. No scene, no significance. This implies that purely verbal dreams (hallucinatory commands, snatches of poetry, etc.) are manifestations of spirit rather than soul.

48. Kerényi, *Heroes*, p. 283.

49. Jung, *Letters*, ed. G. Adler and A. Jaffé, Bollingen Series (Princeton: Princeton University Press, 1973) 1:214.

50. In Jungian therapy, the "initial dream" is the first dream the patient brings to analysis. This dream may have occurred on the eve of the first session, after the first session, be a recent one that the patient recalls or even one from childhood. It is considered of diagnostic and prognostic significance, indicating where the problems lie and what is likely to be made of them. It initiates therapy. Here Jungian practice does begin by putting the patient in his dream; here it precedes anamnesis of consciousness with reminiscence of the dream. But then Jungian practice fails to follow through: though the initial dream is raised to the place of totem or signal image for the whole analysis, the dreams that follow are kept within the context of the patient's life, problems and process of individuation. Eventually, the initial dream comes back down into the context of the others. Originally, it had stood as a pregnant image in relief to the dayworld, possibly only because at the beginning of the analysis the anamnesis had not been established. As that context grows, it swallows the initial dream as one in its series.

The "big dream" in Jungian practice is one that is cosmic, highly symbolic, revelationlike. It presents a suprapersonal challenge to the dreamer and is not considered simply a compensation to his personal life. The sharp distinction between personal life (anamnesis) and the big dream does not, however, give it the status of a psychic image. Rather the "big dream" is treated as a spirit phenomenon. It is handled like a voice of the self, rather than like an image of the soul, responded to more in action than imagination. It does not place the person in his image psychologically. It is not a reflection from the underworld, the dream as a subjective and metaphorical analogy with big reverberations. Instead, the big dream is taken to be a *representation collectif*, as if a symbolic statement for the destiny of the whole tribe, a foretelling and founding of new orientations. It constellates the heroic ego in response, whether challenging it to an extraverted or introverted (shamanistic) task. I treat big dreams in therapy like all others, working with them as images rather than as messages. In fact any dream taken as a message runs the risk of becoming a big dream, turning the person into a big dreamer, inflating him with prophetic, shamanistic, and paranoid singularity.

51. On case history vs. soul history, see my *Suicide and the Soul*, pp. 77–82, and my "The Fiction of Case History" in *Religion As Story*, ed. J. Wiggins (New York: Harper & Row, Colophon Books, 1976).

52. Some schools of therapy have understood Platonic reminiscence in a literal manner, considering the only true anamnesis of personality to require going back in memory, before worldly influences, to uterine waters and recalling prenatal dreams. I am *not* proposing this method, which only further identifies a sacrosanct ego personality with the myth (of the birth) of the divine hero.

BIBLIOGRAPHY

ABBREVIATIONS

Ba *A Study of the Ba Concept in Ancient Egyptian Texts,* by Louis V. Žabkar, Studies in Ancient Oriental Civilization 34 (Chicago: University of Chicago Press, 1968)

BPP *Beyond the Pleasure Principle,* trans. J. Strachey (London: Hogarth Press, 1950)

CP *Collected Papers,* by Sigmund Freud, 5 vols., trans. various (London: Hogarth Press, 1924–50)

Cults *The Cults of the Greek States,* by L. R. Farnell, 5 vols., reprint (New Rochelle, New York: Caratzas, 1977)

CW *Collected Works,* by C. G. Jung, trans. R. F. C. Hull, Bollingen Series XX, vols. 1–20 (Princeton: Princeton University Press, 1953 ff.), paragraph nos.

EI "The Ego and the Id," by Sigmund Freud, in *Standard Edition of the Complete Psychological Works of Sigmund Freud,* vol. 19 (London: Hogarth Press.)

EJ *Eranos Jahrbücher,* vols. 1–38 (Zurich: Rhein-Verlag, 1933–69); from vol. 39 (Leiden: E. J. Brill, 1970 —.)

ERE *Encyclopedia of Religion and Ethics,* ed. James Hastings, 12 vols. (Edinburgh: T. & T. Clark, 1908–21)

ID   *The Interpretation of Dreams*, by Sigmund Freud, trans. J. Strachey; one vol. reprint of vols. 4–5 of the *Standard Edition* (London: Allen and Unwin, 1954)

IL   "Introductory Lectures in Psycho-Analysis I and II," by Sigmund Freud, *Standard Edition* 4.

Lex   *Ausführliches Lexikon der griechischen und römischen Mythologie*, by W. H. Roscher, reprint (Hildesheim: Olms, 1965)

MA   *The Myth of Analysis*, by James Hillman (Evanston, Ill.: Northwestern University Press, 1972); also (New York: Harper & Row, Colophon Books, 1978)

NIL   *New Introductory Lectures in Psycho-Analysis*, by Sigmund Freud, trans. W. J. H. Sprott (London: Hogarth Press, 1933–57)

OD   *On Dreams*, by Sigmund Freud, trans. J. Strachey (London: Hogarth Press, 1952)

OET   *The Origins of European Thought About the Body, the Mind, the Soul, the World, Time, and Fate*, by R. B. Onians, 2d ed. (Cambridge: At the University Press, 1953)

OPA   *The Origins of Psycho-Analysis: Letters to Wilhelm Fliess, Drafts and Notes, 1887–1902* (London: Imago, 1954)

OTL   *An Outline of Psycho-Analysis*, by Sigmund Freud, trans. J. Strachey (London: Hogarth Press, 1949)

PW   August Pauly, ed., rev. by Georg von Wissowa *et alia*, *Realencyclopädie der klassischen Altertumswissenschaft* (Stuttgart: Metzger und Alfred Druckenmüller, 1893—)

RP   *Re-Visioning Psychology*, by James Hillman, The Terry Lectures (New York: Harper & Row, 1975)

TD   "Metaphysical Supplement to the Theory of Dreams," by Sigmund Freud, in *CP* 4:137–51

N.b. HERACLITUS: All *numbering* of Heraclitus' fragments follows the Diels-Kranz arrangement, translated into English by K. Freeman in *Ancilla to the Pre-Socratic Philosophers* (Oxford: B. H. Blackwell, 1948). All *translations* of Heraclitus used in this book are those of M. Marcovich, *Heraclitus: Greek Text With a Short Commentary*, 1st ed. (Merida, Venezuela: Los Andes University Press, 1967), where all the main divergences are represented and discussed. In some cases, other English versions of Heraclitus' fragments are used and so indicated. These are: J. Burnet, *Early Greek Philosophy* (London: A. and C. Black, 1930–48); G. S. Kirk and J. E. Raven, *The Pre-Socratic Philosophers* (Cambridge: At the University Press, 1963); W. K. C. Guthrie, *A History of Greek Philosophy*, vol. 1 (Cambridge: At the University Press, 1962); P. Wheelwright, *Heraclitus* (Princeton, N.J.: Princeton University Press, 1959).

SELECTED REFERENCES

Bachelard, G. *On Poetic Imagination and Reverie.* Translated by C.Gaudin. Indianapolis, Ind.: Bobbs-Merrill, 1971.

Béguin, A. *L'Âme romantique et la rêve.* 2d. ed. Paris: Corti, 1939.

———. *Traumwelt und Romantik.* Translation of *L'Âme romantique,* by J. P. Walser. Bern and Munich: Francke, 1972.

Berry, P. "What's the Matter With Mother?" Lecture No. 190. London: Guild of Pastoral Psychology, 1978.

———. "The Rape of Demeter/Persephone and Neurosis." *Spring 1975.* New York and Zürich: Spring Publications, 1975.

Brandon, S. G. F. *The Judgement of the Dead.* London: Weidenfeld & Nicolson, 1967.

———. "The Personification of Death in Some Ancient Religions." Bulletin John Rylands Library. Manchester, 1961.

Büchenschutz, B. *Traum und Traumdeutung im Alterthume.* Berlin: Calvary, 1868.

Cumont, F. *After Life in Roman Paganism.* New York: Dover Press, 1959.

Dieterich, A. *Nekyia.* Leipzig: Teubner, 1893.

Dietrich, B. C. *Death, Fate and the Gods.* London: Athlone, 1967.

Dodds, E. R. *The Greeks and the Irrational.* Boston: Beacon Press, 1957.

Dumézil, G. *La Religion romaine archaïque.* Paris: Payot, 1966; *Archaic Roman Religion.* Trans. by P. Krapp. Chicago: University of Chicago Press, 1970.

Ellenberger, H. F. *The Discovery of the Unconscious.* London: Allen Lane, 1970.

Farnell, L. R., *Greek Hero Cults and Ideas of Immortality,* Oxford University Press, 1921.

Goodenough, E. R. *Jewish Symbols in the Greco-Roman Period.* New York: Pantheon Books, 1965.

Guthrie, W. K. C. *The Greeks and Their Gods.* London: Methuen, University pb., 1968.

Herzog, E. *Psyche and Death.* Trans. by D. Cox and E. Rolfe. London: Hodder & Stoughton, 1966.

Hillman, James. *Suicide and the Soul.* 2d ed. New York and Zürich: Spring Publications, 1976.

Huidekoper, F. *The Belief of the First Three Centuries concerning Christ's Mission to the Underworld.* New York: James Miller, 1876.

Jones, Ernest. *Sigmund Freud: Life and Work.* 3 vols. London: Hogarth Press, 1953.

Kerényi, K. *The Heroes of the Greeks.* New York: Grove Press, Evergreen edition, 1962. Also London: Thames & Hudson, 1959.

Keuls, Eva. *The Water Carriers in Hades: A Study of Catharsis Through Toil in Classical Antiquity.* Amsterdam: Hakkert, 1974.

Lattimore, R. *Themes in Greek and Latin Epitaphs.* Urbana, Ill.: University of Illinois Press, 1962.

Miller, David L. "Clowns and Christ: Wit and Humor in the Religious Imagination." 1978 Panarion Conference tape. Los Angeles.

Neumann, Eva. *The Masked Dancer,* Philadelphia: St. Joseph's College Press, 1965.

Nilsson, M. P. *Geschichte der griechischen Religion.* 2nd ed. Munich, 1955.

Otto, W. F. *Dionysus.* Translated by R. Palmer. Bloomington, Ind.: Indiana University Press, 1965.

————. *Die Manen.* Darmstadt: H. Gentner, 1958.

Paulson, Ivor. "Untersuchungen über die primitiven Seelenvorstellungen mit besonderer Rücksicht auf Nordeurasien." *Ethnos* 1, no. 2 (1956).

Rohde, E. *Psyche.* Translated by W. B. Hillis. 8th ed. London: Kegan Paul, 1925.

Snell, B. *The Discovery of the Mind.* New York: Harper & Row, Torchbook, 1960.

Steffens, H. *Caricaturen des Heiligsten.* Vol. 2. Leipzig, 1821. Quoted in Béguin, *Traumwelt.*

Wilamowitz-Moellendorf, V. von. *Der Glaube der Hellenen.* Vol. 1. Berlin: Weidmann, 1931.

INDEX